IET COMPUTING SERIES 39

ReRAM-based Machine Learning

Other volumes in this series:

ReRAM-based Machine Learning

Edited by
Hao Yu, Leibin Ni and Sai Manoj Pudukotai Dinakarrao

The Institution of Engineering and Technology

Published by The Institution of Engineering and Technology, London, United Kingdom

The Institution of Engineering and Technology is registered as a Charity in England & Wales (no. 211014) and Scotland (no. SC038698).

The Institution of Engineering and Technology
Michael Faraday House
Six Hills Way, Stevenage
Herts, SG1 2AY, United Kingdom

www.theiet.org

British Library Cataloguing in Publication Data
A catalogue record for this product is available from the British Library

ISBN 978-1-83953-081-4 (hardback)
ISBN 978-1-83953-082-1 (PDF)

Typeset in India by MPS Limited
Printed in the UK by CPI Group (UK) Ltd, Croydon

Contents

Acronyms

ANN	artificial neural network
BCNN	binary convolutional neural network
BNN	bitwise neural network
CNN	convolutional neural network
DNN	deep neural network
DRAM	dynamic random-access memory
FPGA	field programmable gate array
HDD	hard disk drive
IMC	in-memory computing
ML	machine learning
NDC	near-data computing
NVM	nonvolatile memory
ODD	optical disk drive
PCM	phase change memory
PIM	processing-in-memory
ReRAM	resistive random-access memory
ResNet	residual network
SLFN	single-layer feedforward neural network
SRAM	static random-access memory
STDP	spike timing-dependent plasticity
STT-MTJ	spin transfer torque magnetic tunnel junction
STT-RAM	spin transfer torque RAM
TNN	tensor neural network
TSV	through-silicon via
XIMA	crossbar in-memory architecture
1S1R	one selector one ReRAM
1T1R	one transistor one ReRAM

Preface

With the emergence of IoT and handheld devices, the amount of data procured in the data centers have reached nearly exa-scale. Processing such large amounts of data through traditional computing techniques is inefficient due to latency and inefficient resource usage. With the introduction in machine learning (ML) and success in multiple application, ML has been adopted for big data processing.

Despite advancements in terms of processing through ML, transferring and communicating the data to and from the memory and storage units is seen as one of the major bottlenecks. In-Memory Computing (IMC) is seen as a panacea to overcome the challenges of traditional Von-Neumann architectures. For efficient IMC, frameworks such as Hadoop and MapReduce frameworks have been introduced. Such frameworks explore the temporal locality to process such large amounts of data. Despite efficient compared to traditional computing paradigms, existing IMC paradigms are inefficient in terms of power consumption and latency requirements, especially when employed in data centers and other cloud computing platforms.

To address the challenges with CMOS-based IMC, emerging non-volatile memory (NVM) devices are researched in both academia and industry. Such NVM-based IMC architectures are observed to overcome the saturation of Moore's law challenge because of its low power, area and high-density embedded storage benefits. Multiple devices emerging from different materials including resistive random-access memory (ReRAM), phase-change random access memory (PCRAM), magnetic RAM (MRAM), Ferroelectric RAM (FeRAM) and NOR Flash along with traditional DRAMs are introduced and researched. Among multiple emerging NVM devices, ReRAM is the most promising among multiple devices due to its potential of multi-bit storage and compatability with CMOS technology. Such exploration is well-supported by companies such as HP and IBM. Hence, we believe the ReRAM-based IMC will be commercialized with IoT products in the next few years.

This book first introduces existing architectures on IMC such as processing-in-memory (PIM), near-data processing (NDP) and near-data computation (NDC) architectures ranging from general programmable many-core systems to reconfigurable arrays and custom-designed accelerators. A comprehensive analysis on various IMC architectures is discussed and compared. Further, with the emergence of memory devices that support IMC, the authors introduce the ReRAM along with the device modeling and logic circuit design needed for ML operations. ReRAM has been widely deployed for IMC architectures due to minimized leakage power, reduced power consumption and smaller hardware footprint. The authors introduce the design of a crossbar structure with the aid of ReRAM to facilitate matrix multiplications and convolutions that are computationally intensive operations in ML applications. More importantly, they present a true in-memory logic-integration architecture without utilizing I/Os that leads to faster data access and higher throughput with low power. They also present multiple ReRAM-based IMC architectures that can perform other computations of ML and data-intensive applications such as calculation of gradients and L2-norms. Deep learning architectures are heavily growing in terms of depth and leading to an exponential increase in computational complexity. As a case study, the authors discuss how the ReRAM-based IMC can aid in accelerating computations, eventually leading to an increased throughput with high energy efficiency and smaller form factor for a large-scale deep learning network such as residual network (ResNet) and compressive sensing computations.

As the number of elements on a single chip or system are limited, to further enhance the throughputs of data-intensive computations, a distributed computing paradigm has been widely adopted. In this book, the authors introduce techniques to perform distributed computing using IMC accelerators. The emergence of 3D integration has facilitated multiple chips stacked on top of each other, with each chip functioning independently. The authors introduce a 3D CMOS-ReRAM architecture, where ReRAM devices are connected through through-silicon-vias (TSVs) with top-layer wordlines and bottom-layer bitlines. All other CMOS logics are implemented in the bottom layer. They also introduce a multilayer 3D architecture, where multiple ReRAM layers are designed as data buffers.

This book introduces the design of hardware for ML and data-intensive computations. It has been shown by the research community that the mapping of computations is a critical aspect without which the benefits of IMC or hardware accelerator designs cannot be yielded. Thus, to make the design complete, the authors introduce strategies to map ML designs onto hardware accelerators. They also provide data analytics mapping on ReRAM-based IMC architecture for multiple data-intensive applications. The learning and inference procedures of single-layer feedforward neural network (SLFN) have been optimized and partially mapped on a passive binary ReRAM crossbar. In addition, the authors map a binary convolutional neural network (BCNN) on both passive array and One Selector One ReRAM array with different mapping schemes. In addition to traditional 2D integration, this book also introduces how mapping can efficiently be performed for emerging 3D integration-based IMC architectures.

This book is highly motivated by the rapid advancements observed in the ML and hardware design communities, and the lack of a book that provides insights and latest advancements in both these fields, as well as the wide adoption of ML algorithms in a plethora of applications and ever-increasing industrial requirements for enhancing the performance of ML applications. This book can serve as a bridge between researchers in the computing domain (algorithm designers for ML) and hardware designers.

The first chapter introduces the need and motivation to deploy ML algorithms for data-intensive computations. This also introduces the challenges and need for hardware for ML processing. In the second chapter, we present emerging memory devices that can support IMC and the need for IMC is introduced in this chapter. Further, a comprehensive comparison and analysis of different IMC architectures is presented. The architectures include using traditional DRAM to emerging devices such as ReRAM and memristors. In the third chapter, modeling of ReRAM devices is presented followed by the design of crossbar structures that are primarily used for matrix multiplication in ML applications. In addition, design of multibit storage for ReRAMs and other logic functional units with ReRAMs is presented.

The fourth chapter provides the basic information on ML algorithms, computational complexity and the types of operations involved in the ML algorithms, including least-squares method (SVM, ELM), and deep learning (CNN, TNN). Trained quantization (binary, ternary and eight-bit, etc.) will be addressed in this chapter. Additionally, the training mechanisms for deep CNNs and TNNs are focused in this chapter, as they are the time-consuming operations and the performance depends on the training efficiency.

The fifth chapter introduces multiple strategies to map the ML designs on to hardware accelerators. Designing of ReRAM crossbar-based IMC architectures to accelerate ML applications is presented. Further, to accommodate deep DNNs and CNNs, a 3D stacking-based CMOS-ReRAM architecture is introduced. The main focus of this chapter is on the architectural aspects and circuity to support the data-intensive computations with high speed. In Chapter 6, we introduce techniques to map the ML applications for ReRAM and the major challenges and the scope for improvement. The mapping techniques for different ML algorithms for different architectures such as ReRAM cross with traditional 2D and 3D architectures are illustrated.

Case studies for ReRAM-based ML acceleration for different scenarios are presented. Chapter 7 presents ResNet under different scenarios such as DNN with quantization and ReRAM-based acceleration for ResNet. In addition to the ResNet, this book presents ReRAM-based accelerator for compressive sensing application in Chapter 8. For this part, different scenarios such as iterative heuristic algorithm and row generation algorithms are presented. All the case study chapters are presented with substantial amount of experimental results and analysis that aid in replicating the experiments and also prove the efficiency of ReRAM accelerators and its prominence in the design of future hardware accelerators. The last chapter summarizes the ReRAM accelerators and its impact on the ML applications. Furthermore, future directions with ReRAM devices to further enhance the ML computations are presented.

The authors of this book would like to thank the colleagues at Nanyang Technological University, especially members of VIRTUS lab, Hardware architecture and artificial intelligence lab at George Mason University and the affiliated students. We would like also to express my deepest appreciation to the faculty members, Prof. Anupam Chattopadhyay, Prof. Chang Chip Hong, Prof. Shi Guoyong, Prof. Huang Guangbin of Nanyang Technological University and Prof. J. Joshua Yang and Prof. Qiangfei Xia of the University of Massachusetts Amherst for their support. The authors also would like to thank Prof. Amlan Ganguly and Mr. Purab Sutradhar of Rochester Institute of Technology. The authors would also like to thank Dr. Nima Taherinejad and Prof. Axel Jantsch from Vienna University of Technology (TU Wien), Austria.

About the authors

Hao Yu is a professor in the School of Microelectronics at Southern University of Science and Technology (SUSTech), China. His main research interests cover energy-efficient IC chip design and mmwave IC design. He is a senior member of IEEE and a member of ACM. He has written several books and holds 20 granted patents. He is a distinguished lecturer of IEEE Circuits and Systems and associate editor of *Elsevier Integration, the VLSI Journal, Elsevier Microelectronics Journal, Nature Scientific Reports, ACM Transactions on Embedded Computing Systems* and *IEEE Transactions on Biomedical Circuits and Systems*. He is also a technical program committee member of several IC conferences, including IEEE CICC, BioCAS, A-SSCC, ACM DAC, DATE and ICCAD. He obtained his Ph.D. degree from the EE department at UCLA, USA.

Leibin Ni is a Principle engineer at Huawei Technologies, Shenzhen, China. His research interests include emerging nonvolatile memory platforms, computing in-memory architecture, machine learning applications and low power designs. He is a member of IEEE. He received his Ph.D. from the Nanyang Technological University, Singapore.

Sai Manoj Pudukotai Dinakarrao is an assistant professor in the Department of Electrical and Computer Engineering at George Mason University (GMU), USA. His current research interests include hardware security, adversarial machine learning, Internet of things networks, deep learning in resource-constrained environments, in-memory computing, accelerator design, algorithms, design of self-aware many-core microprocessors and resource management in many-core microprocessors. He is a member of IEEE and ACM. He served as a guest editor to *IEEE Design and Test Magazine* and reviewer for multiple IEEE and ACM journals. Also, he is a technical program committee member of several CAD conferences, including ACM DAC, DATE, ICCAD, ASP-DAC, ESWEEK and many more. He received a Ph.D. degree in Electrical and Electronic Engineering from the Nanyang Technological University, Singapore.

Part I

Introduction

Chapter 1

Introduction

1.1 Introduction

In the last two decades, computing paradigms have experienced a tremendous drift with nearly exascale (10^{18} bytes) amount of data being amassed by business units and organizations. The requirements to analyze and respond to such large amounts of data have led to the adoption of machine learning (ML) methods in a wide range of applications ranging from autonomous driving to smart homes.

One of the major challenges to process such large amounts of data is the fetching of data from the memory and writing it back without experiencing the well-known memory-wall bottleneck. To address such concerns, in-memory computing (IMC) and supporting frameworks such as Hadoop and MapReduce have been introduced. This has shown to be highly beneficial as these methods address the challenge of a lack of temporal locality that exists in traditional computing techniques. Undoubtedly, these techniques have helped but the challenges of power consumption and processing delays are still unsolved concerns, especially in macro systems and data centers.

Computing-in-memory methods based on emerging nonvolatile devices are popular in both academia and industry. Many researchers believe that this architecture will be an opportunity to break Moore's law because of its ultra-low power and high-density embedded storage. Various devices including resistive random-access memory (ReRAM), phase-change random-access memory (PCRAM), Magentic RAM (MRAM), Ferroelectric RAM (FeRAM) and NOR Flash have been discussed. ReRAM is the most promising among all these devices due to its potentiality for multilevel resistance and compatibility with CMOS technology. Well-known companies such as IBM and HP have invested in this field, and we believe that this ReRAM-based IMC will be commercialized with Internet-of-things (IoT) products in the next 2–3 years. This chapter introduces the need and motivation to deploy ML algorithms for data-intensive computations.

1.1.1 Memory wall and powerwall

Information technology by new social media such as Google and Facebook is generating a wealth of data at exa-level that is previously unimaginable. For instance, WalMart processes one million transactions per hour, and from these transactions, they collect

2.5 petabytes of information [1], and Facebook users upload 100 terabytes of data and one billion pieces of content every day [2]. In-depth data analytics may become the driving force for the future economic growth in a digital data-oriented society. The main challenge stems from the existing hardware infrastructure built upon the conventional computer architecture and CMOS technology. Moore's law scaling has become slower when compared to the growth of data. There are many recent large-scale research programs such as exascale computing (NSF/DARPA-USA) and Human Brain (European Commission), which are, however, still limited at this singularity point because of the memory bottleneck.

To process and gain insights from such massive collected data, parallel and scalable ML-based solutions that can scale with data are needed. In response, several scalable ML algorithms along with parallel frameworks have emerged: Hadoop [3], Spark [4], Flink [5], [6], Tez [7], Google Dataflow [8], 0xdata H2O [9] and Petuum [10]. Undoubtedly, these frameworks pushed the processing capabilities beyond traditional approaches, but executing these emerging analytic solutions requires a significant amount of computational resources such as power and appropriate processing architectures. Thus, the data centers started to expand by equipping more computational nodes to satisfy the demands of increasing volumes of data [11–14] and the complexity of ML algorithms. While demand for ML-based computational resources continues to grow with the size of data, the semiconductor industry has reached the scaling limits and is no longer able to reduce power consumption in new chips. Current server designs, based on commodity homogeneous processors, ceased to be efficient in terms of performance/watt to process such ML-based data-intensive computations [15–22].

During big-data analytics, the computing systems in data centers or nodes need to process the stored data with intensive memory accesses. Memory access is seen as one of the pivotal obstacles that limit the performance and throughput of the current architectures and data centers. Intensive memory access is seen across the emerging applications including web searching, data mining and also ML applications. The microprocessor needs to process the stored data with the intensive memory access. However, the state-of-the-art data storage and processing hardware still have a bandwidth-wall problem with large I/O congestion, but also powerwall with large static power in advanced CMOS technology. As a result, a design of scalable energy-efficient big-data analytic hardware is highly required. The following research activities [23,24] attempted to alleviate the memory bottleneck problem for big-data storage and processing in the future:

- First, as a promising technology for big-data-oriented computing, the emerging nonvolatile IMC shows a great potential as a high-throughput, energy-efficient solution. The application-specific accelerators can be developed within memory. In this case, before readout by processing unit, data can be preprocessed so that data migration is minimized and the bandwidth wall can be relieved. Moreover, the nonvolatile memory (NVM) devices hold information without using charge such that the leakage current can be significantly reduced with the powerwall relieved as well.

- Second, sparse-represented data by compressive sensing is an effective approach to reduce data size by projecting data from high-dimensional space to low-dimensional subspace with essential feature preserved. Data stored in the memory after compressive sensing can be recovered or directly processed. This procedure reduces data complexity in data storage as well as in data analytics with a further significant power reduction and bandwidth improvement.
- Third, data analytics by ML accelerator can be developed for fast data analytics. Latest ML algorithm on-chip can accelerate the learning process with a potential to realize online training for efficient inference, which is important for applications in autonomous vehicles and unmanned aerial vehicles.

1.1.2 Semiconductor memory

As seen in the previous section, having a memory element close to the processing units can aid plethora of challenges. There exist numerous kinds of memory which are different in terms of their functionality, physical characteristics as well as the benefits they provide. We first review the memory utilized in computer architecture, which will lay basis for the architectural design described in the later chapters.

1.1.2.1 Memory technologies

Traditional semiconductor memories refer to the silicon-based transistor devices (CMOS, BTJ, FINFET and so on) in computer architectures. These memories are applied to store computation instructions as well as data temporarily or permanently. Compared to storage media such as hard disk drive (HDD) and optical disk drive (ODD) with predetermined order of data access due to the limitations of mechanical drive, the semiconductor memories possess the property of random access. It takes almost an identical time to access any data regardless of the data location.

One can further classify all the semiconductor memories into two classes: volatile memory and NVM. In volatile memory, data are stored as electrical signals such as voltage, and it requires uninterrupted power supply. Once the power supply stops, the device is turned off and data are lost. Currently, the most commonly used volatile memories are static random-access memory (SRAM) [25–27] and dynamic random-access memory (DRAM), whose data are indicated by the electrical voltage levels. On the contrary, NVM is able to retain the data even when the device is turned off, as its data are mostly preserved by nonelectrical states. For instance, bits in programmable read-only memory (PROM) are denoted by whether the fuses of individual memory cells are burned. Figure 1.1 briefly introduces the characteristics of the volatile SRAM/DRAM, traditional nonvolatile memories (NVMs) and also emerging NVMs. The memory elements are arranged in terms of the size and access time (the left most elements are present in small quantity/size, but have faster access to the processor, whereas towards the right the elements are in large quantity and have large access time). Three prominent memory technologies are the SRAM, DRAM and flash memory, whose details are presented in the following.

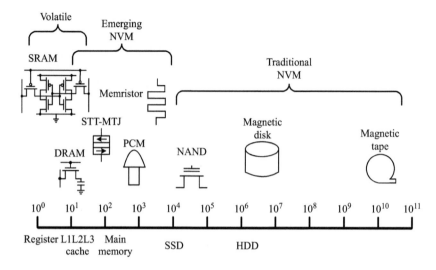

Figure 1.1　Hierarchy of different memories in a computer architecture

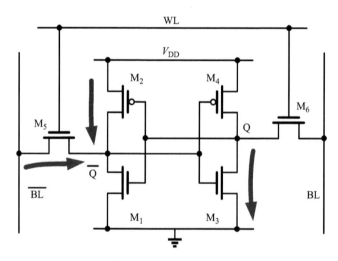

Figure 1.2　A 6T SRAM cell structure with leakage paths in standby state. The BLs are precharged high and assume the stored data is "1" at Q

Static random-access memory

A typical CMOS-SRAM cell consists six transistors, shown in Figure 1.2. The flip-flop formed by M1 to M4 holds the stored bit. The term *static* is derived from the fact that the cell does not need to be refreshed like dynamic RAM, and the data can be retained as long as the power is supplied. The M5 and M6, connected with WL and two bitlines (BLs), are used as access transistors to select target cells.

There are three operation states for an SRAM cell, write, read and stand by. To a write operation, the value to be written needs to be applied on both BLs, namely BL and $\overline{BL}$, in a complementary manner. Assume we wish to write "0" to the cell, i.e., Q to be "0" and $\overline{Q}$ to be "1," the BL is driven low and $\overline{BL}$ high. Once the M5 and M6 are turned on by setting WL "1," the BL drivers will override the previous stored value. In order to easily override the previous state in the self-reinforced flip-flop, the BL drivers are required to be designed stronger than the transistors in flip-flop.

For a read operation, both BLs are precharged high before the start of the read cycle, and the turning on of the wordline (WL) signifies the start of read operation. Because of the opposite voltages at Q and $\overline{Q}$, one of the BLs will be pulled down by the cell, and the discharging of one of the BLs is then detected by the BL sense amplifier. In voltage mode sensing scheme, the sign of BL voltage difference ΔV (V_{BL} minus $V_{\overline{BL}}$) determines the value of stored bit. A ΔV in tens of millivolts is significant enough to efficiently distinguish which BL is being discharged. For example, assume the stored bit is "1" at Q and "0" at $\overline{Q}$, and once the WL is asserted, the $\overline{BL}$ will discharge towards "0"; when a positive ΔV of tens of millivolts is gained, the latch-based sense amplifier will amplify the small voltage difference with positive feedback, and finally output logic "1" as result.

When the WL is connected to ground, turning off the two access transistors, the cell is in the standby state. During the standby state, the two cross-coupled inverters will reinforce each other due to the positive feedback, the value is preserved as long as the power is supplied. One prominent problem regarding SRAM in standby state is severe subthreshold leakage. Subthreshold leakage is the drain-source current of a transistor when the gate-source voltage is less than the threshold voltage. The subthreshold current depends exponentially on threshold voltage, which results in large subthreshold current in deep sub-micron regime. Figure 1.2 shows three leakage paths in one SRAM cell, assuming the stored bit is "1" at Q. Note that the BL and $\overline{BL}$ are always precharged to V_{DD} to facilitate future read operation. Regardless of the stored value, there always will be three transistors consuming leakage power.

Compared to other memory technologies, SRAM is able to provide the fastest access speed, but the advantage comes as a trade-off against density and power. As one SRAM cell requires silicon area for six transistors, SRAM has very limited density and hence is more expensive than other memory technologies. In addition, it is very power consuming due to the leakage problem at standby state. Therefore, SRAM serves best in the applications where high performance is the main concern and the capacity is not significant, namely the caches for processors.

Dynamic random-access memory

The philosophy behind DRAM is simplicity. Unlike SRAM, where one cell is composed of six transistors, each individual DRAM cell consists only one capacitor and one access transistor. The data "0" or "1" is represented by whether the capacitor is fully charged or discharged. However, the electrical charge on the capacitor will gradually leak away, and after a period, the voltage on the capacitor is so low for the sense amplifier to differentiate between "1" and "0". Therefore, unlike SRAM that the data can be retained as long as the power is supplied, the retention time for DRAM is finite and all DRAM cells need to be read out and written back periodically to ensure data integrity. Typically, the cells are refreshed once every 32 or 64 ms. This process is known as *refresh*, and this is how the name of dynamic RAM is derived. Figure 1.3 shows the circuit diagram of such 1T1C structure DRAM cell.

To write a DRAM cell, the BL is first set high or low based on the value to write. After the access transistor is turned on by asserting WL, the capacitor in the selected cell is charged to "1" or discharged to "0." Because the access takes place through an NMOS transistor, there exists a V_{th} drop during the write "1." In order to prevent this V_{th} drop and maintain a long refresh period, the WLs driving voltage is usually boosted to $V_{PP} = V_{DD} + V_{th}$.

To read a DRAM cell, the BL is precharged to $V_{DD}/2$ and then the WL is enabled. Due to the charge sharing, the BL voltage will slightly decrease or increase depending on the voltage that the capacitor was previously charged to, i.e., V_{DD} or 0. If it is previously charged, the charge sharing will slightly boost the BL voltage; otherwise, some charge will be distributed from BL to cell capacitor. In both cases, the voltage of storage capacitor will be changed after read operation; thus, the read operation is called destructive, and an instant write back is required. A slight voltage change on the BL can be calculated by

$$\Delta V = \pm \frac{V_{DD}}{2} \frac{C_{cell}}{C_{cell} + C_{bitline}} \tag{1.1}$$

The sign of ΔV depends on the state of storage capacitor. In modern DRAM devices, the capacitance of a storage capacitor is far smaller than the capacitance of the BL. Typically, the capacitance of a storage capacitor is one-tenth of the capacitance of the long BL that is connected to hundreds or thousands of other cells. The relative capacitance values create the scenario that when the small charge contained in a storage capacitor is placed on the BL, the resulting voltage on the BL is small and difficult to measure in an absolute sense. In DRAM devices, the voltage sensing problem is resolved through the use of a differential sense amplifier that compares the voltage of the BL to a reference voltage.

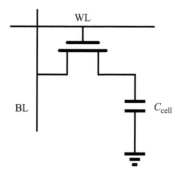

Figure 1.3   The circuit diagram of 1T1C DRAM cell structure

The use of differential sense amplifier, in turn, introduces some requirements on the DRAM array structure. Particularly, instead of a single BL, a pair of BLs needs to be used to sense the voltage value contained in any DRAM cell. In addition, in order to ensure that the voltage and capacitance values on the pair of BLs are closely matched, the BLs must be closely matched in terms of path lengths and the number of cells attached. The above requirements lead to two distinctly different array structures: open BL structures and folded BL structures.

Flash NVM

Flash memory is the most widely used NVM technology today. The key device in this prevailing memory is floating gate (FG) transistors. A figure of cross section of an FG transistor is shown in Figure 1.4. Unlike a metal oxide silicon field effect transistor (MOSFET) transistor, an additional floating gate is added between the control gate and channel. Isolated by oxide layers, floating gate is able to trap charges and keep them for years. Therefore, the FG transistor encodes data based on whether electrons are trapped and is able to retain data without power. That is where "nonvolatile" is derived from.

The principle of read operation can be described as follows. When no charges are trapped in floating gate, the FG transistor has a threshold voltage of V_{th0}; when negative charges are trapped, they attract positive charges of control gate; thus, higher control gate voltage is required to turn on the channel, which produces a higher threshold voltage V_{th1}. By applying intermediate control gate voltage that is between V_{th0} and V_{th1}, and measuring current, the state of device can be known.

The write operation of FG transistor involves injecting or pulling electrons across the oxide barrier. There are two ways to achieve this, quantum tunneling or hot electron injection. In quantum tunneling scenario, high voltage is applied on control gate, quantum tunneling will take place between the floating gate and channel, and electrons can travel across the oxide barrier. For hot electron injection scenario, electrons are accelerated under high electrical field in the channel till its energy is high enough to penetrate the oxide layer. Note that electrons with high energy will damage the oxide lattice, and such damage will accumulate and lead to a limited write cycles, which is typically around 10^5 cycles.

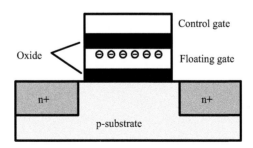

Figure 1.4   The cross section of an FG transistor

There are two common layouts for flash memory, shown in Figure 1.5, NAND flash memory with FG transistors in series and NOR flash memory with FG transistors in parallel. The names NAND and NOR are derived from the fact that their connection fashion in series or parallel resemble a NAND gate or a NOR gate. NAND layout has the density advantage over NOR layout because each row only has one ground connection, and is thus widely used for external storage. NOR layout has lower latency and is thus widely used in embedded systems, where high performance is required. Figure 1.5 also shows how the read of NAND and NOR flash memory can be achieved. The relationship between the different applied voltage magnitude is shown as follows:

$$V_{OFF} < V_{th0} < V_{INT} < V_{th1} < V_{ON} \ll |V_{HIGH}| \tag{1.2}$$

1.1.2.2 Nanoscale limitations

With scaling down of the technology towards nanolevel, there are some challenges and limitations in the traditional memory architecture. Such challenges are caused by physical rules and is summarized from two perspectives. On the one hand, there are functional failures due to the process variation that transistors may have mismatch problems. On the other hand, the thermal runaway failures are caused by positive feedback in an SRAM or a DRAM cell [28]. As a result, NVM is considered as a potential solution for data storage with the scaling technology.

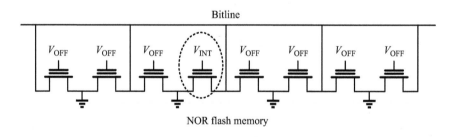

NOR flash memory

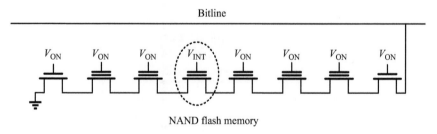

NAND flash memory

Figure 1.5   Two common layouts for flash memory: NOR flash memory and NAND flash memory

1.1.3 Nonvolatile IMC architecture

In the conventional computing architecture, all the data are stored in memory. It is separated from the general processors so that I/O connections are required. As a result, during the data processing, all data need to be read out to the external processor and written back afterwards. However, in data-oriented applications such as ML acceleration, this architecture will incur significant I/O congestions and hence greatly degrade the overall performance [27,29–32]. In addition, significant static power will be consumed because all the data need to be held, even though it does not need to be used at the moment [26,28,33–39].

Theoretically, it is feasible to overcome the bandwidth issue by adding more I/O pins or operating them at higher frequency. Practically, however, the I/O frequency is limited by the signal propagation delay and signal integrity issues, and I/O number is limited by the packaging technology, and thus the bandwidth is nearly saturated.

Besides improving the bandwidth of memory, reducing the volume of data communicating between processor and memory is another feasible option to enhance the performance. Conventionally, the processor only reads raw data from the main memory. If the memory can perform some operations before sending data, the I/O communication requirement can be significantly reduced [40–42]. For instance, if one needs to add eight numbers, one has to load all the eight values into the processor in the conventional way. However, if the addition of two numbers is performed as an in-memory logic operation, one can preprocess the adding inside memory and only four numbers need to be read out.

To perform IMC, implementing logic operations inside the memory is required so that the preprocessing can be done. Such an architecture is called logic-in-memory architecture. In general, the requirement of the ideal logic-in-memory architecture is summarized in Figure 1.6. A big NVM sea is connected with thousands of small accelerator cores through high bandwidth and energy-efficient reconfigurable I/Os.

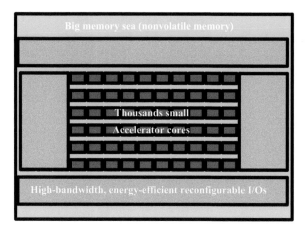

Figure 1.6   Ideal logic-in-memory architecture

Considering the leakage reduction at the same time, logic-in-memory architectures that are associated with NVM are presented in [43–47]. Figure 1.7 shows a logic-in-memory architecture by building CMOS circuits with storage devices. The example shows a full-adder with both *sum* and *carry* logic. However, such a cell-level in-memory architecture has two major problems. First, the CMOS-based logic is built in memory so that it is difficult to be reconfigured. Second, it can only perform low-complex logic operations. In the example, it needs 22 transistors for a simple 1-bit adder. The complexity of memory will be thus greatly increased.

Another in-memory architecture to investigate at the block level in distributed fashion is illustrated in Figure 1.8, which is more effective for traffic reduction. A memory data is usually organized in H-tree fashion, and the data block can be the data array or a number of data arrays that belong to same "H-tree" branch. Instead

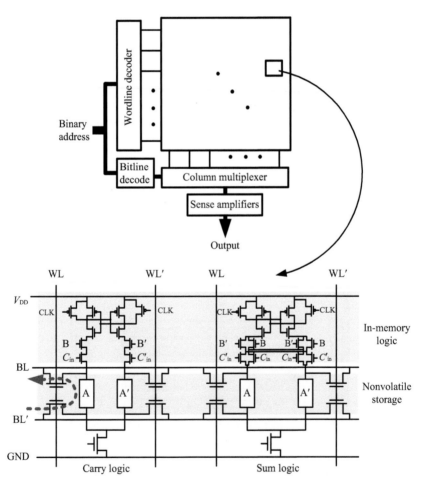

Figure 1.7   IMC architecture at memory-cell level

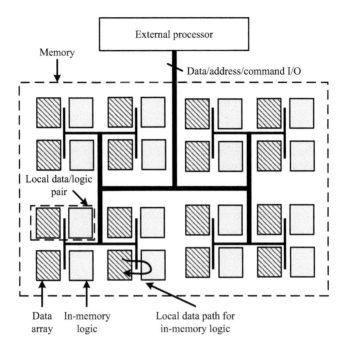

Figure 1.8   IMC architecture at memory block level

of inserting an in-memory logic at memory-cell level inside the data array, the architecture in Figure 1.8 pairs each block of data with in-memory logic (accelerators). Different from the cell level in-memory architecture, the accelerators can be made with higher complexity, and the number of accelerators for each data block can also be customized. The data flow of the block-level in-memory architecture is to read out data from data block to in-memory logic, which performs particular functionality and then writes back the result. The data also needs to be stored in assigned blocks, but it is much more flexible than that of cell level in-memory architecture. The block-level in-memory architecture is very effective to reduce communication traffic between memory and processor. This is because significant operands reduction can be achieved by deploying accelerator with high-level functionality. For example, for face recognition in image processing application domain, instead of transmitting a whole image to obtain a Boolean result, the result can be directly gained through in-memory logic. In other words, the block-level in-memory architecture is suitable for big-data-driven applications where traffic reduction is more beneficial than latency reduction.

In this architecture, the nonvolatile ReRAM is intensively used. Both the memory block and logic block in each pair are purely implemented by ReRAM devices. In addition, energy-efficient in-memory logic units are deployed in the external processor to execute instructions that cannot be accelerated by in-memory logic.

1.2   Challenges and contributions

Future cyber-physical systems require efficient real-time data analytics [48–52] with applications in robotics, brain–computer interface as well as autonomous vehicles. The recent works in [53,54] have shown a great potential for ML with significant reduced training time for real-time data analytics.

Hardware-based accelerator is currently practiced to assist ML applications. In traditional hardware accelerator, there is intensive data migration between memory and logic [55,56] causing both bandwidth wall and powerwall. Therefore, for data-oriented computation, it is beneficial to place logic accelerators as close as possible to the memory to alleviate the I/O communication overhead [57]. The cell-level IMC is proposed in [43], where simple logic circuits are embedded among memory arrays. Nevertheless, the according in-memory logic that is equipped in memory cannot be made for complex logic function, and also the utilization efficiency is low as logic cannot be shared among memory cells. In addition, there is significant memory leakage power in CMOS-based technology.

Emerging ReRAM [58–64] has shown great potential to be the solution for data-intensive applications. Besides the minimized leakage power due to nonvolatility, ReRAM in crossbar structure has been exploited as computational elements [59,65]. As such, both memory and logic components can be realized in a power- and area-efficient manner. More importantly, it can provide a true in-memory logic-memory integration architecture without using I/Os. Nevertheless, the previous ReRAM-crossbar based computation is mainly based on an analog fashion with multilevel values [66] or spike timing-dependent plasticity (STDP) [67]. Though it improves the computational capacity, the serious nonuniformity of ReRAM-crossbar at nanoscale limits its wide applications for accurate and repeated data analytics. Moreover, there is significant power consumption from additional AD-conversion and I/Os mentioned in [67]. Besides ReRAM-crossbar, coupled ReRAM-oscillator can be utilized for analog computing. By mapping fixed-point values to voltages, coupled ReRAM-oscillator can perform an L2-norm calculation. Significant speed-up and energy efficiency can be achieved due to the direct analog computing.

Although the nonvolatile IMC seems to be a promising solution for future data-oriented storage and computing system, the recent emerging ReRAM are still in their infancy due to the following unresolved challenges:

- From circuit level, although there exist some simulators to perform hybrid NVM-CMOS circuit simulation [63,64], the ReRAM-based computation operations have not been fully developed yet. Without the detailed IMC implementation on ReRAM, it is hard to perform a real application on such an ReRAM-based nonvolatile in-memory accelerator.
- From architecture level, it is necessary to explore a detailed implementation for the in-memory architecture. Controllers for conventional memory are not optimal for the ReRAM-based IMC system. The CMOS-based control bus and its communication protocol need to be redefined for such a novel architecture.

- From system level, it is necessary to find out what ML algorithms can be mapped on the in-memory accelerator. For different operations or algorithms, we need to design different accelerators in order to achieve a higher parallelism and a better energy efficiency.

This book presents the idea of exploring the development of ReRAM-based logic operations and NVM in-memory architecture, as well as mapping details of various ML algorithms on such an architecture. For the ReRAM-based IMC implementation, the target is to develop detailed mappings for different operations on ReRAM. We proposed two kinds of ReRAM-based structures for operation accelerating: ReRAM-crossbar and ReRAM oscillator network. Particularly, this book has summarized the following advancements:

- First, the NVM-SPICE is used for circuit-level simulation. The model of drift-type ReRAM is introduced with simulation results. In addition, the measurement results of forming, SET and RESET processes are also shown. For the diffusive-type ReRAM, a sub-circuit model is used for simulation.
- Second, we introduce a binary ReRAM-crossbar for matrix-vector multiplication. Due to the nonuniformity of ReRAM device, the proposed binary ReRAM-crossbar can perform the computation more accurate compared to traditional ReRAM-crossbar in analogue fashion. In addition, three kinds of crossbar structures including passive array, one-transistor-one ReRAM (1T1R) and one-selector-one ReRAM (1S1R) are discussed.
- Third, we describe an ReRAM-based coupled oscillator network for L2-norm calculation. A simple oscillator can be built based on the ON-OFF switching of diffusive ReRAM or the forming process of drift ReRAM. When the basic oscillators form a network, it can perform an L2-norm calculation based on the fitted simulation results.

For the in-memory accelerator, the target is to determine the design of architecture. For the architecture with only ReRAM as computing engine, we design the auxiliary CMOS logic and define the communication protocol between the processor and memory in detail. For the architecture with both ReRAM and CMOS as computing engine, we develop 3D CMOS-ReRAM architecture so that a higher throughput and parallelism can be achieved by introducing the following two topics:

- First, a distributed in-memory computing architecture (XIMA) is described. Despite traditional store and load, we define two more commands: start and wait. In addition, all the logic blocks and data blocks are formed in pairs so that the delay of data-processing communication can be minimized. CMOS logic such as instruction queue and decoders are also designed.
- Second, design space exploration of 3D CMOS-ReRAM architectures is presented. For single-layer 3D architecture, ReRAM devices are via connecting top-layer WLs and bottom-layer BLs. All the other CMOS logics are implemented in the bottom layer. For multilayer 3D architecture, we use two ReRAM layers as data buffer and logic implementation, respectively. In addition, TSVs are used to connect different layers.

For the data analytics mapping on ReRAM-based architecture, the target is to focus on detailed accelerator design for specific applications. In addition, the algorithm requires to be optimized so that all the operations can be fully mapped on the accelerator. We present case studies with several ML algorithms on distributed in-memory architecture (XIMA) and 3D CMOS-ReRAM architectures with significant improvement on bandwidth and energy efficiency.

- First, for the XIMA, we have accelerated three ML algorithms. The learning and inference procedures of single-layer feedforward neural network (SLFN) have been optimized and partially mapped on the passive binary ReRAM-crossbar. In addition, we mapped the binary convolutional neural network (BCNN) on both passive array and 1S1R array with different mapping schemes. Moreover, L2-norm gradient-based learning and inference are also implemented on an ReRAM network with both crossbar and coupled oscillators.
- Second, for 3D CMOS-ReRAM architecture, we also mapped the optimized SLFN algorithm. All the operations in learning and inference stages are implemented so that it can achieve the online learning. In addition, tensorized neural network (TNN) is mapped on both single-layer and multilayer accelerators with different mapping scheme.

For every ML algorithm mapped on XIMA and 3D CMOS-ReRAM accelerator, we evaluate their performance in device, architecture and system levels. All the implementations show higher throughput, bandwidth and parallelism with better energy efficiency.

1.3   Book organization

This book covers the entire flow from device, architecture and learning algorithm to system perspectives for emerging ReRAM. It is organized into the following chapters. The first chapter introduces the need and motivation to deploy ML algorithms for data-intensive computations. It also introduces the challenges and need for hardware for ML processing. In the second chapter, we present emerging memory devices that can support IMC and need for IMC are introduced in this chapter. Further, a comprehensive comparison and analysis of different IMC architectures are presented. The architectures include using traditional DRAM to emerging devices such as ReRAM and memristors. In the third chapter, modeling of ReRAM devices is presented followed by design of crossbar structures that are primarily used for matrix multiplication in ML applications. In addition, design of multibit storage for ReRAMs and other logic functional units with ReRAMs is presented.

The fourth chapter provides the basic information on ML algorithms, computational complexity and the types of operations involved in the ML algorithms, including least-square method (support vector machine (SVM), extreme learning machine (ELM)) and deep learning (CNN, TNN). Trained quantization (binary, ternary, eight-bit, etc.) will be addressed in this chapter. Additionally, the training mechanisms for deep CNNs and TNNs are focused in this chapter, as they are the time-consuming operations and the performance depends on the training efficiency.

The fifth chapter introduces multiple strategies to map the ML designs on to hardware accelerators. Designing of ReRAM crossbar-based IMC architectures to accelerate ML applications is presented. Further, to accommodate deep neural networks (DNNs) and CNNs, a 3D stacking-based CMOS-ReRAM architecture is introduced. The main focus of this chapter is on the architectural aspects and circuit designs to support the data-intensive computations with high speed. In Chapter 6, we introduce techniques to map the ML applications for ReRAM and the major challenges and the scope for improvement. The mapping techniques for different ML algorithms for different architectures such as ReRAM cross with traditional 2D and 3D architectures are illustrated.

Case studies for ReRAM-based ML acceleration for different scenarios are presented. Chapter 7 presents ResNet under different scenarios such as DNN with quantization, ReRAM-based acceleration for ResNet. In addition to the ResNet, this book presents ReRAM-based accelerator for compressive sensing application in Chapter 8. For this part, different scenarios such as iterative heuristic algorithm and row generation algorithms are presented. All the case study chapters are presented with substantial amount of experimental results and analysis that aid in replicating the experiments and also prove the efficiency of ReRAM accelerators and its prominence in the design of future hardware accelerators. The last chapter summarizes the ReRAM accelerators and its impact on the ML applications. Furthermore, future directions with ReRAM devices to further enhance the ML computations are presented.

Chapter 2
The need of in-memory computing

2.1 Introduction

In 1974, Dennard predicted the reduction of switching power with the downward scaling of feature size of transistor [68], and this trend ended around 2004. The operating voltage and current reduction of transistor stagnated despite the ever-shrinking size of transistor because of the increasing leakage current. The increase of the operating frequency and the transistor density further exacerbates the power consumption of a computing system, which generates a large amount of heat and impedes the power efficiency. Another challenge for the power consumption is the intensive data transfer between data processing and memory units in conventional Von Neumann or Princeton computing architecture, so called the "memory wall." In this computing paradigm, the computing unit can only process one task at a certain interval and wait for memory to update its results, because both data and instructions are stored in the same memory space, which greatly limits the throughput and causes idle power consumption. Although mechanisms like cache and branch prediction can partially eliminate the issues, the "memory wall" still poises a grand challenge for the massive data interchanging in modern processor technology.

To break "memory wall," in-memory processing has been studied since 2000s and regarded as a promising way to reduce redundant data movement between memory and processing unit and decrease power consumption. The concept has been implemented with different hardware tools, e.g., 3D-stack dynamic random access memory (DRAM) [69] and embedded FLASH [70]. Software solutions like pruning, quantization and mixed precision topologies are implemented to reduce the intensity of signal interchanging.

The biological neural network (NN) outperforms conventional Von Neumann computing architecture based on central processing unit (CPU) or graphics processing unit (GPU) in term of power efficiency, which consumes only 1–100 fJ per synaptic event when performing intense parallel computing [71,72]. Currently, the synaptic resistive random access memory (ReRAM) has been successfully demonstrated to exhibit low power consumption ($<$pJ) [73]. However, even the two most promising fully CMOS-based brain-inspired chips, the Loihi from Intel and the TrueNorth from IBM, still lag behind in power efficiency, which consume 23.6 and 26 pJ per synaptic event [74,75]. Neuromorphic computing mimics the synaptic dynamics in device and dataflow/connection in NN to perform computing with low power consumption.

The synaptic events, which are directly monitored and precisely adjusted by ion flux in memory devices, have been successfully emulated in the system based on ReRAMs [73]. Neuromorphic computing architecture has less complex peripheral driving circuit and simple weight modification procedure, e.g., fast dot product [76], in comparison with conventional Von Neumann computing architecture, as shown in Figure 2.1 [77]. Neuromorphic computing also emphasizes the imitation of systematic neural architecture, e.g., artificial neural network (ANN) [78], convolution neural network (CNN) [79], spiking neural network (SNN) [75,80] and recurrent neural network (RNN) [81]. Unlike the general purposed processor, NNs are constructed for specified application scenarios. For examples, CNN has segregate layers and modularized kernel for fast and accurate feature recognition; the recycling output of RNNs makes it suitable for speed recognition; SNN is an event-driving system and much more flexible and fault-tolerant. The specialized neuromorphic computing architecture-based system on chip (SoC) usually exhibits several orders of magnitude reduction in power consumption when compared to the systems based on conventional Von Neumann architecture. For instance, the Intel-produced Loihi chip [75], which is based on asynchronous SNN, outperformed a single CPU by three orders of magnitude in both power efficiency and area.

Conventional computer systems based on Von Neumann architecture and Si CMOS technologies offer much faster data processing speed and higher computing accuracy than human brain, but still significantly lag behind in terms of power consumption. For example, the Google-produced supervised deep learning machine, Alpha Go, consists of up to 1,202 CPUs and 176 GPUs to defeat the world champion of game Go, while it consumes $1,000\times$ time energy than human brain. Recent advances on the algorithms of neuromorphic computing, involving effectively solving complex tasks like the human brain, such as pattern recognition, data classification and object detection, make it close to practical applications. However, the hardware implementation of these neuromorphic computing algorithms based on Si CMOS technologies for parallelism and weight adaption reasons poises great challenges in terms of computation, memory and communications, and gives rise to high power consumption. It is highly imperative to make breakthrough in the hardware implementation for neuromorphic computing systems.

2.2   Neuromorphic computing devices

As today's computing becomes more and more data intensive, the computing paradigm is transferring from computation center to data center. Neuromorphic computation (e.g., vector matrix multiplication) requires the device characteristics with linear and symmetric tuning, long retention, low stochastic behavior (blind updates) and low energy tuning. Emerging nonvolatile memories (NVMs) can potentially meet these requirements, e.g., instantaneous writing/reading ($\sim$ns), low operation voltage (<1 V) and power consumption ($<$pJ per synaptic event) [82]. Here, we briefly describe the working mechanisms of the ReRAM, spin-torque-transfer-magnetic random-access memory (STT-MRAM) and phase-change memory (PCM).

The widely used static random access memories (SRAMs) and DRAMs store information through charge and require a constant wave of operating voltage to maintain or update their states, by charging or discharging a capacitor. Emerging NVMs of ReRAM is non-charge-based device, which is free from the constrain of capacitor for data storage. A small operating voltage (<1 V) is sufficiently large for the operation ReRAM, and no subsequent power is required for maintaining the states.

Today's deep learning applications require unprecedented amount of data for dynamic data analysis. Conventional CPU/GPU has to fetch data from cache memory through programmed procedures, which usually results in the standby of processor due to the lack of useful data. Because data interchanging is costly in latency and power consumption, the most direct optimization methodology is data localization, which minimizes the physical distance between processor and cache. ReRAM has good compatibility with CMOS, which makes them ideal for 3D stacking. The 3D-stacked ReRAMs can be mounted on the top of processor and can shorten the data traveling path and enable high-density memory, due to thickness. The 3D-stacked ReRAM memory can substantially reduce data traveling, enlarge data reuse and ultimately improve power efficiency. Compared with the current popular memories, STT-MRAM excel SRAM in cell size and power efficiency, ReRAM outclassed FLASH in power consumption, read/write speed and endurance. In STT-MRAM, retention time is in trade-off with operating or switching power. Unlike other NVM devices with retention time over 10 years, retention of STT-MRAM has a one-to-one relation with stimulating pulse. And as substitution of RAM, long retention time of STT-MRAM is irrelevant to performance and thus retention is reduced (e.g., second) for lower power consumption.

As a memory, reading/writing is essential for computing. Unlike the traditional state holding units, ReRAM can be read out and modulated in crossbar separately with high power efficiency. Because during reading/writing process, the one-transistor one ReRAM (IT1R), for instance, only the targeted unit is assigned and all other units would remain idle.

2.2.1 Resistive random-access memory

The resistance switching property of ReRAM was first studied in 1960s [82]. The device configuration of ReRAM is a sandwich-like structure with an insulating material between two metal electrodes. It includes the top electrode (TE), the middle layer of oxides and the bottom electrode (BE). Generally, the ReRAMs are two-terminal devices, which have two resistance states, a high-resistance state (HRS, or OFF state) and a low-resistance state (LRS, or ON state). The resistance states are manipulated by applied electrical potential and stimuli duration. The resistive switching mechanism is a result of the formation/rupture of conductive filament in metal oxide caused by the generation and drift of oxygen vacancies. It exhibits symmetric behavior or Lissajous I/V curve in SET/RESET process. The non-charge-based ReRAM possesses a long-term plasticity characteristics, which keeps the weight (conductance) stable in certain period, even without cycling operating power.

The *I–V* characteristic of ReRAM is presented according to (2.1):

$$I = I_0 \exp\left(-\frac{g}{g_0}\right) \sinh\left(\frac{V}{V_0}\right) \tag{2.1}$$

where I_0 ($\sim$1 mA), g_0 ($\sim$0.25 nm) and V_0 ($\sim$0.25 V) are constants, determined based on the material properties. The HRS resistance has exponential co-relationship with distance (g) and large amount of V ($>$0.5 V). The ReRAM resistance not only responds to electrical stimuli but also depends on the duration of applied stimuli, as shown in (2.2):

$$\frac{dg}{dt} = -V_0 \left[\exp\left(-\frac{qE_{ag}}{kT}\right)\cdot\exp\left(\frac{\gamma a_0}{L}\frac{qV}{kT}\right) - \exp\left(-\frac{qE_{ar}}{kT}\right)\cdot\exp\left(-\frac{\gamma a_0}{L}\frac{qV}{kT}\right)\right] \tag{2.2}$$

where $\frac{dg}{dt}$ is vacancy generating speed and is determined by the discrepancy between generation and recombination rate. The mathematic model of ReRAM is similar to biological synapse and exhibition of nonvolatile behavior with ultra-low power computing, [83,84], which makes ReRAM an ideal candidate for the building block of neuromorphic computing. Spiking time-dependent plasticity, a vital characteristic of biological synapse for array-level neuromorphic computing, e.g., SNN, has been successfully demonstrated in ReRAM [85].

As a two-terminal nonvolatile device, ReRAM crossbar has inherent advantage in power efficiency and switching speed. When ReRAM crossbars are fabricated in large scale with CMOS integration, ReRAM devices are sandwiched by two perpendicular electrode wires at every cross point. Thus, a matrix-like dense array of nanoscale ReRAM is relatively easy to implement. Since nonvolatile and two-terminal ReRAM enables in-memory computing (IMC) and requires only a small amount of operating voltage, the processing unit based on ReRAM crossbar outperform CPU or GPU with conventional Von Neumann architecture in energy consumption, scalability and process speed.

2.2.2   *Spin-transfer-torque magnetic random-access memory*

The STT-MRAM contains three layers to form magnetic tunneling junction (MTJ), the free layer for data storage, the pined layer for reference and the tunnel barrier for magnetic insulation and data reading procedure [86,87]. The tunnel barrier defines the energy barrier (E_B) for switching ON and OFF states. The magnetic field direction of free layer is deterministic to the electrical resistance of the memory cell. When the magnetic moments of free layer and tunnel layer are in parallel, the STT-MRAM shows low resistance. The STT-MRAM exhibits HRS in antiparallel configuration. By introducing opposite magnetic field into free layer, the STT-MRAM can exhibit multiple resistance states [87]. An insulation domain wall is placed between the two opposite magnetic domains and adjusted by STT phenomenon. As the retention time is associated with E_B and switching power, the STT-MRAM has the smallest power consumption in all NVMs and operating speed with its full exploited nonvolatility.

2.2.3 Phase change memory

In PCM, the transition from HRS to LRS is represented by the phase change from amorphous to crystalline state of switching layer. In RESET procedure, the crystallized phase change material is melted to amorphous phase by electrically generated heat. A smaller current is required to SET the phase change material back to LRS.

The NVM devices exhibit great advantages in terms of endurance, power consumption and speed over SRAM and FLASH in data storage. A ReRAM-based hybrid system can work as a memory and processor simultaneously, which can eliminate redundant data movement. With the boost of dot-product engine [76,89], an array of ReRAM can solve some complex task by simply using Ohm's law and Kirchhoff's current law in a very short time, e.g., the multiplication and summation of matrix.

PCM possesses similar synaptic plasticity with ReRAM. Compared to other NVM devices, PCM has a relatively large range of switching resistance, which makes it ideal for synaptic analog computing with modulation scale of 1% per event. By using a gradually increasing amplitude and customized duration of stimulating impulse, PCM are reported to have over 200 adjusting levels from LRS to HRS [90]. As shown in Figure 2.1, plasticity or weight updating of PCM is time dependent. The different arrivals of pre- and post-synapse event determine the direction of modulation. Like neuro-synapse, PCM exhibits accumulative behaviors in response to a string of continuous spikes and can be described as according to (2.3):

$$\Delta w = Ae^{-\Delta t/\tau} \tag{2.3}$$

where Δw is the synaptic weight to be updated, Δt is the arrival time variance of pre/post-synapse events, A is scaling factor and τ stands for the constants of STDP

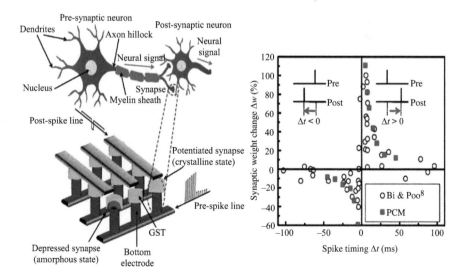

Figure 2.1   Simulation of PCM to neural cell, and spiking time-dependent plasticity of biological synapse [88] and PCM

curve. PCM-based synapse exhibits lower power consumption compared with CMOS and capacitor-based synaptic device, which consumes only ~50 and 0. 675 pJ for RESET and SET process and can be further reduced as PCM device shrinks down. But the CMOS and capacitor-based synaptic devices require consumption of ~10^{-9} J per synaptic event for proper functionality [91].

2.3   Characteristics of NVM devices for neuromorphic computing

The desirable characteristics of neuromorphic device for computing include linear/symmetric tuning, scalability, multilevel resistance state, long retention time, stochastic behavior and low energy consumption.

1. Linear/symmetric tuning: Because weight updating follows a time-dependent mechanism, the linear and symmetric relationship between weight carrier and stimulating pulse facilitates the less computing operation and power consumption. Most of the aforementioned NVMs possess relatively linear *I/V* electrical characteristics. For instance, the linearity of TaO_x/TiO_2 ReRAM can be enhanced by applying a string of varying-duration impulse, as shown in Figure 2.2.

2. Scalability and stackability: The downward scaling of memory device enables high-density integration. Most of the NVM devices have been successfully fabricated in approximately 10 nm scale level. To further increase the integration density and shorten the distance between memory and process, emerging NVM devices are implemented in three-dimensional (3D) stacking and embedded into processor.

3. Multilevel resistance state: Because the weights in biological synapses are processed in analog form, it requires multilevel resistance states in neuromorphic

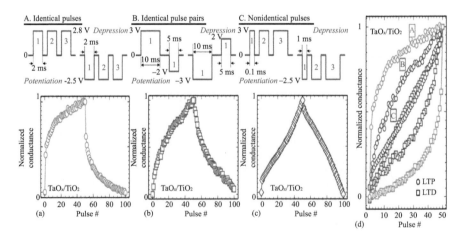

Figure 2.2   Modulation of TaO_x/TiO_2 ReRAM stimulating pulse for better linearity [92]

devices. A great amount of bioinspired algorithms require multilevel of states than inferenced 0/1 state [92].

4. Longtime retention: During the implementation process of computation, the continuous updating of weights has limited requirements on retention time. But after the operation, the long retention time of NVMs is required to ensure that the stored weight remains even if NVM devices are switched to idle (power-off). Therefore, extra power could be saved as a global updating of weights is no longer required in NVM-based system.

5. Low stochastic tunneling: NVMs still suffer from device variation and switching ambiguity, e.g., abrupt decrease of resistance in ReRAM and PCM. The stochastic switching property of NVM is still an open research and hinders commercial applications. Recently, there are a few works about NNs [92,93], which reveals great resistance to device variations. However, such NNs sacrifice in architecture and accuracy.

2.4   IMC architectures for machine learning

Therefore, an increasing amount of research in alternative non-Von Neumann computer architectures such as in-memory and near-memory computing is being carried out in order to overcome the existing challenges of traditional Von Neumann architecture [20,94]. IMC or processing-in-memory (PIM) bridges the separation between memory and processor by implementing processing units inside the memory chip itself [95,96]. Due to fabrication limitations of the memory chips, these processing elements can achieve only limited functionalities [97]. However, they can leverage the bitline-level parallelism inside memory chip to construct a massively parallel single-instruction multiple data (SIMD)-like processing architecture that also enjoys the very high-bandwidth and low-latency data communication through the memory bitlines. IMC makes a viable candidate for implementing ML applications, most importantly the CNN algorithms in which convolution operations alone accounts for the largest fraction of a CNN computation time when implemented in GPUs and CPUs [94,98]. IMC architectures can achieve dramatic performance optimization at unmatched power efficiency in CNN/DNN applications.

A vast amount of research has been carried out over the past decade in designing CNN/DNN inference and training machines on different memory platforms including the traditional memory platforms of SRAM and DRAM as well as novel nonvolatile resistive RAM (ReRAM), PCM and MRAMs such as STT-MRAM and spin orbit torque MRAM (SOT-MRAM) technologies. It has been found that a satisfactory level of accuracy can be retained even despite performing various levels of quantization/downscaling of data parameters in CNN algorithms [99–103]. This opens up an exploration space for high performance and low power CNN implementations for IoT and mobile applications. The IMC paradigm is also capitalizing on this data downscaling technique [94,103–111].

Given the importance of memory technology in the design of IMC systems, we first categorize IMC architectures w.r.t. the memory technology that the IMCs are built on. The memory technologies can be classified into conventional memory (SRAM and DRAM) and emerging memory (ReRAM, STT-MRAM and SOT-MRAM). Recent works on the IMC based on the memory technology is provided next.

2.4.1   Operating principles of IMC architectures

2.4.1.1   In-macro operating schemes

The basic principle of IMC is to perform computation in memory devices/macros, and there are a variety of implementations. In general, IMC implementation from most of the literature can be summarized into four schemes, shown in Figure 2.3.

Figure 2.3(a) shows the most common scheme of IMC. Users have to write operand 2 into the memory devices and array first, and then convert operand 1 as input signals. In this scheme, operand 1 can be altered very fast while operand 2 needs to retain in memory. Most of the literature map weights as operand 2, and feature maps as operand 1 to accelerate NN applications. Because this scheme does not require high endurance, it is suitable for various memory devices including SRAM, ReRAM, PCM, Flash, etc.

Scheme in Figure 2.3(b) is more like "computing by-memory" instead of in-memory. In this scheme, both operands 1 and 2 are originally stored in registers (outside memory array). They need to be written into memory array first, and then peripheral circuits generate a specific waveform to let the memory perform computation. After that, circuits like sense-amps are required for result readout. Potentially, this scheme can be used to replace traditional CMOS digital logic circuits.

In Figure 2.3(c), the basic assumption is that both operands 1 and 2 are pre-stored inside the memory array. This usually happens in SRAM-based cache in Von Neumann architecture: feature maps from the last layer and weights in this layer are

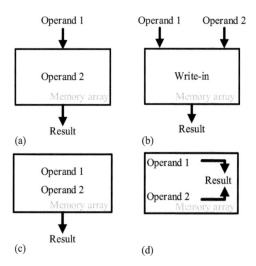

Figure 2.3   IMC schemes

stored in the same cache, and users want to do some preprocessing before sending all data in the processor.

Scheme in Figure 2.3(d) shows an ultimate idea of IMC: both operands are originally stored inside the memory, and the result will be automatically written in memory after the computation process. This scheme unifies the data format of input and output, just like the voltage-level representation of the state-of-the-art CMOS logic.

2.4.1.2 Architectures for operating schemes

From an architectural perspective, operating schemes in Figure 2.3 are suitable for different architectures. Dataflow-like [112] and cache-like architectures [113] are the most common architectures for IMC. These two architectures can be simplified as shown in Figure 2.4. Obviously, dataflow-like architecture is good for scheme in Figure 2.3(a), and cache-like architecture is good for schemes in Figure 2.3(b) and (c).

As a deep neural network (DNN) hardware accelerator, we can find that dataflow-like architecture can be used for CNN and multilayer perceptron (MLP) which require multiplication-and-accumulation (MAC) for large matrices. Cache-like architecture performs better for small matrices operations with large iterations, such as RNN, gate recurrent unit (GRU) and long short-term memory (LSTM).

In the following sections, we will mainly discuss the in-macro scheme in Figure 2.3(a) and dataflow-like architecture in Figure 2.4(a).

2.4.2 Analog and digitized fashion of IMC

To perform computation inside memory, computing circuit should be customized in the memory macro. In the view of memory designers, the operating scheme in an ordinary memory macro can be summarized into three steps:

- Step 1: receive read/write command and address in digital domain;
- Step 2: pre-charge bitlines, enable wordlines, sample bitcell voltage (for SRAM) or measure resistance (for NVMs) in analog domain;
- Step 3: perform readout operation with sense amplifier, the output the result in digital domain.

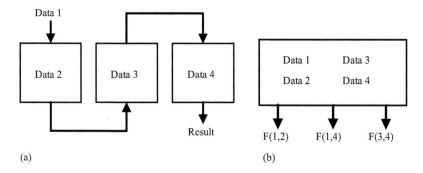

(a)   (b)

Figure 2.4   General architectures for IMC: (a) dataflow architecture; (b) cache architecture

Even in an ordinary memory macro access procedure, part of the process is done in the analog domain. As a result, the key of computing-in-memory is to perform different operations in analog domain. In most of literature, it is achieved by enabling multiple wordlines or bitlines simultaneously. Figure 2.5 shows the comparison of ordinary memory macro and computing-in-memory macro.

Next, we will discuss the detailed implementation of analog and digitized IMC. We can roughly categorize analog and digitized fashion with the following conditions:

- Input resolution: The input digital signal can be directly used or converted into analog.
- Memory device resolution: The memory device can be used as single-level cell (SLC) or multilevel cell (MLC).
- Readout accurateness: Computing operation is performed in analog domain, and the circuit can read it out in an accurate fashion or inaccurate fashion.
- Output resolution: The output signal can be readout with ADC/quantizer for multibit readout, or with SA/comparator for single-bit readout.

We also summarize analog and digitized computing-in-memory fashion in Table 2.1. In the categorization, the computing-in-memory fashion can only be called "digitized" when it is using digital(binary) input, SLC device, accurate readout and digital output.

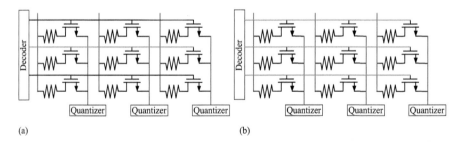

(a)   (b)

*Figure 2.5 Comparison of (a) ordinary memory macro with one wordline enabled;
(b) computing-in-memory macro with multiple wordlines enabled*

Table 2.1 Categorization of analog and digitized computing in-memory

Input	Memory device	Readout accurateness	Output	Fashion
A	SLC or MLC	Accurate or inaccurate	A or D	Analog
D	MLC	Accurate or inaccurate	A or D	Analog
D	SLC	Inaccurate	A or D	Analog
D	SLC	Accurate	A	Analog
D	SLC	Accurate	D	Digitized

2.4.3 Analog IMC

2.4.3.1 Analog MAC

Analog IMC for multiplication: The most common scheme of analog IMC performs computation in the current domain. Figure 2.6 shows two schemes of multiplication in analog computing-in-memory. Figure 2.6(a) assumes that the memory device can operate as a two-terminal resistor, resulting a voltage-in-current-out computing scheme. On the contrary, Figure 2.6(b) assumes that the memory device can operate as a three-terminal transistor-like device, resulting a current-in-current-out computing scheme. It is obvious that these two operating schemes are suitable for different memory devices.

    Analog IMC for MAC: Most of the literature perform MAC-like traditional analog adder design as shown in Figure 2.7. Here we use voltage-in-current-out scheme in Figure 2.6(a) as an example. Each input signal is converted into analog voltage, and a multiplication is performed with the memory device value, characterized as a resistor. Here the multiplication result is represented by the current. After multiplication, summation among all currents is performed with Opamp and feedback resistor or trans-impedance amplifier (TIA). As a result, the output voltage can be formulated as the following equation:

$$V_{\text{out}} = \left(\frac{V_1 - V_{\text{ref}}}{R_1} + \frac{V_2 - V_{\text{ref}}}{R_2} + \frac{V_3 - V_{\text{ref}}}{R_3} \right) \times R_f \tag{2.4}$$

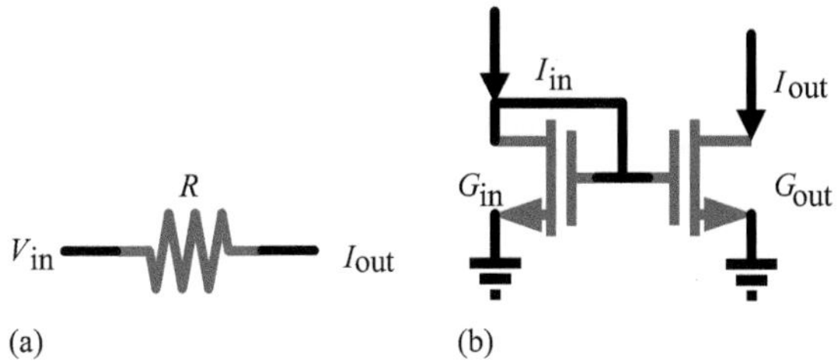

(a)   (b)

Figure 2.6   *Analog multiplication in memory device with (a) voltage-in-current-out scheme; (b) current-in-current-out scheme*

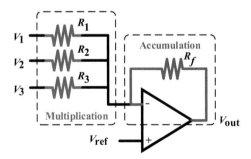

Figure 2.7   *Matrix multiply and accumulate operation by analog IMC with Opamp-based summation circuit*

If R_1, R_2 and R_3 are implemented by memory devices, we can achieve analog computation by memory devices. This computing scheme can be extended from device to array or macro as shown in Figure 2.8.

Besides current-domain-based IMC mentioned above, time-domain-based analog IMC [114] and charge-domain-based analog IMC [115] are also proposed. However, because these two schemes mainly utilize circuitry outside memory array to perform computation, we will not discuss them in detail in this book.

2.4.3.2   Cascading IMC macros

Computation is performed in voltage-in-current-out or current-in-current-out scheme as shown in Figure 2.6. If we want to design it in a normal way, i.e., make IMC macro as a universal processing core, we need digital-to-analog converters (DACs) and analog-to-digital converters (ADCs) for input and output, which consumes a lot of power. However, if we want to have a dedicated processor core, we can cascade several IMC cores in serial for higher energy efficiency, as shown in Figure 2.9.

It is obvious that Figure 2.9(a) is more flexible in the architecture level. Users can perform different operations between arrays like floating-point multiplication, summation, division and nonlinear activation functions (Tanh, Sigmoid, etc.) for machine-learning algorithms. But for Figure 2.9(b), it can only support limited activation functions between layers like ReLU. Moreover, the analog computation error will be accumulated till ADC is used, resulting no error correction can be used in all-analog domain.

If cascading is considered directly, current-in-current-out scheme in Figure 2.6(b) is better than voltage-in-current-out in Figure 2.6(a) because it has a uniform input-output representation. For the other one, TIA is still needed for current–voltage conversion in each array.

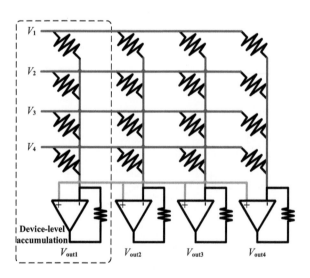

Figure 2.8   Analog IMC by Opamp-based summation circuit

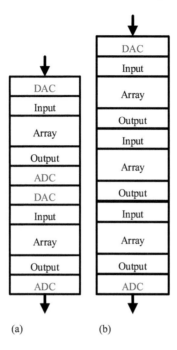

(a)   (b)

*Figure 2.9   Cascading IMC macros with (a) DAC and ADC for each array; (b)
DAC and ADC for multiple arrays*

2.4.3.3   Bitcell and array design of analog IMC

In this section, we want to discuss bitcell and array design, which greatly influence feasibility and competitiveness of IMC solutions. However, they are ignored in many works. For example, the dimension of customized SRAM bitcell in standard analog design rule (before shrink) can have smaller transistor variation, leading a better accuracy performance in simulation or test-chip measurement. However, it may be 2 to 3 times larger than foundry's bitcell (after shrink). For example, works in [116–119] directly use foundry's SRAM bitcell or slightly modify the layout in compact rule, resulting area competitiveness when comparing with traditional architecture.

As for emerging memories such as RRAM, PCM and MRAM, because 1T1R or 1T1M is normally used in logic process, bitcell design may not be a problem for IMC. However, if multilevel input is used, the array layout design may be different from foundry's design for storage, as shown in Figure 2.10.

Figure 2.10(a) is parallel-sourceline-bitline scheme and Figure 2.10(b) is vertical-sourceline-bitline scheme. For higher energy efficiency and throughput IMC core design, most of works use vertical scheme because it supports analog voltage input. However, some challenges exist in this scheme. First, this scheme needs DACs at input, resulting in extra power consumption. Meanwhile, this DAC should have a large driving capability because all the current through memory device comes from DAC.

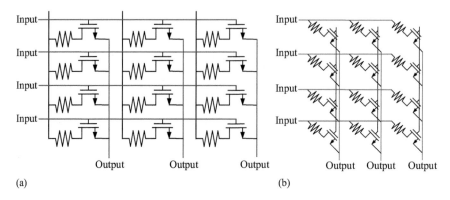

Figure 2.10   Comparison for 1T1R array with (a) parallel sourceline and bitline; (b) vertical sourceline and bitline

In this case, it is challenging to design a DAC with both high resolution and large output current. Second, because the array needs to perform parallel program, IR drop may incur some problems. For example, the last cell in one row may not be fully programmed. However, for parallel sourceline and bitline scheme in Figure 2.10(a), each sourceline and bitline only needs to program one device. Therefore, it is less likely to have the device program problem.

As what we observe, most of the works use vertical scheme in Figure 2.10(b), and works from [120,121] use parallel scheme in Figure 2.10(b).

2.4.3.4   Peripheral circuitry of analog IMC

A brief overview of analog IMC macro is shown in Figure 2.11. It is composed of digital input buffer, input circuit, memory array, readout peripheral, digital controller, program circuit and output buffer.

- The digital input module receives commands and data from modules outside IMC core, and it needs to do two tasks: (1) to buffer input data and send to input peripheral; (2) to analyze commands and send to compute-in-memory (CIM) digital controller.
- The input peripheral converts input data into analog voltage with large driving capability, performs sample-and-hold (if time division multiplexing is used).
- The CIM digital controller is the core module which determines the mode (program, verify, computing, testing, etc.) of CIM core, input peripheral converts input data into analog voltage with large driving capability, performs sample-and-hold (if time division multiplexing is used) and performs significant controlling (such as pulse width and amplitude for programming an MLC device).
- The program peripheral generates voltage signals required for both programming and computing. For SRAM, it can be simplified as a write driver, but for RRAM or NOR Flash, charge pump and linear dropout regulator may be used. What is more, if MLC is required in programming procedure, it needs to have trimmer or DAC to generate very precise voltage or current.

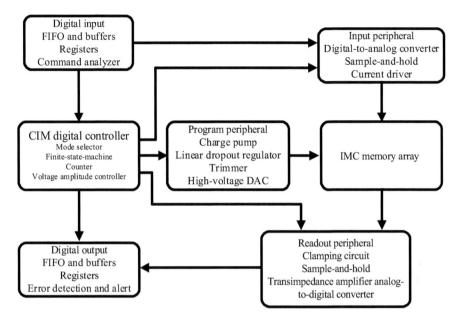

Figure 2.11   Analog IMC by Opamp-based summation circuit

- The readout peripheral focuses on how to measure output current or voltage signals. It should be with high accuracy, large dynamic range and fast readout.
- The digital output module works as an output buffer, and it also needs to send alert signal outside when necessary.

2.4.3.5   Challenges of analog IMC

Although analog IMC has shown great potential for a low-power high-throughput solution for machine learning, it still needs to overcome several challenges in some perspectives.

First, in the architecture level, IMC core can only be used as accelerator of MAC operation. As a result, it can show the best advantage for applications with massive MAC operations. However, some large-scale machine learning algorithms are not full of MAC operations, but have some activation and division operations. In addition, IMC core is good for large-scale MAC, i.e., $1,024 \times 1,024$. If the dimension of matrix is only 16×16, it may not be more energy-efficient than GPU or tensor processing unit (TPU). Also, the architecture flexibility of IMC is worse than general processors.

Second, in the application level, most of high-throughput scenarios require very powerful computation capacity for both training and inference. IMC has shown its high-throughput potential in inference stage, but the endurance and write speed become limitation in training stage. As a result, most companies or startups are going to use IMC in edge devices.

Third, the accuracy loss is difficult to evaluate in analog computation. As far as we know, analog IMC composes the following error sources:

- Input error: The error occurred in DACs.
- Device error: The conductance or resistance variation of the memory device. Note that analog 8-bit does not equal to digital 8-bit, and an analog MLC will show a specific distribution, resulting, in calculation error.
- Array error: Accuracy loss due to large-array effects, including IR-drop, cross talk, and so on.
- Output error: The error occurred in ADCs.

2.4.3.6   Trade-offs of analog IMC devices

We summarize the ideal specification of IMC devices in Table 2.2. It would be perfect if a device can have SRAM-like write/read speed, endurance and on/off ratio, MRAM-like on-state variation and retention, RRAM-like cell density, NOR Flash-like resolution and linearity.

However, some specifications listed in Table 2.2 are contradictory. For example, a device must be trimmed and run through a long write–verify scheme to be programmed to 8 bits or more. Similarly, a multilevel sensing circuit is required for a high-resolution device, resulting in longer readout time.

2.4.4   Digitized IMC

As shown in Table 2.1, digitized IMC should have everything binarized including input, memory cell and output. As a result, it is very similar with a normal memory array but with limited numbers of wordlines/bitlines enabled simultaneously. For example, works in [113,122] only enable two wordlines inside memory array.

It is obvious that the digitized IMC can have better accuracy compared to analog fashion. In addition, error correction code (ECC) techniques can be used in this scheme and the computation is reversible. However, apparently this fashion can only gain 1 to 2 times energy efficiency, compared to normal memory macro.

2.4.5   Literature review of IMC

The IMC architectures are categorized based on the memory node type, mapping, access and quantization type, as presented in [303].

2.4.5.1   DRAM-based IMCs

AMBIT: AMBIT [123] is an IMC that performs bulk bitwise AND & OR operations based on charge sharing across bitlines by simply activating three operand rows (wordlines) concurrently. Additionally, AMBIT performs NOT operations by a novel mechanism which is facilitated by enhancing one row of cells in a subarray with two access transistors (2TC1) formation. Although AMBIT does not have a machine learning-aimed application domain, it establishes the basis for two other CNN accelerators DRISA [104] and DRACC [105].

Table 2.2 Vital specification of IMC device

Specification	Ideal value	Remarks and reason
Resolution	8 bits or more	Directly determines what algorithm can be implemented in CIM
On/off ratio	1,000× or more	For "real-zero" in CIM
On-state variation	< 1%	For "uniformed-one" in CIM
Retention	10 years@125°C	Determines the refresh period
Endurance	Unlimited	Can be used in training scenario
Linearity mismatch	<1%	Determines the input resolution
Write speed	~ns	Can be used in training scenario
Current density	<1 μA	Reduce the impact from wire resistance, also for low-power and easy-circuit implementation
Read speed	~ns	For low-latency scenario
Area	$4F^2$	High-density on-chip
3D-stack	Yes	For higher-density on-chip
Process	BEOL	Can be integrated in advanced technology node
Yield	100%	N/A

DRISA: DRISA [104] is a DRAM-based in-situ CNN accelerator that performs CNN inference on 8-bit binary weighted neural network (BWNN). DRISA leverages a 3T1C memory cell formation from older DRAMs for implementing NOR logic and also the regular 1T1C DRAM cell formation for AND, OR & NOT operations, whose mechanisms are borrowed from AMBIT. Additionally DRISA features a shifting layer, which together with the logic layer forms a re-configurable in-memory processing layer that can implement selection, ripple carry addition, carry–save addition and complete multiplication on large data. The DRAM memory organization is completely revamped through the resizing of parallel-operable banks and subarrays and also an additional hierarchical stage above banks called a Group.

DrAcc: DrAcc [105] is a DRAM-based CNN accelerator that performs ternary weighted neural network (TWNN) inference where the convolution operations are reduced to accumulation (addition). It too follows AMBIT's mechanism for bitwise AND/OR logic operations but its key feature is the carry look-ahead adder implemented by modifying the sense-amplifier circuit. With an additional shifting layer, DrAcc can implement all CNN layers such as pooling, quantization–normalization and activation inside the memory. Furthermore, three data partitioning and mapping strategies as well as three different performance modes are proposed, which offer maximum throughput, minimum latency and maximum power efficiency, respectively.

SCOPE: SCOPE [124] is an in-situ DNN (CNN/RNN) accelerator that utilizes stochastic computing (H2D algorithm) to simplify computation-intensive multiplication operations into bitwise AND operations. It's a bulk bitwise IMC/PIM architecture that can perform AND/OR operations. The subarray sense-amplifiers are modified to facilitate logic circuitry, register, shifter and stochastic number generator unit (SNG) for stochastic conversion. It can perform carry–save addition by combining the bitwise logic operations and capable of both inference and training of CNN with 8-bit fixed point precision.

pPIM: Programmable PIM (pPIM) [125] is a look-up table (LUT)-based novel PIM architecture implemented inside DRAM chip. It is primarily designed to perform ultra-low power and low latency CNN/DNN acceleration. pPIM processing units are called "cores," each of which contain one 8-bit LUT and consequently can perform computations and logic operations by reading from the pre-calculated entries. These LUTs can be programmed and re-programmed to perform virtually any operation on a pair of 4-bit operands. However, nine pPIM cores are grouped together and interconnected through a sophisticated routing fabric in order to form a "cluster." Each of such cluster can perform operations such as MAC on 8-bit data operands by following a nine-step operation combining stages of operand decomposition, multiplication and addition. Due to its programmability, it is also capable of executing other CNN/DNN layers such as fully connected, activation and pooling layers. Alongside, pPIM can support operations with lower data precision, such as 4-bit scaled precision MAC. pPIM clusters are placed in rows in-between memory subarrays of DRAM banks. For inter-cluster communication, pPIM leverages the local bitlines of memory subarray, with the enhancement of subarray-interlinks that join bitlines of adjacent subarrays in order to facilitate fast data travel. pPIM cores are mostly implemented using transmission gates to minimize area overhead. Simulations show that this architecture can achieve 2,000×, 657.5× and 1.46× improvement in inference throughput per unit power consumption compared to state-of-the-art conventional processor architecture, GPU and a prior hybrid LUT-logic based PIM, respectively. Furthermore, 4-bit precision scaling improves the energy efficiency of the pPIM approximately by 1.35× for representative operations over its baseline 8-bit precision mode.

LAcc: LAcc [98] is a DRAM-based PIM CNN accelerator that leverages the memory cells in a DRAM subarray to implement LUTs which store pre-calculated outputs of multiplication operations. Together with an XOR-based adder implemented on modified sense amplifiers, LAcc can perform 16-bit convolution operations. Since LUTs expand quadratically with the operands' size, LAcc leverages matrix decomposition to keep LUTs smaller. For further LUT reduction, it proposes fixing of either weights or inputs. LAcc performs convolution with 16-bit precision with impressive power and performance figures.

2.4.5.2   NAND-Flash-based IMCs

AMBIT: AMBIT [123] is an IMC that performs bulk bitwise AND & OR operations based on charge sharing across bitlines by simply activating three operand rows (wordlines) concurrently. Additionally, AMBIT performs NOT operations by a novel mechanism which is facilitated by enhancing one row of cells in a subarray with two access transistors (2TC1) formation. Although AMBIT does not have a machine learning-aimed application domain, it establishes the basis for two other CNN accelerators DRISA [104] and DRACC [105].

2.4.5.3   SRAM-based IMCs

Neural cache: Neural cache [122] is an SRAM based in-memory DNN inference (primarily focused on CNNs) engine made by re-purposing cache memory. It can implement convolution, pooling, quantization and fully connected layers at 8-bit data precision. Its base functionalities are bitwise AND & NOR operations which are performed simply by concurrently activating the operand rows. It can perform bit-serial addition, subtraction, multiplication, comparison, search and copy on larger data, aided by carrying latches appended to the sense amplifiers. A transpose memory unit provides hardware support to reorganize data in bit-serial format inside the memory.

IMAC: IMAC [126] is a CNN inference engine that leverages ReRAM-like analog MAC to perform convolution of multibit data. Memory cells in a row contain multibit weights. Analog version of the input signals are driven through the wordlines of that row and the corresponding analog voltage signals on the bitlines are aggregated to perform MAC operations. Peripheral converters (DAC/ADC) perform digital-to-analog conversion and vice versa. It can implement fully connected layers and activation (ReLU) function too.

XNOR-SRAM: XNOR-SRAM [106] is an in-memory binary/ ternary convolution macro for accelerating NNs. Binary/ternary CNN reduces convolution operations to a XNOR operations [101] followed by accumulation (XAC). XAC is performed by driving binary/ternary input signals through the wordlines in analog form which causes the 8T-SRAM cells that contain the binary weights to produce XNOR output signals on the read bitlines (RBL). Analog accumulation of XNOR outputs takes place on the RBL, followed by digitization in the ADC.

2.4.5.4   ReRAM-based IMCs

ISAAC: ISAAC [127] is a ReRAM crossbar array structured CNN/DNN in-situ accelerator that maps synaptic weights in the form of analog resistance values in the memory cells. In ISAAC, input bits are driven in serial through the wordlines in the form of analog voltage pulses. The corresponding current magnitudes in the bitlines represent the accumulated products of the input bits with all the weights (cells) connected along the respective bitlines. These partial products are digitized, shifted and then accumulated for complete MAC operations. Weights are represented in 2's complement to account for both positive and negative ones. ISAAC has a sophisticated hierarchical architecture including MAC, ADC/DAC, sigmoid and max pool units in each processing "tile". ISAAC maps all the layers of a CNN in different tiles and adopts a pipelined dataflow.

PRIME: PRIME [112] is an IMC architecture on ReRAM platform. It is created by modifying a portion of ReRAM crossbar array that can either act as host memory or an NN accelerator. It performs analog MAC in the crossbar array in a mechanism resembling that of ISAAC, except that separate crossbars are dedicated to positive and negative analog weights. It modifies default ReRAM micro-architecture heavily to also facilitate sigmoid, ReLU, max pooling, ADC/DAC and precision control unit and also a buffer subarray. PRIME features bank-level parallelism and offers software and API support for programming and data mapping.

PipeLayer: Pipelayer [128] is a ReRAM-based accelerator which leverages spike-based signals and introduces batch level intra-layer parallelism through an inter-layer pipeline implementation. To improve throughput, this accelerator supports tiled architecture which combines computation and data encoding together in order to process data in parallel in the in-ReRAM crossbar array. The accelerator analyzes data dependencies between layers to improve the effectiveness of pipelining and inter-layer parallelism.

BCNN accelerator: Tang *et al.* [108] present a BCNN accelerator that focuses heavily on optimizing CNN inference on the ReRAM crossbar platform. It considers a binary data storage in analog ReRAM cells to ensure maximum robustness from process variations. An elaborate matrix splitting scheme is presented for mapping large CNNs across multiple crossbar units. Different layers of the CNN including convolutional, fully connected and max-pooling layers are mapped to different ReRAM crossbar blocks, and the execution of the layers is pipelined. A sophisticated buffer (Line-Buffer) ensures the fastest and the most efficient transition of data from one layer to the next.

Atomlayer: Atomlayer [129] is a ReRAM-based accelerator that leverages atomic layer computation in which one layer of an NN is processed at a time to eliminate pipelining. It addresses ISSAC's [127] limitation in performing NN training and the low power-efficiency issue of Pipelayer [128]. In order to reduce the pipeline bubbles, this design utilizes a large DRAM main memory to store initial and intermediate data generated in the NN inference or training. It uses rotating crossbars as the key components to perform atomic layer computations. It also uses row disjoint filter mapping to distribute filter rows across its multiple processing elements to ensure maximum data reuse and reduces the DRAM bandwidth.

XNOR-ReRAM: XNOR-ReRAM [107] is a binary NN (MLP) inference engine implemented on ReRAM. Since the inputs and weights are binary (1-bit), the convolution operations are reduced to bitwise XNOR operations. A dual complementary cell setup is used to perform the XNORs. A worldline switch matrix replaces the row decoder in the ReRAM synaptic architecture that enables parallelism across memory rows. Operand matrices are split and distributed across bitlines. Partial sums are generated at multilevel sense amplifiers (MSLAs) on each bitline and then quantized accumulated and undergo binary activation to obtain output.

2.4.5.5   STT-MRAM-based IMCs

Binary CNN: Pan *et al.* [109] showed that binary CNN is a BCNN accelerator implemented on STT-MRAM. It uses multilevel STT-MRAM cell structure (ML-STT) where two asymmetric cells are fused together to contain 2 bits. It is capable of bulk bitwise AND/NAND, OR/NOR through multirow activation and also XOR and ripple–carry addition through modified sense amplifiers. Auxiliary processing unit (APU) peripheral to the memory bank performs other CNN operations such as batch normalization and pooling. This work is evaluated on XNOR-NET [101].

MRIMA: MRIMA [110] is an IMC device implemented on STT-MRAM platform and is aimed at two different application domains: CNN inference and AES data encryption. Both applications are facilitated by in-memory compute arrays that can either act as memory devices or perform bulk bitwise AND, NAND, NOR (on either 2 or 3 operands) & XOR/XNOR operations by leveraging multirow activation and using different reference currents for the sensing of each of the logic outputs. MRIMA can perform BWNN and low bit-width CNN inferences. Convolutions are simplified by performing column decomposition of input and kernel matrices, followed by generating partial products by bitwise parallel AND operations between input and kernel columns and finally shifting and accumulating those partial products. MRIMA has its own instruction set architecture (ISA) and can be connected as a co-processor through the PCIe port.

MRAM-DIMA: MRAM-DIMA [130] is an MRAM-based crossbar array MAC engine aimed at DNN applications. Weights are mapped in column major format across bitlines, and inputs are provided through the wordlines in pulse-width-modulated (PWM) form. Analog vector multiplication takes place in the MRAM cells in parallel and partial products are generated on the bitlines, later to be accumulated by a digital processor. MRAM-DIMA is also capable of performing clipped ReLU activation.

2.4.5.6   SOT-MRAM-based IMCs

Binary CNN: Fan *et al.* [131] is a binary CNN accelerator based on SOT-MRAM platform. BCNN inference reduces convolutions to simple in-memory bitwise AND operations, followed by accumulation in peripheral bit-counter. A DPU (digital processing unit) performs batch normalization, scaling, multiplier and pooling operations.

IMCE: IMCE [94] is a SOT-MRAM-based IMC device that can perform CNN inference and training at different data precision combinations by leveraging a binary convolution mechanism. This mechanism involves column decomposition of the input f-map and the kernel (weight matrix) bitwise convolution of those columns and finally shifting and accumulation of those partial products through peripheral counter, shifter and adder to obtain the output feature map. An in-memory DPU executes quantization, batch normalization, pooling and activation filters.

CMP-PIM: CMP-PIM [132] is a SOT-MRAM IMC that performs comparator-based DNN inference. Here the pixel-wise convolution operations in a convolutional layer are replaced by depth-wise separable convolutions which are a combination of binary pattern feature extraction (depth-wise convolution) and binary point-wise (bitwise) convolutions. The depth-wise convolution leverages fixed ternary kernel which is implemented through multibit comparison and accumulation in this paper. The bulk bitwise IMC architecture of CMP-PIM can perform AND/NAND, OR/NOR, XOR/XNOR operations. The point-wise convolution stage is implemented through bitwise AND, followed by bit-count, shifting and accumulation operations. Quantization, batch normalization and activation take place in in-memory DPU.

2.5   Analysis of IMC architectures

Table 2.3 presents a qualitative comparison of different IMC techniques. Figure 2.12(a) and (b) presents the comparison of the area of the IMCs based on traditional and emerging memory platforms, respectively. DRAM CNN/DNN accelerators are centered around a baseline area of 60 mm^2 except for SCOPE whose area is more than four times that of a commodity DRAM chip. SRAM-based neural cache's smaller footprint is due to its very low memory capacity (35 MB). ISAAC and PRIME have the highest areas among the ReRAM IMCs. This can be attributed to their large data precision (16-bit). However, AtomLayer also has 16-bit data precision and yet it has a significantly smaller area because it employs

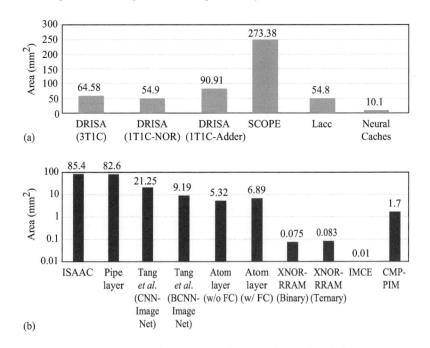

Figure 2.12   Area for IMC architectures with (a) traditional and (b) emerging memory technologies

Table 2.3 *Prominent IMC architectures and their characteristics*

Name	Memory	Interfacing	ML algorithm	Data precision	Large data mapping	In-memory bitwise op.	In-memory large data op.	Data set, neural network architecture
DRISA [104]	DRAM	Co-Processor	CNN,RNN (Inf.)	BWNN	Bit-parallel	AND, OR, NOR, shift	Add(CSA* & RCA*), mul.*	AlexNet, VGG-16, VGG-19 & ResNet-152
DrAcc [105]	Cache (SRAM)	Co-Processor	CNN (Inf.)	TWNN	Bit-parallel	AND, OR, NOT	Add (CLA)	Mnist, Cifar10, AlexNet, VGG-16 & VGG-19
LAcc [98]		Co-Processor	CNN (Inf.)	16-bit	LUT	N/A	Addition	Lenet-5, AlexNet, VGG16, VGG19 & ResNet-152
SCOPE [124]		Co-Processor	CNN/RNN (Inf. & Train)	8-bit (INT8)	Bit-parallel	AND/OR	Add*, mul. (stochastic)*	AlexNet(train.), VGG-16, ResNet-152 & Vanilla RNN
Neural cache [122]		Co-processor	CNN (Inf.)	8-bit	Bit-serial	AND, NOR	Add/sub*, mul*, comp*	Inception V3
IMAC [126]	SRAM	Memory device	CNN (Inf.)	5-bit	Crossbar (analog)	N/A (analog)	MAC	Lenet-5, VGG
XNOR-SRAM [106]		Memory device	CNN(Inf.)	BCNN/TCNN	Crossbar (analog)	XNOR	N/A	Custom MLP; VGG-like CNN & ResNet-14
ISAAC [127]	ReRAM	Co-processor	CNN/DNN (Inf.)	16-bit Fixed	Crossbar (analog)	N/A (analog)	MAC (analog)	VGG-(1,2,3,4), MSRA-(1,2,3), deepface
PRIME [112]		Memory device	CNN/MLP (Inf.)	6-bit (In.) & 8-bit (Wt.)	Crossbar (analog)	N/A (analog)	MAC (analog)	VGG-D, CNN-(1,2) & MLP-S/M/L (3 layers)
Pipelayer [128]		Co-processor	CNN (Inf. & Train)	16-bit	Bitline-wise kernel/X-bar	N/A	MAC (analog)	AlexNet, VGG-(A,B,C,D,E)
Tang et al. [108]		Co-processor	CNN (Inf.)	BCNN (analog)	Crossbar (analog)	MAC (analog)	N/A	LeNet, AlexNet
Atomlayer [129]		Co-processor	CNN Inf.	16-bit	Disjoint row kernel/X-bar	N/A (analog)	MAC (analog)	VGG-19 & DCGAN(Inf.), VGG-19 & ResNet-152 (train.)
XNOR-ReRAM [107]		Co-processor	CNN/BNN (Inf.)	BNN(1-bit)	Crossbar	XNOR	N/A	Custom MLP & CNN
Pan et al. [109]	STT-MRAM	Memory device	CNN (Inf.)	BCNN	N/A	AND/NAND, OR/NOR, XOR*	ADD (RCA)	XNOR-NET
MRIMA [110]		Co-processor	DNN/CNN (Inf.)	Low-width/ BWNN	Bit-parallel	(N)AND,(N)OR (2/3), X(N)OR	ADD (RCA), MAC*, shift	CNN(ISCAS85)
MRAM-DIMA [130]		Co-processor	DNN(Inf.)	4-bit(In.) & 5-bit(Wt.)	Crossbar (col. major)	N/A	MAC	LeNet-300-100 on MNIST, 9 layer CNN on CIFAR-10
Fan et al. [131]	SOT-MRAM	Memory device	CNN (Inf.)	BCNN	Bit-parallel	AND/OR	Binary MAC	AlexNet-BCNN
IMCE [94]		Memory device	CNN (Inf. & Train)	BCNN/var. width	Bit-parallel	AND/OR	Bin/multibit MAC*	AlexNet
CMP-PIM [132]		Memory device	DNN (Inf.)	8-bit/var. width	Bit-Parallel	AND/OR/XOR	Comparison*, mac*	CMP-NET (ResNet based)

*Operations formulated by combining bitwise functionalities of the IMC.

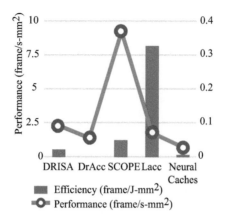

Figure 2.13　Benchmarked on AlexNet for traditional memory IMCs

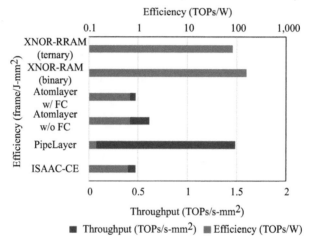

Figure 2.14　Emerging memory IMCs

massive resource re-utilization aimed at reducing processing area. The two data pre-cision configurations of Tang *et al.* (CNN and BCNN) and the binary precision of XNOR-ReRAM also reflect the same pattern of area being proportional to data precision. Similar observations can also be made for MRAM (STT-MRAM and SOT-MRAM)-based works—IMCE with binary data precision and CMP-PIM with 8-bit data precision where CMP-PIM has a larger footprint.

Figure 2.13 presents performance (throughput per unit chip area) and efficiency (output per unit energy consumption) benchmark on AlexNet for volatile memory-based (DRAM and SRAM) IMCs. SCOPE presents splendid performance figures, albeit at a rather low efficiency which can be attributed to its stochastic method for multiplication operations. LAcc, thanks to its LUT implementation, ensures the maximum efficiency among these works. Neural cache's lowest efficiency and lowest performance figure can be traced back to its comparatively inefficient SRAM platform and smaller capacity (35 MB), respectively.

Figure 2.14 presents throughput (as Tera operations per second (TOPS) per unit area) and efficiency (as TOPs per unit power) comparison for NVM IMCs. Pipelayer has dramatically higher throughput but the lowest energy efficiency compared to ISAAC and Atomlayer because it leverages massive intra-layer data parallelism to maximize pipeline throughput. Although Atomlayer has the advantage of training capability, it does not outperform ISAAC in the field of efficiency. Due to very low data precision (binary/ternary precision), XNOR-ReRAM is the most efficient ReRAM IMC under comparison.

Chapter 3
The background of ReRAM devices

In this chapter, we will first introduce the characteristics of resistive random-access memory (ReRAM) devices. Post-characterization of the ReRAMs, we introduce the structural design of the ReRAMs followed by a few applicational designs of ReRAM-based devices.

3.1 ReRAM device and SPICE model

In this section, we illustrate two types of the ReRAM devices depending on the diffusion of the charge particles: drift-type and diffusive-type. The model and usage of these devices are introduced in [24,133] and are described with sufficient details in the following.

3.1.1 Drift-type ReRAM device

The existence of ReRAM, also named as memristor, was first predicted by Leon Chua in 1976 [60], but not until nearly 30 years later was it first re-discovered and utilized in nanoscale devices at HP Labs [62]. The name memristor is derived from the fact that its resistance is determined by the current passed through it in the present and past as if it can remember its history. The memory effect specifically is the time integral of the current flowing through the device: when current flows in one direction through an ReRAM, its electrical resistance increases; while resistance decreases when the current flows in the opposite direction; similarly, when the current flow is stopped, the ReRAM retains its previous resistance, thus retaining or memorizing the (resistance) state. The bistable states of the device are defined as HRS and LRS. The write operation is achieved by applying large current, which changes its resistance rapidly. To read the cell, small current is applied to detect its resistance without significantly changing its resistance. The foundation of the fourth element ReRAM proposed by Leon Chua is shown in Figure 3.1. In 2008, the first physical realization of an ReRAM was demonstrated by HP Labs: the memristive effect was achieved by moving the doping front along a TiO_2 thin-film device [62]. The materials at the different sides of the doping have different resistivity, and the overall resistance is calculated as the resistance of having two resistors in series. The diagram of TiO_2/TiO_{2-x}-based ReRAM cell structure is shown in Figure 3.2. In addition, HP Labs has released

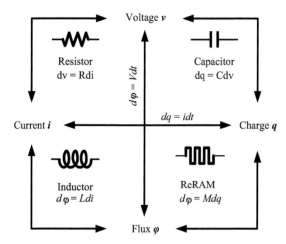

Figure 3.1　The voltage–charge–current relationship among the basic three elements (resistor, capacitor and inductor) and the prediction of the fourth element: ReRAM [60]

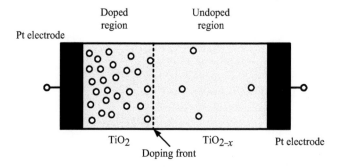

Figure 3.2　The diagram of TiO_2/TiO_{2-x}-based ReRAM cell structure

the scanning electron microscope (SEM) photograph of ReRAM array (the ReRAM crossbar structure) in [61], as shown in Figure 3.3.

A comprehensive dynamic ReRAM model which takes charge-induced-drifting effect, slowdown effect and strong-electric-field effect into consideration is illustrated in Figure 3.4(a) with doping and un-doping regions. The term doping ratio (w) is introduced to numerically represent the ratio of doping region (W) over the whole thickness of ReRAM film (D). As there is a large difference of resistivity in doping and un-doping regions, the total resistance is changing with respect to the doping ratio. For instance, when $w = 1$, the ReRAM is at LRS, where the resistance is nearly a thousand times smaller than the resistance at LRS with $w = 0$.

The operating principle of ReRAM device can be summarized as follows: charge-induced state (doping-ratio w) shifting. As illustrated in Figure 3.4(a), the ReRAM

Figure 3.3   Photograph of fabricated ReRAM array from HP

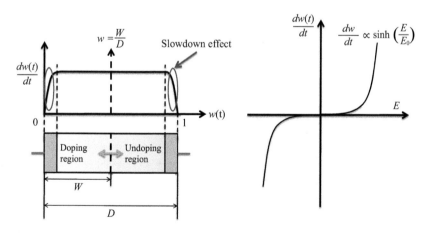

Figure 3.4   Structure of ReRAM and nonlinear effects for dynamic model:
(a) slowdown effect at boundary; (b) exponential relation between drift
velocity and electric field

can be seen as two regions in series, doping region and undoping region. The domain wall that separates two regions can be shifted by electric charge that flows through. When the positive charge flows towards the right-hand side of ReRAM junction, the domain wall shifts rightward, and thus the doping ratio (w) increases and the resistance reduces accordingly, and vice-versa for the charge flowing in the reverse direction. Traditionally, this mechanism can be described as a generalized voltage-controlled memristive system [60], mathematically defined as follows:

$$v(t) = R(w, v)\, i(t) \tag{3.1}$$

$$\frac{dw(t)}{dt} = f(w, v) \tag{3.2}$$

where R is the resistance of ReRAM and f is the explicit function of w and applied voltage v; dw/dt is the normalized drift velocity determined by w and external voltage v. Note that the complementary current-controlled memristive system can be defined similarly. The drifting velocity of ReRAM is a function of applied current that can be initially modeled in the following piecewise linear form [62]:

$$\frac{dw(t)}{dt} = \begin{cases} \mu \frac{R_{LRS}}{D^2} i(t) & \text{model1} : \text{normal} \quad \text{operation} \\ 0 & \text{mode2} : w = 0 \quad \text{or} \quad 1 \\ 0 & \text{mode3} : |v| < V_{\text{th}} \end{cases} \tag{3.3}$$

In addition, strong-electric-field effect stands for the exponential increase in the drift velocity under a strong electrical field condition (>1 MV/cm) [134]. It usually happens in the nanoscale devices such as newly fabricated ReRAM at the scale of 20 nm. As illustrated in Figure 3.4(b), the phenomenon can be approximated by a sinh function, as described in [134]:

$$\frac{dw(t)}{dt} = \frac{\mu E_0}{D} \sinh\left(\frac{E}{E_0}\right) \tag{3.4}$$

where $E = v(t)/D$ is the applied field strength, and definitions of remaining variables are shown in Table 3.1.

Moreover, the slowdown effect of ReRAM is illustrated in Figure 3.4(a), when w is approaching the boundaries where $w = 0$ or 1, the drift velocity drops quickly and is no longer linear with the current applied. This nonlinear dynamic effect can be characterized by either of the following window functions [135,136]:

$$F(w) = 1 - (2w - 1)^{2p} \tag{3.5}$$

$$F(w) = 1 - [(w - u(-i(t)))^{2p}] \tag{3.6}$$

Therefore, the complete nonlinear dynamic ReRAM model relevant to doping-factor w considering charge-induced-drifting effect, slowdown effect and strong-electric-field effect can be obtained from (3.2) to (3.6):

$$\frac{v(t)}{i(t)} = R_{\text{HRS}} - (R_{\text{HRS}} - R_{\text{LRS}})\, w(t)$$

$$\frac{dw(t)}{dt} = \frac{\mu E_0}{D} \sinh\left(\frac{v(t)}{DE_0}\right) F(w(t)) \tag{3.7}$$

Table 3.1 Definitions of variables used for drift-ReRAM device

Variable	Definition
M	Resistance of ReRAM
G	Conductance of ReRAM
Φ	Magnetic flux
q	Charge
W	Length of the doped region
D	Thickness of ReRAM film
$w(t)$	Doping ratio (W/D), $w(t) \in [0, 1)$ (nonvolatile state variable)
$dw(t)/dt$	Normalized drift velocity
R_{LRS}	Resistance of low-resistance state (LRS)
R_{HRS}	Resistance of high-resistance state (HRS)
$F(x)$	Window function defining the boundary condition of $w(t)$
μ	Mobility at small electric field
E_0	Characteristic field for a particular mobile atom in the crystal

Incubating (3.5)–(3.7) derived in the ReRAM dynamic function described in modified nodal analysis (MNA) matrix, the following Jacobian terms can be derived, as presented in the following:

$$G = \begin{bmatrix} G & -G \\ -G & G \end{bmatrix}; S = \begin{bmatrix} v_n \times \frac{dG}{dw_m} \\ -v_n \times \frac{dG}{dw_m} \end{bmatrix}$$

$$K_v^F = \begin{bmatrix} -c_1c_2F(w_m)\cosh(c_2v_n) & c_1c_2F(w_m)\cosh(c_2v_n) \end{bmatrix}$$

$$K_s^F = -c_1\sinh(c_2v_n) \times \frac{dF(w_m)}{dw_m}; K_v^G = 0; K_s^G = 1$$

where G is the conductance and $\frac{dG}{dw_m}$ is the nonvolatile state variable derivative of conductance; $c_1 = \frac{\mu E_0}{D}, c_2 = \frac{1}{DE_0}$ are constants; and $F(w)$ is the window function. Recall that the other parameters are defined in Table 3.1. Therefore, all Jacobian terms required for the linearized system equation can be established, with which the ReRAM device simulation considering the nonvolatile state variables can be implemented in the SPICE-like simulator accordingly.

In order to verify the dynamic ReRAM models and functionality, a simulation to generate ReRAM hysteresis loop is required. The efficiency of the model-based operational characteristics is validated against experimental measurement in [62] for efficiency evaluation. The device parameters are set as $d = 10$ nm, $R_{LRS} = 200$ Ω, $R_{HRS} = 3,800$ Ω; the initial resistance $R_{init} = 3,790$ Ω, $\mu = 1 \times 10^{-17} m^2/(V \cdot s)$, $E_0 = 1$ MV/cm; and Joglekar window function is applied with $p = 2$. The dynamic behavior is investigated under the driving voltage of $v(t) = -0.2 + \sin(200\pi t)$. As shown in Figure 3.5, simulation result can well capture the experiment results reported in [62].

Apart from the modeling and simulation results, this chapter presents some measurements of the drift-ReRAM device. To perform this, one needs to perform a forming process of the ReRAM first, as shown in Figure 3.6. Compliance current is set to 50 μA in our experiment.

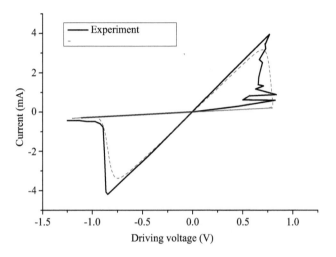

Figure 3.5   ReRAM device simulation with Joglekar window function: I–V curve, which is consistent with the measured results reported

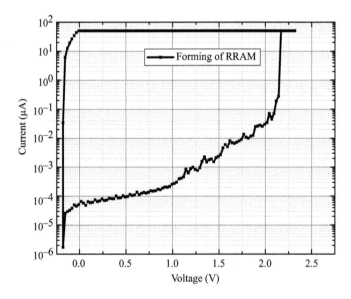

Figure 3.6   Measurement results of voltage and current of a drift ReRAM in forming process

After forming process, an analysis with some experiments for the SET and RESET of the ReRAM device is analyzed here. First, a DC measurement with 17 times of SET and 18 times of RESET is studied, and the behavior of ReRAM shows a hysteresis loop as shown in Figure 3.7. For the SET process, we use 10 μA as the compliance current.

In addition, transient measurements are of interest to study. For this purpose, consider three pulses are used that the first and third pulses are for read propose, and the second voltage pulse is for SET or RESET. The transient measurement results use 1 μs as time interval. First, Figure 3.8 depicts the SET operation and illustrates how the resistance of ReRAM changes from 1 MΩ to 50 kΩ. Here, a 0.5 V pulse is for read operation while 2.5 V is for write. We can see the SET delay is in ~μs so that we can hardly see the procedure of resistance change. Second, we use Figure 3.9 to show the RESET operation, and the resistance of ReRAM changes from 680 Ω to 100 kΩ. A 0.5 V pulse is for read operation while −2 V is for write operation.

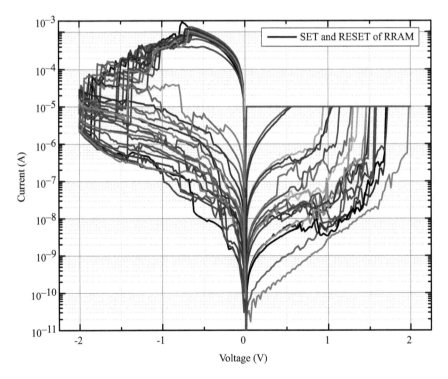

Figure 3.7   Measurement results of an ReRAM hysteresis loop drift in SET and RESET processes

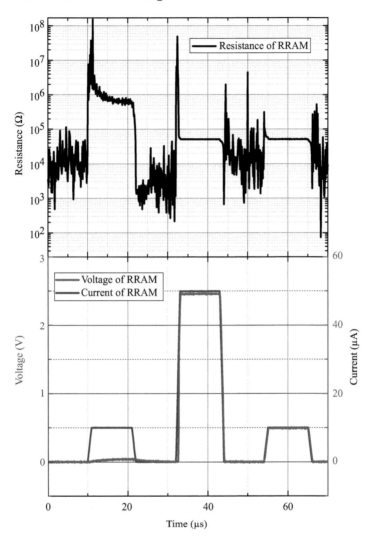

Figure 3.8   Transient measurement results of resistance, voltage and current of a drift ReRAM in SET operation

3.1.2   Diffusive-type ReRAM device

The recent research studies [137,138] have reported a diffusive-type ReRAM device. Different from the common drift-type ReRAM, the initial state of diffusive ReRAMs is always HRS with $\sim G\Omega$ when no external voltage or current is applied. When the input voltage exceeds a threshold value $V_{th,on}$ for a while (e.g., 1 ms), the diffusive ReRAM will switch to LRS with $\sim k\Omega$. After the device switches on, the resistance

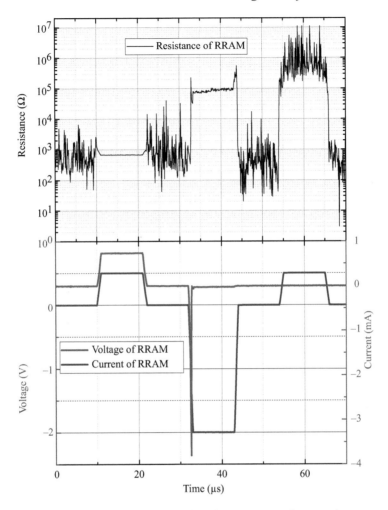

Figure 3.9 *Transient measurement results of resistance, voltage and current of a*
drift ReRAM in RESET operation

will slowly recover back to HRS if the applied voltage drops below another threshold $V_{th,off}$ for about 20 ms. Such a device shows great potentials as an automatically ON/OFF selector. In the following, we use R_{on} and R_{off} to represent the two states of diffusive-type ReRAM.

In most applications, the diffusive ReRAM is connected to a drift ReRAM serially, forming a one-selector-one-ReRAM (1S1R) structure. Such a diffusive ReRAM can work as the synapse emulator [137] and also the selectors [138]. We use SPICE simulation to characterize both of the ReRAMs in Figure 3.10. Here we set $R_{LRS} = 500$ kΩ, $R_{HRS} = 5$ MΩ according to [139] for drift-type ReRAM, and

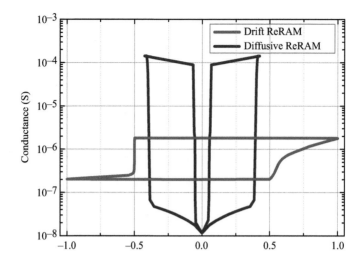

Figure 3.10 Characterization of drift ReRAM and diffusive ReRAM

$R_{on} = 9$ kΩ, $R_{off} = 90$ MΩ, similar to the [138] for diffusive-type ReRAM. In the following sections, the SPICE model is used for 1S1R performance evaluation.

3.2 ReRAM-crossbar structure

As mentioned above, ReRAM is a two-terminal device that can be observed in sub-stoichiometric transition metal oxides (TMO$_s$) sandwiched between metal electrodes. Such a device can be used as nonvolatile memory with state of ion resistance, which results in two nonvolatile states: HRS and LRS. One can change the state from HRS to LRS or vice versa by applying a SET voltage (V_w) or a RESET voltage ($-V_w$).

The two states RHS and LRS represent 0 and 1, respectively. To read a ReRAM cell, one can apply a read voltage V_r to the ReRAM. The V_r and V_w follow

$$V_w > V_{th} > V_w/2 > V_r \tag{3.8}$$

where V_{th} is the threshold voltage of the ReRAM.

Because of the high density of ReRAM device, one can build a crossbar structure as the array of ReRAM [59,140–144]. Such crossbar structure can be utilized as memory for high-density data storage. The memory array can be read or written by controlling the voltage of wordlines (WLs) and bitlines (BLs). For example, we can apply $V_w/2$ on the ith WL and $-V_w/2$ on the jth BL to write data into the ReRAM cell on ith row, jth column.

3.2.1 Analog and digitized ReRAM crossbar

This section introduces the traditional analog ReRAM crossbar and the digitized ReRAM crossbar in the following. The I/O interface and the number of ReRAM device resistance value are different in these two structures.

3.2.1.1 Traditional analog ReRAM crossbar

ReRAM is an emerging nonvolatile memory based on two-terminal junction devices, whose resistance can be controlled by the integral of externally applied currents. The fabric of crossbar intrinsically supports matrix–vector multiplication where vector is represented by row input voltage levels and matrix is denoted by the mesh of ReRAM resistances. In order to calculate the matrix–vector multiplication $y = \Phi x$. As shown in Figure 3.11, by configuring Φ into the ReRAM crossbar and setting x as the crossbar input, the analog computation can be achieved by ReRAM crossbar directly with output y.

However, such an analog ReRAM-crossbar has two major drawbacks. First, the programming of continuous-valued ReRAM resistance is practically challenging due to large ReRAM process variation. Specifically, the ReRAM resistance is determined by the integral of current flowing through the device, which leads to a switching curve as shown in Figure 3.12(a). With the process variation, the curve may shift and leave intermediate values very unreliable to program, as shown in Figure 3.12(b). Second, the analog-to-digital converter (ADC) and digital-to-analog converter (DAC) are both time-consuming and power-consuming. In our simulation, the analog-to-digital and digital-to-analog conversion may consume up to 85.5% of total operation energy in 65 nm as shown in Figure 3.13.

3.2.1.2 Digitalized ReRAM crossbar

To overcome the aforementioned issues, a fully digitalized ReRAM crossbar for matrix-vector multiplication. First, as ON-state and OFF-state are much more reliable

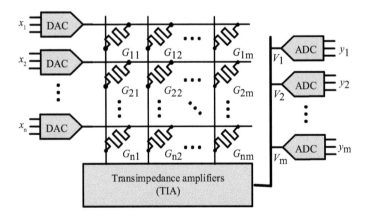

Figure 3.11 Traditional analog-fashion ReRAM crossbar with ADC and DAC

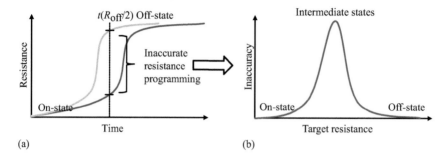

Figure 3.12   (a) Switching curve of ReRAM under device variations.
(b) Programming inaccuracy for different ReRAM target resistances

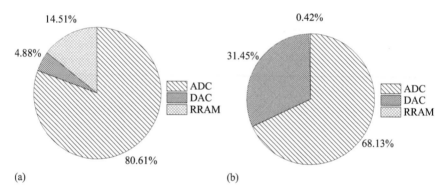

Figure 3.13   (a) Power consumption of analog-fashion ReRAM crossbar. (b) Area consumption of analog-fashion ReRAM crossbar

than intermediate values shown in Figure 3.12, only binary values of ReRAM are allowed to reduce the inaccuracy of ReRAM programming. Second, a pure digital interface without A/D conversion is deployed.

In ReRAM crossbar, We use V_{wl}^i and V_{bl}^j to denote voltage on ith WL and jth BL. R_{LRS} and R_{HRS} denote the resistance of LRS and HRS, respectively. In each sense amplifier (SA), there is a sense resistor R_s with fixed and small resistance. The relation among these three resistance is $R_{HRS} \gg R_{LRS} \gg R_s$. Thus, the voltage on jth BL can be presented by

$$V_{bl}^j = \sum_{i=1}^{m} g_{ij} V_{wl}^i R_s \tag{3.9}$$

where g_{ij} is the conductance of R_{ij}.

The key idea behind digitalized crossbar is the use of comparators. As each column output voltage for analog crossbar is continuous-valued, comparators are used to digitize it according to the reference threshold applied to SA

$$O_j = \begin{cases} 1, & \text{if } V_{bl}^j \geq V_{th}^j \\ 0, & \text{if } V_{bl}^j < V_{th}^j \end{cases} \tag{3.10}$$

However, the issue that rises due to the digitalization of analog voltage value is the loss of information. To overcome this, three techniques can be applied. First, multi-thresholds are used to increase the quantization level so that more information can be preserved. Second, the multiplication operation is decomposed into three suboperations that binary crossbar can well tackle. Third, the thresholds are delicately selected at the region that most information can be preserved after the digitalization.

Compared to the traditional analog ReRAM-crossbar [145,146], the advantages of the digital ReRAM-crossbar are the following:

- It has better programming accuracy of the ReRAM device under process variation with no additional ADC conversation as well.
- Since only LRS and HRS are configured in digital ReRAM crossbar, it does not require high HRS/LRS ratio so that low-power (high LRS) device [139] can be applied. In addition, the wire resistance affects little on IR-drop when using the low-power ReRAM device.
- The binary input voltage has a better robustness on the IR-drop in large-size crossbar.

However, the area and energy consumption of ReRAM devices will increase in the digital ReRAM-crossbar implementation. It will also be discussed in Section 5.

3.2.2 Connection of ReRAM crossbar

There are three approaches for the connection of ReRAM crossbar: direct-connected ReRAM, one-transistor-one-ReRAM (1T1R), and 1S1R. These approaches are described in-detail along with the differences among them.

3.2.2.1 Direct-connected ReRAM

Direct-connected ReRAM, also known as the passive ReRAM array, which is a crossbar structure with only ReRAM devices. Every WL and BL are connected with a single drift-type ReRAM. The structure of direct-connected ReRAM is shown in Figure 3.14(a), and here we use ith WL (WL_i) and jth BL (BL_j) as an example. To perform a write operation, one needs to apply a write voltage V_{write} between WL_i and BL_j. In this case, the ReRAM connecting them ($R_{i,j}$) can be precisely configured.

However, a problem exists in this structure that sneak path may occur. In this example, the purple path is the ideal current path we want to have, but there may be another path identified by green. This path consists of $R_{i-1,j}$, $R_{i-1,j-1}$ and $R_{i,j-1}$ so that we can see a V_{write} is also applied on the serial of these three ReRAMs. In some of the cases, two of them are in LRS and one of them is in HRS, causing a very large voltage applied on the ReRAM device in HRS. In this case, the status of this ReRAM may also be configured, which we do not want it happens.

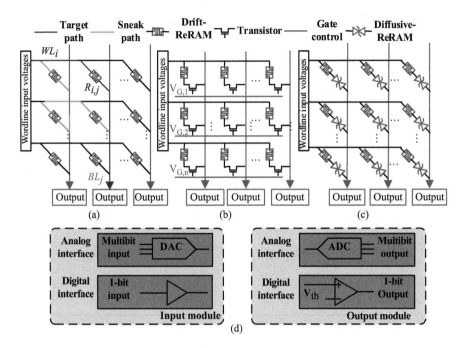

Figure 3.14 Comparison of ReRAM-crossbar implementation among (a) direct connection with sneak path; (b) 1T1R with extra control signals; (c) proposed sneak-path-free 1S1R without extra control signals; (d) comparison of analog and digital interfaces

To overcome the sneak-path issue, a solution is proposed in [147–149] that we can applied a constant voltage on the rest of WLs and BLs. Here, the target WL and BL are applied with $2/V_{\text{write}}$ and $-2/V_{\text{write}}$, respectively. Meanwhile, we also apply 0 V on all the inactive lines. This solution has two requirements for the device and controller design:

- The nonlinearity of ReRAM device should be very good since the device cannot be configured with a $2/V_{\text{write}}$ drop.
- The external CMOS controller needs to output multiple voltages for all lines at the same time. In addition, the amplitude of voltage of all the lines should be independent.

3.2.2.2 One-transistor-one-ReRAM

In 1T1R structure, an NMOS transistor in connected with each ReRAM device serially indicated in [145]. As a result, each WL is connected to a BL with one transistor and one ReRAM, as shown in Figure 3.14(b). The NMOS transistor is used as a voltage-controlled selector so that we can configure the connectivity of each ReRAM cell. The major benefit of 1T1R is to avoid the sneak path in the direct-connected structure.

In Figure 3.14(b), we use one signal to control the transistors connecting to the same WL. It is clear that we only need to apply voltage on the target WL_i, BL_j and only put $V_{G,i}$ to high, only the target cell can be configured. The metric of this structure can be summarized as follows:

- Low requirement on the nonlinearity of ReRAM device because voltage is only applied on the target cell.
- The controller design is much more easier than the direct-connected structure.

However, the 1T1R structure still has a disadvantage that the crossbar array area depends on the transistor, which is not scalable compared to ReRAM device. Therefore, it is not a good option when the size of ReRAM crossbar is large.

3.2.2.3 One-selector-one-ReRAM

A sneak-path-free digital ReRAM-crossbar is shown in Figure 3.14(c). In this architecture, every drift-ReRAM is connected in serial with a diffusive ReRAM as selector. Compared to the previous two implementations, the 1S1R can remain good scalability and eliminate sneak path without additional controllers. Compared to [150], the R_{on} of selector can only affect little to the operation on digital ReRAM. Since $R_{off} \gg R_{HRS}$ as shown in Figure 3.10, the static resistance of 1S1R is almost equal to R_{off}. In addition, the majority of applied voltage is on the selector device when it is OFF. Since each sneak path will connect to at least three 1S1Rs, the operating voltage V only needs to satisfy the following equation to eliminate the sneak path:

$$3V_{th,on} > V > V_{th,on} \tag{3.11}$$

We will further discuss about the simulation results regarding the sneak-path-free effect in Section 7.5.

3.3 ReRAM-based oscillator

Oscillatory behavior in ReRAM device has been observed in [151,152], and it is performed by the forming process of a drift-type ReRAM. The recent diffusive-type ReRAM [137,138] shows the feasibility as oscillators. The ReRAM-based oscillator can be built as shown in Figure 3.15(a). In this ReRAM-based oscillator, a physical resistor R_s is in series with the ReRAM device. The output voltage will depend on the proportion of R_s and ReRAM resistance R_M. With the charge/discharge of capacitor C_M, the output voltage V_{out} will be approaching $\frac{V_{DD} \cdot R_M}{R_M + R_s}$. To make the oscillation work, we have the following requirements for the ReRAM device in the structure:

- At a relatively high voltage V_h, the resistance of the ReRAM R_M decreases significantly to R_l.
- If we drop the voltage to a low value V_l, R_M will increase to R_h.

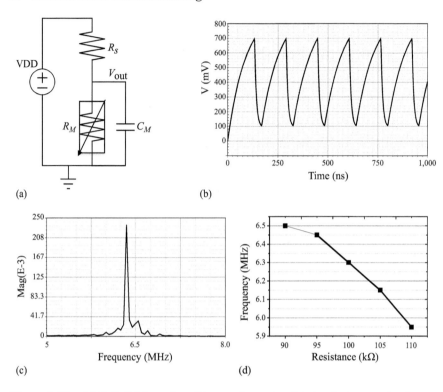

Figure 3.15   (a) ReRAM-based oscillator schematic; (b) simulation result of oscillator; (c) DFT analysis of oscillator; (d) oscillatory frequencies vs. different R_s values

Therefore, we can build up the oscillation if all the parameters in Figure 3.15(a) are well-fitted, following

$$\frac{R_l}{R_l + R_s} < V_l < V_h < \frac{R_h}{R_h + R_s} \qquad (3.12)$$

where R_l and R_h are, respectively, the low resistance and high resistance of the ReRAM device. As a result, R_M and V_{out} cannot be in a static state with the condition stated in (3.12). When the ReRAM turns from R_l to R_h or vice versa, a negative resistance effect is performed. Moreover, the oscillatory frequency is determined by the value of R_s. The ReRAM model for oscillator according to [153] is built for case study, and one can observe the oscillation result in Figure 3.15(b). Figure 3.15(c) shows the Discrete Fourier transform (DFT) analysis of Figure 3.15(b). Figure 3.15(d) shows the oscillatory frequencies vs. different R_s values. With higher R_s, there is less current passing through the oscillator such that the charge/discharge will be slower, resulting in lower oscillatory frequency.

3.4   Write-in scheme for multibit ReRAM storage

3.4.1   ReRAM data storage

Electrical engineers are quite familiar with circuits which include the three basic passive circuit elements—resistor, capacitor and inductor. However, for the first time, in 1971 Leon Chua proposed a fourth circuit element, describing the relation between charge (q) and flux (ϕ) [60]. The resistance of the so-called memristor device depends on the total charge passed through the device [60,154]. In this chapter, we use the terms ReRAM and memristor interchangeably. The device characteristics of the memristor open the floor for many new fields of application [155–159]. One of the most important applications is, as expected, using it as a memory element. For example, [160–162] and others have invested considerable effort in studying the design of memristor-based memory units. The main advantage of using memristors is given by the fact that in a modern chip, the number of transistors required to store data (e.g., in an SRAM) has a significant—and increasing—impact on the total transistor count [163]. In consequence, implementation of new memory architectures by using memristors would decrease the total amount of device leakage current dramatically [161].

Since HP developed the first passive memristor in 2008 [62], there have been works on single-bit [160–162,164] and multibit [165,166] memory storages. The unique $\phi–q$ characteristic of memeristors, however, leads to a nonlinear $v–i$ characteristic, which makes it difficult to determine the pulse size for achieving a certain state [165,166]. Therefore, it has been seen as a problem for multilevel memory designs [165,166]. To overcome this problem, researchers have developed methods, some fairly complicated, which use analog circuits and Opamps for both reading and writing [165,166]. Using Opamps and analog circuits for readout seems to be inevitable [160,165,166]. However, as we will present, the aforementioned characteristic can be taken advantage of, to store more than one bit in memristors, using circuits which are compatible with digital designs. These circuits are hence less complex. Although digital bit streams have been used for setting synaptic values [167], the exact stored value and recovery of the stored value are not of high importance in such applications. In memory applications, on the other hand, this is of paramount importance. Therefore, in this chapter, we discuss the reliability of the storage and readout, as well as how encoding can help improving these parameters.

The rest of this chapter is organized as the following: In the next section, we briefly review the aforementioned unique characteristics of memristor and show how it can be taken advantage of, in order to store more than one bit in each memristor. In Section 3.4.3, we present the digital writing method for storing two bits of data on a single memristor, as well as the readout circuit. Then, in Section 3.4.4, we show the results of our simulations which confirm the feasibility of the proposed approach. In Section 3.4.5, we improve the reliability of the storage, and the number of stored bits, using different proposed encoding schemes, especially regarding practical implementations and further verification of the proposed approach.

3.4.2　*Multi-threshold resistance for data storage*

It is a well-established phenomenon in the literature that the resistance of a memristor depends on the charge flown through it [60,168]. This can be modeled in various ways, one of the most prominent of which is [168]:

$$R(q(t)) = R_{\text{off}} + \frac{R_{\text{on}} - R_{\text{off}}}{e^{-4k_m(q(t)+q_0)} + 1} \tag{3.13}$$

where R_{off} and R_{on} are the maximum and minimum resistance of the memristor, and $q(t)$ is the charge flown through the memristor with the initial value of q_0. Finally, k_m is a constant which represents physical characteristics of the device such as doping of the semiconductor and its size.

According to (3.13), not only the resistance, but also changes of the resistance in a memristor due to identical voltage pulses depend on its current state [165,169]. This characteristic seen as a hardship [165,166] can be turned into an opportunity based on the following theorem.

Theorem: *Distinct output resistances correspond to distinct input patterns, which allows storage of more than one bit in a single memristor.*

Short Proof*: Assume two distinct states A and B, seen in Figure 3.16, with unequal resistance of R_x, where $x \subset \{A, B\}$. Now, we are interested in finding out the ratio of resistance change at these two points, due to the application of an input voltage pulse with the amplitude of V and width of T. Based on Ohm's law, we have

$$V = R(q(t))\frac{dq}{dt} \tag{3.14}$$

where $R(q(t))$ of the memristor is given by (3.13). Solving this equation is rather complicated and out of the scope of this chapter. Therefore, in a simplified manner, we estimate the changes of resistance at each point by its slope, m_x. In other words, in the vicinity of point x, we estimate (3.13) by

$$R(q) = -m_x q + R_x \tag{3.15}$$

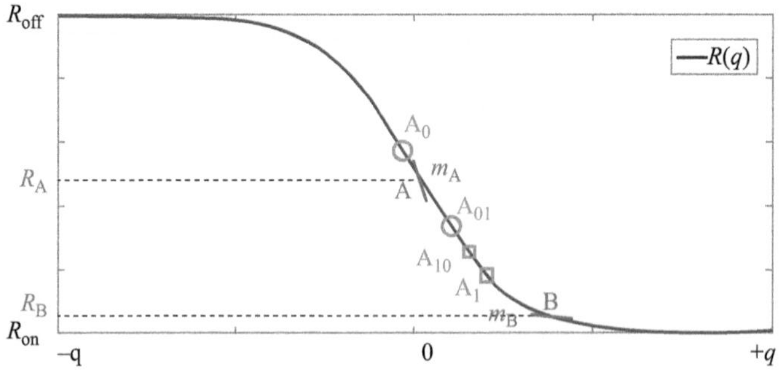

Figure 3.16　Resistance of a memristor as a function of the charge stored in it

---

*The full proof is provided in [169]. We kindly ask the readers to refer to that paper for more information on details.

By substituting (3.15) into (3.14), and integrating over the period, T, we have [169]

$$\rightarrow \quad Vdt = Rdq = (-m_x q + R_x)dq$$

$$\rightarrow \quad \int_0^T Vdt = \int_0^{dq_x} (-m_x q + R_x)dq$$

$$\rightarrow \quad VT = \frac{-m_x}{2}(dq_x)^2 + R_x dq_x \tag{3.16}$$

Solving (3.16), we obtain

$$dq_x = \frac{R_x}{m_x}K_x \tag{3.17}$$

where

$$K_x = 1 + \sqrt{1 - \frac{2m_x VT}{R_x^2}} \tag{3.18}$$

On the other hand, we can easily infer from (3.15) that $\frac{dR_x}{dq_x} = -m_x$. Based on this, the ratio of resistance change due to charge change at point A and B is

$$\frac{dR_A}{dq_A} \bigg/ \frac{dR_B}{dq_B} = \frac{m_A}{m_B} \rightarrow \frac{dR_A}{dR_B} = \frac{R_A K_A}{R_B K_B} \tag{3.19}$$

This shows how the change of resistance of memristors at different stages due to identical pulses depends on its state (resistance) at the time. This ratio could be further simplified and approximated to the resistance ratio only [169].

Now, assuming that a positive pulse presents "1" and a negative pulse presents "0," if a memristor is fed by a positive input pulse followed by a negative input pulse ("10"), it will reach a different state ("A_{10}"), compared to the case where the negative pulse is applied before the positive pulse ("01" and hence A_{01}). The rationale behind it is that the resistance change due to an initial negative pulse (A to A_0) is different compared to the resistance change due to the same pulse, once the state of memristor has changed due to a previous positive pulse (A_1 to A_{10}). The same holds for changes due to positive pulses in two different states (A_0 to A_{01} versus A to A_1). Therefore, we can conclude that, since the states of the memristor after application of "01" and "10" are different, based on the state of the memristor, its original input can be retrieved [169]. This will be verified in the next section.

3.4.3 Write and read

Based on the aforementioned concept, in this section, we present our read and write method and simulate them in Section 3.4.4, to test the feasibility of successfully recovering a data value which was stored through digital streaming. For the array architecture, isolation and access to the memory cell, a 1T1R architecture similar to [166] is assumed. Since the Opamp (comparator) is the crucial part of the circuit determining the feasibility and reliability of this implementation, we have used a model of an existing off-the-shelf Opamp, namely LT1012, which takes into account nonideal characteristics such as offset.

3.4.3.1   Write-in method

As previously discussed in order to distinguish the "1" input and "0" input, respectively, positive and negative pulses are used, which can be implemented through simple switches to reference voltages. This eliminates the need for the complex circuit proposed in [165] or the DAC used in [166]. The magnitude of these pulses for the current experiment is 0.5 V and the pulse widths are 10 ms. The inputs were applied based on the most-significant-bit first and the least-significant-bit last.

Table 3.2 shows the data to be stored and the resulting state of the memristor (resistance) due to these inputs. This table shows that, as expected, different input data patterns lead to different states for the memristor. Similar to [166], the thermometer readout codes at this column can be later converted to the normal binary representation (similar to the left-most column) using simple digital logic circuits. Only one instance of such a circuit will be necessary for each memory block containing hundreds to thousands of memristor cells. Therefore, the cost of the additional hardware is negligible.

3.4.3.2   Readout method

For retrieving the stored data, [160] uses an Opamp-based circuit, [166] uses an ADC, and [165] uses a circuit inspired by ADCs. In this chapter, as shown in Figure 3.17, we also use a circuit inspired by flash ADCs. In this circuit, after the inputs are applied and the data are stored in the memristor, the input source is disconnected. Then, after applying a controlled current pulse (here a rectangular pulse with the magnitude of 1 µA and width of 1 ms), the resulting voltage across the memristor is buffered and fed to three comparator circuits (only one of which is shown at the bottom of Figure 3.17, for simplicity). The voltage across the memristor is then compared with the voltage produced by applying a similar current pulse to predetermined resistance values. If the voltage across the predetermined resistors (R_i) is greater than the voltage read from the memristor, the comparator will flip to high output and a "1" will be stored in the respective flip-flop output (RD_i). This implies that the resistance of the cell is below the respective resistor, R_i.

We note that the readout current pulse is chosen to be significantly smaller than input pulses, so that it would have a smaller effect on the state of the memristor. Nevertheless, however small this effect is, it needs to be compensated for. Therefore, similar to [160,166], by applying another controlled pulse in the reverse direction, this

Table 3.2   *Data to be stored on the memristor, resulting states and expected unencoded readouts*

Data	R_{mem} (kΩ)	Exp. readout
"00"	5.213	"000"
"01"	5.108	"001"
"10"	4.890	"011"
"11"	4.778	"111"

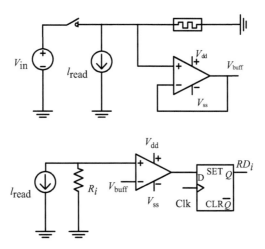

Figure 3.17 For reading out, V_{buff} is fed to three comparators connected to D flip-flops which provide RD_i bits (for simplicity, only one set is depicted)

effect can be compensated for. The advantage of using current pulses, compared to the voltage pulses used in [160,166], is that the effect of positive and negative current pulses on the resistance change will be similar, whereas as proved in Section 3.4.2, it is not the case for voltage pulses. That is, a negative voltage pulse, due to inherent characteristics of the memristor and its nonlinear voltage–current relationship, cannot precisely compensate a positive voltage pulse and will leave residual extra charges (positive or negative). Therefore, the state of memristor needs to be checked and more often refreshed to compensate the residual charges as well.

Using current sources, as proposed here, the complex method of readout effect elimination is reduced to an automatic compensation through a reverse current pulse, which is considerably simpler than the one used in [165]. Automatic refreshing may lead to extra power consumption; however, it eliminates the state-read operation or counting process for the refreshing proposed in [166]. Therefore, it is going to be simpler. We note that this technique may not prove efficient for all types of memristor technologies (e.g., for non-TiO$_2$ memristors) or scenarios (e.g., for power-constrained applications). Therefore, in order to compensate for the destructive effect of uncompensated readouts (for power critical applications or where this technique is not efficient), other scenarios, as discussed in [166], can be employed to compensate for the readout effect.

3.4.4 Validation

In order to evaluate the practicality of the proposed approach in storing data in memristors, we have simulated the proposed circuit in LTSPICE. We have used the most prominent model (namely, Biolek's [168]) of TiO$_2$ memristors, described by

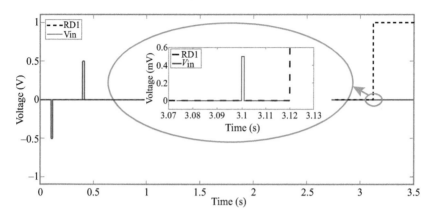

Figure 3.18   Simulation results for "01" input. Shortly after applying the readout current at 3.1 s (zoomed in), the output of RD_1 flips to "1" representing the stored data. RD_0 and RD_2 remained zero and are not shown for simplicity

(3.13). The following values were used for the model parameters (as given by the authors [168]); $R_{on} = 100$ Ω, $R_{off} = 10$ kΩ, $k_m = 10,000$ and $R_{init} = 5$ kΩ. Input signals last 10 and 1 ms, respectively, for input voltages and readout current pulses. The amplitudes are ±0.5 V for "1" and "0" input pulses and −1 µA for readout current pulses. The value of R_i resistors used in this set of simulations are 5,170, 5,130 and 5,010 Ω for i =1, 2 and 3, respectively.

Comparators and their precision play a crucial role in the practical implementation of the readout circuit, which determine to what level the small differences between states can be distinguished. To account for their nonidealities, we have used the model for an off-the-shelf Opamp, namely LT1012 (with 25 µV maximum offset). This ascertains that the assumed values for parameters such as offset are realistic and accounted, i.e., this circuit can—in practice also—perform as expected.

Figure 3.18 shows the result of simulation for a sample case, namely "01" input. In this figure, the blue curve shows the voltage across the memristor (namely V_{in}) and the black curve shows the RD_1 output. For simplicity, RD_2 and RD_3 which as expected remained zero during the whole simulation are not shown. As we can see, shortly after applying the readout current at 3.1 s (zoomed-in area) the output of RD_1 turns to "1."

This and other simulations for all outputs satisfied the expected outputs as shown in Table 3.2, where the expected outputs represent "RD_3 & RD_2 & RD_1" combination. Once these values are obtained, different inputs are distinguished properly and with simple logic circuits, these outputs can be turned into binary values once again. This proof of concept confirms the feasibility of digital streaming approach for storing, and successfully retrieving two bits of information on a single memristor.

Table 3.3   Resistance for memristors with different ranges of
memristance. M_1: 0.1–10 $k\Omega$ and M_2: 0.5–100 $k\Omega$

Input	R_{M_1} (kΩ)	R_{M_2} (kΩ)
"000"	7.2453	47.2428
"001"	5.8991	28.9629
"010"	5.8997	28.9710
"011"	3.9089	5.0033
"100"	5.8990	28.9600
"101"	3.9078	4.9898
"110"	3.9088	5.0014
"111"	1.0396	0.5000

3.4.5   Encoding and 3-bit storage

In this section, we present the impact of the range of the memristor and the encoding of data on the reliability of the readout.

3.4.5.1   Exploration of the memristance range

Trying to store 3 bits or more in a single memristor can have a negative impact on the reliability of the readout, due to smaller differences between resistances at different states. Expanding the range of the memristor (between R_{on} and R_{off}) helps in reducing the relative sensitivity. Although the relative difference in memristance between inputs with the same number of ones or zeros can be thus improved, this improvement is not necessarily proportional to the expansion of the range.

For example, in a memristor with a range of 100 Ω–10 kΩ, if the difference between "10" and "01" is 10 Ω, in a memristor with a range of 1–100 kΩ, the difference—according to our simulations—can be 17 Ω. This is validated in our simulations, where two memristors are considered: memristor 1 (M_1) with the range of 0.1–10 kΩ and memristor 2 (M_2) with the range of 0.5–100 kΩ. The pulse width is set to 100 ms, and the amplitudes are set to ± 0.5 V for "1" and "0" inputs. Initial state of memristor is assumed to be 5 kΩ. Table 3.3 presents the memristance value for different 3-bit data patterns.

For instance, the memristance difference between "011" and "101" is 1 Ω for M_1, whereas it is 14 Ω for M_2. This indicates that inputs with the same number of ones or zeros can be differentiated easier in the memristor with a wider resistance range.

Although in this way the difference is increased, it is yet small and requires complex complementary circuits, such as the one used in [165], to set the values precisely. It also needs precise comparators, such as the one assumed in [166], to read the values out. To alleviate the problem of close resistance at different states, and in order to improve reliability without using analog write-in circuits or extra circuits with extensive complexity for the readout operation, we propose two encoding schemes. These techniques lead to a significantly higher relative memristance difference between inputs with the same number of ones and zeros. As the number of memristors are not increased with encoding, the area of the memory remains constant, except for the addition of an encoder for the whole system (which is a memory block with hundreds to thousands of memory cells). Therefore, the area used for the encoder is considerably negligible.

3.4.5.2   Uniform input encoding

In the first scheme, we employ a simple encoding method. In this technique, we append the most significant bit (MSB) to the end of the input, as shown in Figure 3.19. In other words, input "100" is encoded as "1001." The simulation setup is the same as stated values earlier in Section 3.4.4, with memristor M_1 chosen for simulation, and initial memristance set to 5 kΩ. Tables 3.4 and 3.5 show the effect of encoding for 2-bit input and 3-bit input data, respectively.

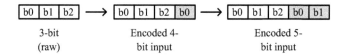

Figure 3.19   Uniform input encoding of 3-bit input data to 4-bit and 5-bit data

Table 3.4   Memristance for 2-bit input with uniform encoding

Input	Raw (kΩ)	Encoded value (kΩ)	Encoding scheme
"00"	6.6384	7.2453	"00**0**"
"01"	5.0005	5.8998	"01**0**"
"10"	4.99955	3.9079	"10**1**"
"11"	2.5919	1.0396	"11**1**"

Bold represent additional encoded bits.

Table 3.5   Memristance for 3-bit input with two different uniform encoding schemes

Input	Raw (kΩ)	Encoded to 4-bit (kΩ)	Encoding scheme	Encoded to 5-bit (kΩ)	Encoding scheme
"000"	7.2453	7.7431	"000**0**"	8.1511	"000**00**"
"001"	5.8991	6.6384	"001**0**"	7.2451	"001**00**"
"010"	5.8997	6.6389	"010**0**"	5.9002	"010**01**"
"011"	3.9089	5.0004	"011**0**"	3.9095	"011**01**"
"100"	5.8990	4.9996	"100**1**"	5.8968	"100**10**"
"101"	3.9078	2.5906	"101**1**"	3.9073	"101**10**"
"110"	3.9088	2.5919	"110**1**"	1.0404	"110**11**"
"111"	1.0396	0.1000	"111**1**"	0.1000	"111**11**"

Table 3.4 presents the memristance for raw input data and encoded data. Originally, the memristance difference between "01" and "10" is nearly 1 Ω, whereas when encoded to 3 bits, the relative memristance is nearly 1.9 kΩ. As such, larger implementation errors (such as inaccuracy of reference values) and variations (of fabrication, implementation or between different cells) can be tolerated. In [166], a potential of up to 6% physical variation in fabrication process is observed and in [165], 10% memristance variation is assumed. However, given that the minimum distance between the memristance states after the proposed encoding is 19% (whereas it was 0.2% before), a flawless operation despite those variations is expected.

Similarly, the effect of encoding on 3-bit data is presented in Table 3.5. Here, we show the memristance when the 3-bit data is encoded to 4-bit, and 5-bit (N.B., in this case first *two* MSB bits are appended to the end of the data). From Table 3.5, we can see that the memristance difference between the two inputs of "001" and "100" for the raw (3-bit), encoded to 4-bit and encoded to 5-bit data, is, respectively, 0.1 Ω, 1.64 kΩ and 1.4 kΩ. However, if we notice, the relative memristance difference between "001" and "010," when encoded to 4-bit, is <1 Ω. This is because the appended bits for both are the same. This difference is larger between these two inputs in the case of 5-bit encoded data. Simply because the appended bits in this case are not the same anymore. Nonetheless, in some instances, the values are still significantly close to each other which endangers a reliable retrieval of the stored data. Hence, further improvements as it follows are necessary.

3.4.5.3 Nonuniform encoding

To address the problem of close values and similar appended bits in the uniform encoding scenario, we propose another encoding scheme, shown in Table 3.6. In this scenario, appendices were selected not based on the two MSBs, but rather such that the distance between all states is maximized. To this end, some bits are appended with two bits, some with one and some with none.

As we see in Table 3.6, using the new encoding scheme, the minimum difference between all inputs is increased to 905.6 Ω, whereas it was previously only 0.5 Ω in the 4-bit encoding scheme and 2.2 Ω in the 5-bit encoding scheme shown in Table 3.5.

Table 3.6   Memristance for 3-bit input with nonuniform encoding, where "−" presents no input application

Input	Raw (kΩ)	Encoded value (kΩ)	Encoding scheme
"000"	7.2453	8.1511	"00000"
"001"	5.8991	5.8991	"001--"
"010"	5.8997	7.2455	"01000"
"011"	3.9089	3.9089	"011--"
"100"	5.8990	4.9996	"1001-"
"101"	3.9078	2.5906	"1011-"
"110"	3.9088	1.0404	"11011"
"111"	1.0396	0.1000	"1111-"

This minimum distance being always larger than 11% shows that potential physical and fabrication variations mentioned in [165,166] can be tolerated by the system. Hence, using this nonuniform encoding scheme, three bits of data can be digitally streamed to a single memristor and the stored values can be reliably recovered using the readout circuit presented in Section 3.4.3.

3.5   Logic functional units with ReRAM

Based on the characteristics of the ReRAM, we construct the logic gates using ReRAMs. This section first presents the logic OR gate, followed by AND gates.

3.5.1   OR gate

Inspired from [170,171], a logic OR gate is presented here. The logic OR gate using ReRAMs consists of two forward polarized memristor (FPM) ReRAMs, with one input for each ReRAM and the "minus" nodes of ReRAMs are joined together with a load at the output. The ReRAM-based OR gate is shown in Figure 3.20(a). The ReRAMs act as voltage divider circuit for the input, whose output voltage is given by (3.20) [171].

$$V_{\text{out}} = \frac{M_b}{M_a + M_b} V_a + \frac{M_a}{M_a + M_b} V_b \qquad (3.20)$$

where M_a and M_b are the memristance of ReRAM A and B, respectively, and V_a and V_b represent the input voltages for ReRAMs A and B, respectively. The operation of gate is explained using the following three cases.

    Case 1: Input "00": When the input on ReRAMs A and B are logic 0, both the ReRAMs will be in HRS due to FPM characteristics (R_{OFF}). The output voltage becomes same as the input, i.e., logic 0.

    Case 2: Input "01": When the input at the ReRAM A is logic 0 ($V_a = 0$), ReRAM A will be in HRS, i.e., OFF state (R_{OFF}) and the input logic 1 at ReRAM B ($V_a = 1$) makes the ReRAM to ON state, i.e., R_{ON}. The output voltage based on (3.20) is modified to

$$V_{\text{out}} = \frac{M_a}{M_a + M_b} V_b \approx V_b \qquad (3.21)$$

Thus, the output voltage is high. A similar operation is expected for "10" input.

    Case 3: Input "11": When both the inputs are high, the ReRAMs will be in LRS (R_{ON}) and a logic one (input) appears at the output load, as per (3.20).

3.5.2   AND gate

Logic AND gates are designed similar to OR gates, but the ReRAMs are placed in RPM condition. Figure 3.20(b) shows the construction of AND gate using ReRAMs. The output voltage is given by (3.20). Similar to OR gate, the operation of AND gate is explained under three cases.

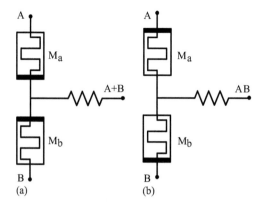

Figure 3.20   Logic gates: (a) OR gate; (b) AND gate

Case 1: Input "00": When the input "0" is applied to a ReRAMs in RPM, both the ReRAMs are forced to switch ON simultaneously and has a resistance of R_{ON}. The output voltage becomes same as the input, i.e., logic "0."

Case 2: Input "01": When logic input "0" is applied to ReRAM A and logic "1" to ReRAM B, ReRAM B will be OFF state ($M_b=R_{OFF}$) and ReRAM A in ON state ($M_a=R_{ON}$). As such, the first term in (3.20) is neglected and the output voltage is given by

$$V_{out} = \frac{M_a}{M_a + M_b} V_b \approx 0 \qquad (3.22)$$

As $R_{OFF} \gg R_{ON}$, the output voltage is close to zero, i.e., logic 0. If the negative voltage indicates logic 0, the value of V_{out} will be $-V_b$, which indicates logic zero. The same is applicable for input "10."

Case 3: Input "11": When both the inputs are high, output voltage becomes input voltage as per (3.20), i.e., logic 1.

It needs to be noted that the presented logic gates are inspired from [170,171]. In [170], the output load is not considered in the circuit, which has quite significant impact on the behavior. Whereas, in [171], the outputs are distinguished as logic "1" or "0" based on the state of ReRAM (R_{ON}, R_{OFF}) rather than the output voltages.

3.6   ReRAM for logic operations

As mentioned in the Introduction, using an memory element for storing as well as processing (logic) will help in reducing area overhead and increase in on-chip memory. In this section, we propose such a circuit, which will be used for logic as well as for storage purpose. The designed circuit is based on the logic circuits designed in Section 3.5. As an illustrative example, we show the ReRAM-based OR gate-cum-memory here.

Figure 3.21 shows the OR gate with two ReRAMs, which can be used for multi-purpose, i.e., as a ReRAM for data storage and as an OR computational element for the data stored in ReRAMs. The input for the ReRAMs is provided by the sources V_1 and V_2. To perform the logic operation (OR in this case), switches S_1 and S_2 are closed and with disconnected current source. The output of the OR gate can be clearly observed across the load, resistor R_1. The load resistor R_L can be replaced with another ReRAM-based circuit.

To use the ReRAMs for the purpose of storage, switches S_3 and S_4 are left open (disconnect). It needs to be noted that source (V_1, V_2) must be connected to ReRAM before performing read operation. The stored data can be read from by disconnecting sources and connecting the current source. To optimize the design, one readout circuit voltage-controlled capacitors can be used to connect to ReRAMs and data can be read in time-multiplexed manner. It needs to be noted that, for the purpose of illustration, OR-based circuit is presented, and in the similar manner, other gates can also be realized.

3.6.1 Simulation settings

A wide variety of models are proposed to characterize the ReRAM operation; however, in this chapter, we use the model proposed in [168,172], which is built based on the physical construction. The threshold-switching type model in [172] is stated to be tolerant to variations [173]. The α, β, R_{on}, R_{off} and R_{init} for the threshold model in [172] is set as 1e6, 0, 100, 390 and 100, respectively. It needs to be noted that R_{on}

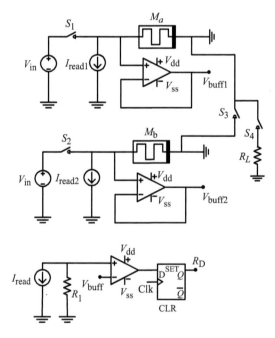

Figure 3.21   Two input ReRAM OR gate output

and R_{off} denote the values in terms of charge, which is different from the resistance states. For the ideal ReRAM model in [168], the R_{on}, R_{off} and R_{init} are set as 100 Ω, 10 kΩ and 5 kΩ, respectively. The Opamp used for reading out the ReRAM is LT1012. The simulations are performed in PSPICE and LTSPICE on a CPU running at 2.66 GHz with 8 GB RAM. To demonstrate the working capability of the ReRAM, we considered the pulse widths of 5 and 10 ms. Simulations can as well be performed at ns scale, but with the proper tuning of the parameters. Majorly α needs to be tuned, as suggested by Vourkas, who built the threshold-switching ReRAM model.

3.6.2 ReRAM-based circuits

In this subsection, we will present the operational characteristics of ReRAM-based logic gates and readout circuit.

3.6.2.1 Logic operations

The ReRAM-based OR gate is simulated in PSPICE. The load resistor is set as 10 kΩ. The pulse width of input is set as 5 ms. The output of the ReRAM-based OR gate is shown in Figure 3.22.

In a similar manner, the simulation result for ReRAM-based AND gate is presented in Figure 3.23. It needs to be noted that the pulse width is kept sufficiently long for better understanding.

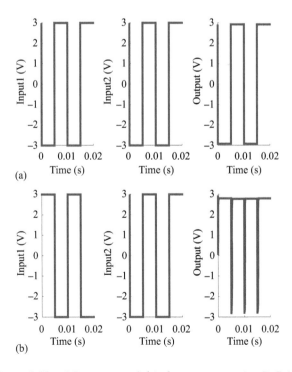

Figure 3.22   OR gate-cum-2-bit data storage using ReRAMs

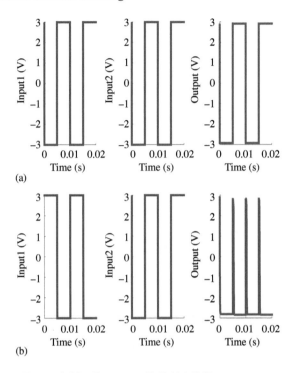

Figure 3.23 Two input ReRAM AND gate output

3.6.2.2 Readout circuit

Here we will present the output of the readout circuit proposed in Section 3.4.3.2. The simulations are carried out in LTSPICE with ideal ReRAM model developed in [168]. The same can be carried out using the threshold switching ReRAM model in [172]. However, due to large number of variables, users need to take care of convergence issues and SPICE can take longer time.

For the purpose of readout, the input current pulses of smaller amplitude −1 μA is used, so that the data stored in ReRAM is not changed. The pulse width is set to 10ms. Logic "1" and "0" are set as +3 V and −3 V, respectively. The output of readout circuit in case of Logic "0" and "1" is shown in Figure 3.24. One needs to observe that when the input is logic "1," the output obtained is +1 V, whereas when the stored bit is logic "0," the output is 0 V. These output values can be predetermined and the Opamp can be tuned to provide those voltage levels for corresponding logic "1" and "0."

3.6.3 ReRAM as a computational unit-cum-memory

For the ease of understanding, the simulation results of ReRAM as OR gate-cum-memory is presented here. Simulation results using the ideal model of a ReRAM is

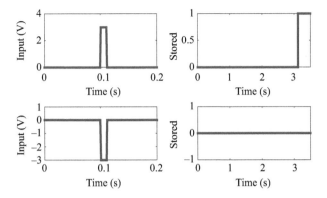

Figure 3.24   Value obtained from read-out circuit for logic 1 and 0

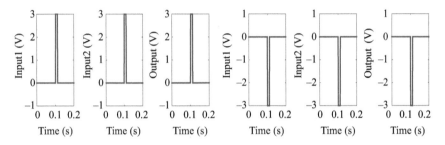

Figure 3.25   OR gate operation with ReRAM for inputs '11' and '00'

shown, for the ease of replication by the readers and face no convergence issues due to large number of variables in threshold-type switching models. The input data is provided to the ReRAM during first 0.5 s, i.e., logic 1 is provided to one of the ReRAM and logic 0 to the other, as represented by waveforms *inp1*, *inp2* in Figure 3.25. The logic operation is performed first, and the corresponding result is shown by the waveform *op1*. The readout of ReRAM is then carried out, and the readout data from each of ReRAMs is represented in waveforms *Rop1* and *Rop2*, which indicates logic 1 and 0, respectively.

It needs to be noted that the readout is performed after logic operation, to show that the readout operation by the proposed circuit did not destroy the stored data. Further, with the proper alignment of readout switches, one readout circuit can be used to read multiple ReRAMs in a serial manner.

Part II

Machine learning accelerators

Chapter 4

The background of machine learning algorithms

This chapter provides an introduction to the machine learning algorithms along with the optimization techniques. We first introduce support vector machines (SVMs) followed by neural networks and their variants. The applications considered as basis to illustrate these algorithms are the classification problems.

4.1   SVM-based machine learning

SVM is a supervised learning model with associated learning algorithms that analyze data used for classification and regression analysis. Given a set of training samples, each marked for belonging to one of two categories (considering binary classification problem), an SVM training algorithm builds a model that assigns new examples into one category or the other, making it a non-probabilistic binary linear classifier. An SVM model is a representation of the samples as points/coordinates in space, mapped so that the samples of the separate categories are distinguished with an observable/separable boundary that is as wide as possible. New incoming samples are then mapped onto the same space and predicted to belong to a category based on which side of the boundary they fall on.

In a nutshell, SVM is a binary classifier (can be extended to multiclass) that seeks the maximum-margin separating hyperplane from training samples. The type of SVMs may be different depending on the property of data. For a data that can be linearly separated, a linear SVM as shown in Figure 4.1(a) can be applied, where one can observe the distinguishing boundary. Otherwise, if the data cannot be linearly separated, a nonlinear SVM in Figure 4.1(b) is required. Nonlinear SVMs can efficiently distinguish complex data sets compared to techniques such as regression.

As traditional SVM only provides binary classification, it is not feasible to classify multiple labels with one SVM. Therefore, multiple SVMs are needed for complex applications such as fingerprint recognition, as shown in Figure 4.2. The test images need to go through several classifiers before SVM provides the classification result. To achieve higher performance, every SVM (at different stages) needs to provide the correct classification. This indicates the requirement to have high precision SVMs at each stage.

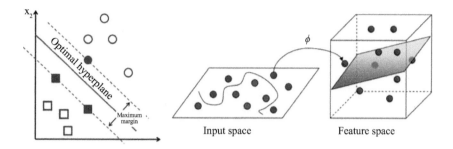

Figure 4.1   Demonstration of (a) linear SVM; (b) nonlinear SVM

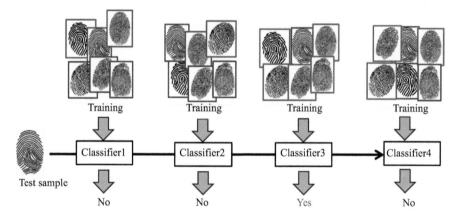

Figure 4.2   Fingerprint recognition by multiple SVMs

4.2   Single-layer feedforward neural network-based machine learning

In addition to SVM, there exist numerous techniques for multiclass classification. One of the prominent techniques that achieved significant success in analyzing and classifying complex data sets is the neural network. The neural networks are considered to be mammalian brain-inspired technique stemming through the utilization of artificial neurons and exploiting their interconnectivity to perform complex tasks. Given numerous available variants of neural networks, we describe prominent and widely utilized architectures and techniques here.

4.2.1   Single-layer feedforward network

Present-day data analytics is mainly based on machine learning algorithms to build a model to correlate the input data with targeted output. Feature extraction from the data is performed through the neurons and their connectivity to extract the key information for data analytics in a neural network. Neural network is a popular model to utilize for data analytics applications [174] and usually has two computational phases: training and testing. In the training phase, the weight coefficients of the neural network model, i.e., weights determining the connectivity between neurons are determined by minimizing the error between the trial and the targeted using the training input data through backpropagation technique. In the testing phase, the neural network with determined coefficients is utilized for the classification of the new testing data.

However, the input data could be of high dimension with redundant information. To facilitate the training and minimize the redundancy in the information, feature extraction is usually needed performed to represent the characteristic data with redundancy and/or dimension reduction.

Despite reduction in the features, the training time of neural networks when applied with large amounts of data is extremely high. To speed up the training process, one needs to tackle the challenges from two perspectives. First, a general incremental machine learning architecture with the minimal tuning of parameters is seen as a solution to speed up the training phase. The proposed single-layer feedforward network (SLFN) is shown in Figure 4.3, which is mainly based on incremental least-squares (LS) solution. Second, analyzing the key complexity of each learning step and optimizing towards a hardware friendly algorithm to explore the parallelism with minimized hardware operational complexity is another solution towards enhancing the training process. As the computations on hardware are much faster compared to that of software, exploiting the parallelism in hardware significantly speeds up the training process. Feature extraction from the input data is a pivotal process in performing classification and prediction operations, followed by learning of the data distribution.

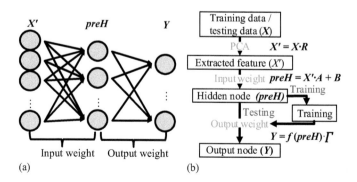

Figure 4.3 (a) *Single-layer neural network.* (b) *General flow of neural network training and testing*

4.2.1.1 Feature extraction

In general, the features from the original data $\mathbf{X}$ are extracted by projection,

$$\mathbf{X}' = \mathbf{R} \cdot \mathbf{X} \tag{4.1}$$

where $\mathbf{X}'$ is the extracted feature. The projection matrix $\mathbf{R}$ can be found with the use of principal/singular components, random embedding or convolution [175]. Projection matrix $\mathbf{R}$ is computed off-line and used for dimension reduction. One can treat $\mathbf{R}$ as a new basis to represent the columns of $\mathbf{X}$, and remove those small redundant values to minimize the total squared reconstruction error as

$$\min \|\mathbf{X}' - \mathbf{R} \cdot \mathbf{X}\|_2 \tag{4.2}$$

One can observe intensive matrix–vector multiplications during the feature extraction as shown in (4.1).

This chapter also introduces a different feature extraction approach in this section. As a step towards feature extraction, the first step is to compress raw data with reduced complexity. Image patches (subset of an image) represent small groups of nearby pixels, which are commonly used for image feature extraction. For instance, a 6×6 square pixel patch is moving across the whole input image with a step of 1 pixel and further is encoded by unsupervised learned dictionary $\mathbf{D}$ to form patches-based image representation. Pooling is performed by summing up the quarter of encoded patches to form image features for classifier. Here, the presented analysis is mainly based on SLFN but it can be also extended to linear classifiers such as LS-SVM.

The learning dictionary $\mathbf{D}$ is determined from sparse coding, based on orthogonal matching pursuit (OMP) technique, where the key complexity arises from the incremental LS problem. After building the dictionary $\mathbf{D}$, encoding for image patch x is performed based on soft threshold α as follows:

$$f_j = \{\max(0, \mathbf{D}^T x - \alpha), \ \max(0, -\mathbf{D}^T x - \alpha)\} \tag{4.3}$$

where $j \in [0 \ k]$ and n is the number of basis of learning dictionary $\mathbf{D}$. α is a fixed threshold and $\{f_0, f_1, \ldots, f_k\}$ forms a patch in image representation. Therefore, in the feature learning, one can observe that the matrix–vector multiplication and sorting are the major computations.

4.2.1.2 Neural network-based learning

After feature extraction, one can perform various machine learning algorithms [53, 176,177] for data analytics. As shown in Figure 4.3, for a typical neural network model, one needs to determine the network weights from training and then perform testing (inference). Let n represent the number of features with training input $X_f \in R^{N \times n}$, where N is the training data size. The extracted feature will be input to the neural network with the following relationship for the first layer output **preH**:

$$\mathbf{preH} = \mathbf{X}_f \mathbf{A} + \mathbf{B}, \ \mathbf{H} = g(\mathbf{preH}) = \frac{1}{1 + e^{-\mathbf{preH}}} \tag{4.4}$$

where $\mathbf{A} \in \mathbb{R}^{n \times L}$ and $\mathbf{B} \in \mathbb{R}^{N \times L}$ are randomly generated input weight and bias formed by a_{ij} and b_{ij} between $[-1, 1]$; $\mathbf{H}$ is the hidden-layer output matrix generated from the Sigmoid function $g(\cdot)$ for activation.

The intention of training a neural network is to minimize the error with an objective function, mathematically defined as

$$\min_{\Gamma} \; ||\mathbf{H}\Gamma - \mathbf{T}||_2^2 + \eta |||\Gamma||_2^2 \tag{4.5}$$

where η is the regularized parameter and $\mathbf{T}$ is the label of training data.

One can solve (4.5) either by iterative backward propagation method [178] or direct L2-norm solver method for LS problem [53]. The output weight can be obtained as $||\tilde{\mathbf{H}}\Gamma - \tilde{\mathbf{T}}||$, and can be solved as

$$\Gamma = (\tilde{\mathbf{H}}^T \tilde{\mathbf{H}})^{-1} \tilde{\mathbf{H}}^T \tilde{\mathbf{T}} = (\mathbf{H}^T \mathbf{H} + \eta \mathbf{I})^{-1} \mathbf{H}^T \mathbf{T}$$

$$\text{where } \tilde{\mathbf{H}} = \begin{pmatrix} \mathbf{H} \\ \sqrt{\eta} \cdot \mathbf{I} \end{pmatrix}, \quad \tilde{\mathbf{T}} = \begin{pmatrix} \mathbf{T} \\ \mathbf{0} \end{pmatrix} \tag{4.6}$$

Here $\tilde{\mathbf{H}} \in \mathbb{R}^{(N+L) \times L}$ is formed based on $\mathbf{H}$ and $\mathbf{I}$. For matrix Γ, it is the solution of an LS problem, where one can adopt Cholesky decomposition to solve it [179]. In addition, this book also analyzes the major computations of Cholesky decomposition for LS problem, which will be discussed in Section 7.5.

As a result, in the testing phase, output node $\mathbf{Y}$ is calculated by already determined hidden node value and output weight value as

$$\mathbf{Y} = \mathbf{H} \cdot \Gamma \tag{4.7}$$

The index of the maximum value in $\mathbf{Y}$ represents the class that the test data belongs to. Based on the computation analysis on feature extraction and neural network, one can observe that matrix–vector multiplication is the dominant operation as shown in (4.1), (4.6) and (4.7). As such, a hardware accelerator to facilitate the matrix–vector multiplication is indeed the critical requirement for the efficient machine learning-based data analytics.

4.2.1.3 Incremental LS solver-based learning

The objective function in (4.5) is an LS problem and can be solved using backwards propagations (BPs) or direct solution based on matrix operations. Since the target is to have incremental learning with latest training samples, iterative gradient-based BP is slow comparing to pseudo-inverse solutions [53], BP will not be elaborated in details. In fact, as discussed in the next sections, the discussed three-dimensional (3D) multi-layer complementary metal oxide semiconductor (CMOS)-resistive random-access memory (ReRAM) architecture can accelerate the matrix–vector multiplications, which will also benefit BP-based neural network training method.

Equation (4.6) shows how to obtain the output weight Γ. The symmetric positive definite matrix $\tilde{\mathbf{H}}^T \tilde{\mathbf{H}}$ is decomposed into $\mathbf{Q}\mathbf{P}\mathbf{Q}^T$.

$$\tilde{\mathbf{H}}^T \tilde{\mathbf{H}} = \mathbf{Q}\mathbf{P}\mathbf{Q}^T \tag{4.8}$$

$\mathbf{Q}$ is a lower triangular matrix with diagonal elements $q_{ii} = 1$ and $\mathbf{P}$ is a positive diagonal matrix. Such method can maintain the same memory space as Cholesky factorization but need not perform square root extraction, as the square root of $\mathbf{Q}$ is resolved by diagonal matrix $\mathbf{P}$ [180]. Here, we use $\mathbf{H}_l$ to represent the matrix decomposition at l iteration (where $l \leq L$) as follows:

$$\tilde{\mathbf{H}}_l^T \tilde{\mathbf{H}}_l = [\tilde{\mathbf{H}}_{l-1} \; h_l]^T [\tilde{\mathbf{H}}_{l-1} \; h_l]$$

$$= \begin{pmatrix} \tilde{\mathbf{H}}_{l-1}^T \tilde{\mathbf{H}}_{l-1} & \mathbf{v}_l \\ \mathbf{v}_l^T & g \end{pmatrix} \tag{4.9}$$

where $(\mathbf{v}_l, g)$ is a new column generated from new hidden node output $h_l^T h_l$, compared to $\tilde{\mathbf{H}}_{l-1}^T \tilde{\mathbf{H}}_{l-1}$. Therefore, one can determine

$$\mathbf{Q}_l \mathbf{P}_l \mathbf{Q}_l^T = \begin{pmatrix} \mathbf{Q}_{l-1} & 0 \\ \mathbf{z}_l^T & 1 \end{pmatrix} \begin{pmatrix} \mathbf{P}_{l-1} & 0 \\ 0 & p \end{pmatrix} \begin{pmatrix} \mathbf{Q}_{l-1}^T & \mathbf{z}_l \\ 0 & 1 \end{pmatrix} \tag{4.10}$$

As a result, the $\mathbf{z}_l$ and scalar p for Cholesky factorization can be calculated as

$$\mathbf{Q}_{l-1} \mathbf{P}_{l-1} \mathbf{z}_l = \mathbf{v}_l, \; p = g - \mathbf{z}_l^T \mathbf{P}_{l-1} \mathbf{z}_l \tag{4.11}$$

where $\mathbf{Q}_l$ and $\mathbf{v}_l$ is known from (4.9), which means we can continue use previous factorization result and update only according part. Please note that Q_1 is 1 and P_1 is $\tilde{\mathbf{H}}_1^T \tilde{\mathbf{H}}_1$.

As a conclusion, this section presents an elaborated basic learning problem on neural network and optimize Cholesky decomposition to solve the incremental LS problem. In addition, this section indicates the major computations in an SFLN are matrix–vector multiplications such as layer output in (4.4) and (4.7) and also Cholesky decomposition in (4.9), (4.10) and (4.11). Therefore, this book presents a 3D multilayer CMOS-ReRAM architecture, which is designed to accelerate matrix–vector multiplication, and can be also extended to BP-based training method, where matrix–vector operation is the major computation [181].

4.2.2 L2-norm-gradient-based learning

4.2.2.1 Multilayer neural network

A multilayer neural network-based machine learning is known for its success in many data analytic application domains ranging from prediction to image classification [182]. It typically has two computational stages: training stage and testing stage. During the training stage, features are extracted as aforementioned, and a neural network is built to map features to its class with trained input to determine the network coefficients. During the testing stage (inference stage), based on the trained network, the new input data are classified by choosing the closest label value of the class. The main computational bottleneck is actually from the training stage.

Given a neural network with D inputs and M outputs as shown in Figure 4.4, a training set $(x_1, t_1), (x_2, t_2), \ldots, (x_N, t_N)$ is given with N number of training samples, D dimensional input features and M classes, and x_i and t_i represent ith data sample and the corresponding class, respectively. There can be multiple hidden layers of neurons

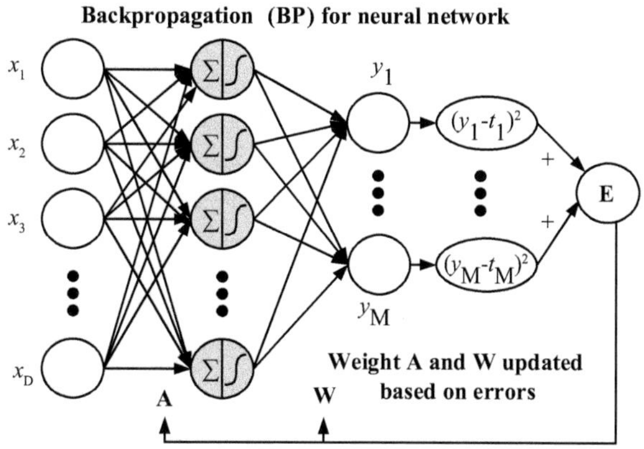

Figure 4.4   *L2-norm-gradient-based multilayer neural network for machine learning*

with a target error function in the form of L2-norm. During the training stage, the aim of neural network is to minimize the L2-norm error function with determined weights of A and W: the input weights and output weights, respectively.

Usually, the hidden layer can be described with a nonlinear sigmoid activation function which maps all the values in the range $[-1, 1]$ calculated as

$$\mathbf{preH} = \mathbf{XA} + \mathbf{B}, \; \mathbf{H} = \frac{1}{1 + e^{-\mathbf{preH}}} \tag{4.12}$$

where $\mathbf{A} \in \mathbb{R}^{D \times L}$ and $\mathbf{B} \in \mathbb{R}^{N \times L}$ are trained input weights and bias; $\mathbf{H} \in \mathbb{R}^{N \times L}$ is the sigmoid function for activation. The output of the neuron network $\mathbf{Y}$ is

$$\mathbf{Y} = \mathbf{HW} \tag{4.13}$$

where $\mathbf{W} \in \mathbb{R}^{L \times N}$ is the trained output weight. The index with the maximum value will become the class during the testing stage.

The training objective function can be generally formulated a L2-norm minimization problem:

$$E = ||\mathbf{T} - \mathbf{Y}||_2^2 \tag{4.14}$$

Therefore, the error objective E can be minimized using an iterative gradient-descent method [177] with the gradient of L2-norm respecting to each weight calculated as

$$\nabla E = \left(\frac{\partial E}{\partial a_{11}}, \frac{\partial E}{\partial a_{12}}, \dots, \frac{\partial E}{\partial a_{DL}}, \frac{\partial E}{\partial W_{11}}, \frac{\partial E}{\partial W_{12}}, \dots, \frac{\partial E}{\partial W_{LM}} \right) \tag{4.15}$$

Each weight can be updated as

$$a_{dl} = a_{dl} - \beta * \frac{\partial E}{\partial a_{dl}}, \quad d = 1, 2, \dots, D, \quad l = 1, 2, \dots, L \tag{4.16}$$

where β is the learning constant that defines the step length of each iteration in the negative gradient direction. As a summary, the L2-norm-gradient-based machine learning training/testing algorithm can be observed in Algorithm 4.1.

4.2.2.2 Direct-gradient-based L2-norm optimization

As shown in Algorithm 4.1, it requires to compute the partial derivative of each weight using one forward pass through the network, following by one backward pass of the network [177]. Such a method is very efficient when the derivative of each weight is known. However, for a hardware-based training, the derivative is usually unknown a priori. In this algorithm, based on the L2-norm calculation, a direct-gradient computation can be realized on hardware as follows:

$$\frac{\partial E}{\partial a_{dl}} \approx \frac{E(a_{dl} + \Delta) - E(a_{dl})}{\Delta} \tag{4.17}$$

where Δ is a small positive change compared to a_{dl}. This technique is simple and accurate enough for the hardware evaluation of the L2-norm-based error functions. In the following sections, this book shows that by utilizing a coupled oscillator network and crossbar structures in ReRAM devices, forward passing through the neuron network and also the evaluation of the L2-norm error function can be extremely fast with possibly done in one clock cycle.

Algorithm 4.1: Backpropagation training for neural network

Input: Training matrix $X \in \mathbb{R}^{N \times D}$, target matrix $T \in \mathbb{R}^{N \times M}$, number of hidden nodes L and learning rate β

Output: Neuron network input weight A and output weight W

1: Initial guess: A^0 and W^0; initial set $k = 1$, learning rate β
2: Perform feedforward operation, the input X is fed into the network as (4.12) and (4.13).
3: Calculate training error on each neuron $E^{k-1} = ||\mathbf{T} - \mathbf{Y}^{k-1}||_2^2$.
4: Calculate gradient $\frac{\partial E^{k-1}}{\partial a_{ij}^{k-1}}$ and $\frac{\partial E^{k-1}}{\partial w_{ij}^{k-1}}$.
5: Update a_{ij}^{k-1} and w_{ij}^{k-1}.
$$a_{dl}^k = a_{dl}^{k-1} - \beta * \frac{\partial E^{k-1}}{\partial a_{dl}},$$
$$w_{lm}^k = w_{ij}^{k-1} - \beta * \frac{\partial E^{k-1}}{\partial w_{lm}}.$$
6: Calculate the training error E^k with the updated weights.
7: If $E^k - E^{k-1}$ is larger than threshold, repeats from Step 3 and $k = k + 1$.

4.3   DCNN-based machine learning

In addition to multilayer neural networks, deep neural networks and deep convolutional networks have obtained higher performance when performing data-intensive and image analysis as well as complex data sets.

4.3.1   *Deep learning for multilayer neural network*

Although the SLFN can achieve a desirable accuracy with small inference and training time, it has not been proved to handle the complex benchmarks. For instance, the recent research in [183] only shows an efficient performance on University of California Irvine (UCI) data set [184], which is still far away from the real-life problems. The study in [185] shows that deep learning can be applied to train a neural network with multiple layers. A simple deep learning diagram is shown in Figure 4.5. In this figure, there are $(n + 1)$ weight matrices connecting with adjacent nodes. When the output of neural network is obtained, one can update all the weights in the multilayer neural network.

The architectures of deep learning include various deep neural networks, deep convolutional neural networks (DCNNs), deep belief networks and recurrent neural networks. In the following sections, the details on the DCNN with binary weights and neurons are described.

4.3.2   *Convolutional neural network*

Figure 4.5 illustrates a multilayer neural network with all fully connected layers. However, usually the simple fully connected layers cannot extract enough information from input signals and hidden nodes. Therefore, the basic structure of convolutional neural network (CNN) [186] is applied in [187] and the DCNN is formed. In this architecture, the convolution layers are used to replace the fully connected layers in Figure 4.5. In each layer, there are several convolution cores to extract different information of one input pattern.

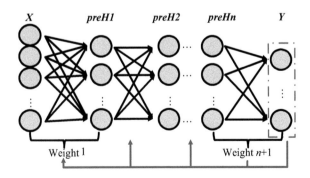

Figure 4.5   Diagram of simple deep learning with full-connect layers

Figure 4.6 shows a layer of image classification by CNN with a 3×3 convolution core as an example. The dimension of input feature is 10×8 and all the pixels are real valued. In this example, the multiplication between two 9×1 vectors is performed for 63 times. For the whole algorithm, there are many convolution cores and layers so that the computation complexity is large. As such, the binary convolutional neural network (BCNN) is developed to lower the bit width in the operation.

4.3.3 Binary convolutional neural network

As discussed in Section 4.3.2, the traditional direct mapping of CNN to hardware would require large and unnecessary hardware resources with poor parallelism. The recent work in [188] suggests a CNN using binary constraints during training. This section discusses generating a CNN model with bitwise parallelism for convolution, batch normalization, pooling function and activation function.

4.3.3.1 Bitwise convolution

The convolution operation is the most time-consuming and computation-intensive operation in CNN. The binary convolution in [188] uses $\{-1, +1\}$ for both input features and weights, so that the floating-point matrix–vector-multiplication operation is not required. However, the negative binary weights cannot be directly realized on hardware. To avoid the negative weights, recent work [189] uses bitwise XNOR and bit-count operation with $\{0, 1\}$ for hardware implementation. Thus, the bitwise CNN (bitCNN) can be mathematically represented as follows:

$$s_k(x,y,z) = \sum_{i=1}^{w_k} \sum_{j=1}^{h_k} \sum_{l=1}^{D_k} w_k^b(i,j,l,z) \otimes \quad a_{k-1}^b(i+x-1, j+y-1, l) \quad (4.18)$$

where $w_k^b \in \{0,1\}^{w_k \times h_k \times D_{k-1} \times D_k}$ and $a_{k-1}^b \in \{0,1\}^{W_{k-1} \times H_{k-1} \times D_{k-1}}$ are the binary weights in kth block and the binary input feature map, respectively. The s_k is the output of the binary convolution and $\otimes$ is defined as bitwise XNOR operation. Comparing to a real-valued CNN in the single-precision data format, since the elements of weights and feature maps can be stored in 1-bit, logic and memory resources requirement for binary convolutional (BinConv) layer can be greatly reduced. Meanwhile, it can lead to a higher parallelism as well as greater energy-efficiency improvement.

4.3.3.2 Bitwise batch normalization

Next, batch normalization is required to stabilize and accelerate the training process. In the inference stage, the normalization is retained to match training process. The output of the normalization can be represented by

$$a_k(x,y,z) = \frac{s_k(x,y,z) - \mu(x,y,z)}{\sqrt{\sigma^2(x,y,z)}} \gamma(x,y,z)$$
$$+ \beta(x,y,z) \quad (4.19)$$

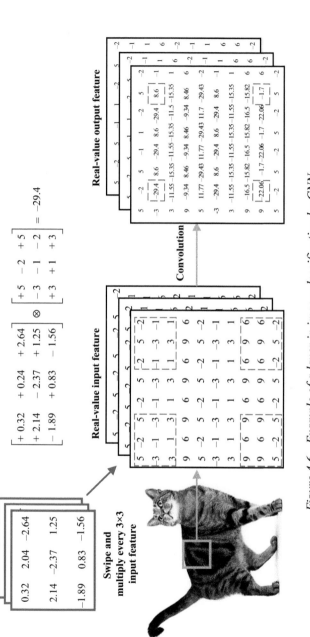

Figure 4.6 Example of a layer in image classification by CNN

where $\mu \in \mathbb{R}^{W_k \times H_k \times D_k}$ and $\sigma^2 \in \mathbb{R}^{W_k \times H_k \times D_k}$ are the expectation and variance over the mini-batch, while $\gamma \in \mathbb{R}$ and $\beta \in \mathbb{R}^{W_k \times H_k \times D_k}$ are learnable parameters [190] that scale and shift the normalized value. During the inference stage, μ, σ^2, γ and β are all fixed to normalize the convolution output, determined during the training stage.

4.3.3.3   Bitwise pooling and activation functions

To minimize the computational complexity, the pooling layer performs a downsampling across an $M \times M$ contiguous region on the feature map output by normalization layer. Pooling is used for selecting the most significant information from the features. It also provides translation invariance and reduces the computation intensity. Two kinds of pooling schemes are commonly used in CNN. One is the max-pooling, which takes the maximum value in the pooling region. The other is average-pooling, which takes the mean value of the pooling region. The binary max-pooling for binary CNNs is applied as follows:

$$a'_k(i,j) = \text{Max}\{a_k(Mi + k, Mj + l)\}, (k, l \in (0, M)) \tag{4.20}$$

where a_k and a'_k are the features before and after pooling, respectively. The binary non-linearity can be represented as The activation function to process the output of max-pooling in a binary CNN is called binarization (Binrz), which can be represented as

$$a_k^{b'}(i,j) = \begin{cases} 0, & a'_k(i,j) \leq 0 \\ 1, & \text{otherwise} \end{cases} \tag{4.21}$$

where a_k is the output of the max-pooling layer and a_k^b is the binarized activation generated by the kth binarized layer.

To summarize pooling and binarization, the aforementioned two steps are designed to find out the sign of the maximum number in the pooling region. As such, one can do the binarization for all the numbers in the pooling region first, and then determine the maximum among them. Since the results from binarization become only 0 or 1, the pooling process only needs to detect whether there are any 1s in the region. An example with the exchange of pooling and binarization for a 2×2 region is shown as follows:

$$\begin{bmatrix} +0.70 & -0.42 \\ -0.21 & +0.35 \end{bmatrix} \Longrightarrow \begin{cases} \begin{bmatrix} 1 & 0 \\ 0 & 1 \end{bmatrix} \Longrightarrow 1 \\ 0.70 \quad \Longrightarrow 1 \end{cases} \tag{4.22}$$

Here, the 2×2 real-value matrix denotes the output of batch normalization. The first path in (4.22) is doing binarization first, then max-pooling, while the second path is doing it conversely. It is clear that exchanging the max-pooling and binarization will not affect the final output in the inference stage.

4.3.3.4   Bitwise CNN model overview

The overall working flow of a bitwise-parallelized CNN model is shown in Figure 4.7(b). Each BinConv layer takes the binary feature map generated from the previous layer as input and conducts a bitwise convolution between binary feature

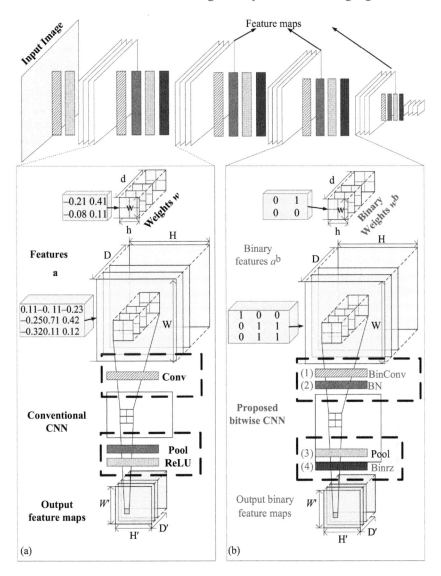

Figure 4.7   Computation flow comparison between (a) conventional CNN and (b) bitwise-parallelized CNN

maps and binary filter weights. The convolution output is further processed by the normalization layer before downsampling by the max-pooling layer. The downsampled feature maps are subsequently fed into Binrz layer that produces binary nonlinear activations according to the input sign.

The training flow in Algorithm 4.2 can be summarized as follows. In the training stage, all the weights are stored in a real-valued format w_k and binarized to w_k^b during the forward pass (Line 1–7). After the forward pass, the error signal C is generated by comparing the output of the network $\hat{Y}$ with the corresponding label Y (Line 9). Then the error signal C is backpropagated to each previous layer to compute the weight's gradient $g_{w_k^b}$ and feature's gradient $g_{a_k^b}$ (Line 13–18). Note that instead of using the real-valued weights w_k to compute the feature's gradient of previous layer, the binarized weight is applied for gradient computation, which is indicated in Line 17. On the other hand, the value of w_k is constrained in the range of -1 to $+1$ at each iteration to ensure the convergence (Line 21). It is different from the conventional update scheme that directly updates the weights without limiting their amplitudes.

The key difference between the bitwise CNN and the direct-truncated CNN using less precision bit [191] is illustrated as follows. The direct-truncated CNN is obtained

---

Algorithm 4.2: Training flow of BNN. L is the number of layers, Binrz($\cdot$) defines the binarization, BinConv($\cdot$) defines the binary convolution, BatchNorm($\cdot$) defines the normalization and MaxPool($\cdot$) defines the 2×2 max-pooling.

0: {Forward pass:}
1: **for** $k = 1$ *to* L **do**
2:      $w_k^b = \text{Binrz}(w_k)$
3:      $s_k = \text{BinConv}(a_{k-1}^b, W_k^b)$
4:      $a_k = \text{BatchNorm}(s_k)$
5:      $a_k = \text{MaxPool}(a_k)$
6:      $a_k^b = \text{Binrz}(a_k)$
7: **end for**
8: $\hat{Y} = \text{softmax}(a_L)$
9: $C = Y - \hat{Y}$
10: $g_{a_L} = C$
11: $g_{s_L} = \text{BackBatchNorm}(g_{a_L})$
12: $g_{a_{L-1}^b} = g_{s_L} * w_L^b$
12: {Backward pass:}
13: **for** $k = L - 1$ *to* 1 **do**
14:     $g_{a_k} = g_{a_k^b} \circ 1_{|a_k| \leq 1}$
15:     $g_{s_k} = \text{BackBatchNorm}(g_{a_k})$
16:     $g_{w_k^b} = g_{s_k} * a_{k-1}^b$
17:     $g_{a_{k-1}^b} = g_{s_k} * w_k^b$
18: **end for**
18: {Weights update:}
19: **for** $k = 1$ *to* L **do**
20:     $w_k = w_k + \eta g_{w_k^b}$
21:     $w_k = \max(\min(w_k, 1), -1)$
22: **end for**

---

by reducing the numerical precision in post-training phase while the bitwise CNN developed here is obtained by training with binary constraints [188]. As such, the direct-truncated CNN that suffers from accuracy loss in general, but the bitwise CNN retains most of the accuracy with the lowest precision. In the inference stage, only the binarized weights w_k^b will be retained for much smaller storage, faster inference, higher parallelism as well as higher energy efficiency.

4.4 TNN-based machine learning

Previously discussed neural network compression is simply performed either by precision-bit truncation or low-rank approximation [192–195], which cannot maintain good balance between network compression and network accuracy. By representing dense data in high-dimensional space with natural sparsity, tensorized data formatting can significantly compress the neural network complexity without much accuracy loss [196]. Contrastingly, this section discusses a tensor-train-formatted neural network [197] during the training. The tensor-train-based decomposition and compression will be first introduced. Then, a tensorized neural network (TNN) will be discussed based on the extension of general neural network. Finally, a layer-wise training of TNN using modified alternating LS (MALS) method is further proposed. For simplicity, we illustrate the idea based on a single hidden-layer neural network and later extend it to a multilayer neural network. A tensor-train-based neural network training method is also developed with the consideration of model compression using MALS method with complexity analysis provided.

4.4.1 Tensor-train decomposition and compression

Tensors are natural multidimensional generation of matrices. Here, we refer one-dimensional data as *vectors*, denoted as v. Two-dimensional (2D) arrays are *matrices*, denoted as V and higher-dimensional arrays are *tensors* denoted as shown in Figure 4.8. To refer one specific element from a tensor, this chapter uses calligraphic upper letters $\mathcal{V}(i) = \mathcal{V}(i_1, i_2, \ldots, i_d)$, where d is the dimensionality of the tensor $\mathcal{V}$. One can effectively reshape a 2D matrix into a four-dimensional (4D) tensor as shown in Figure 4.8.

A d-dimensional $n_1 \times n_2 \times \cdots \times n_d$ tensor $\mathcal{V}$ is decomposed into the tensor-train data format if the tensor core G_k is defined as $r_{k-1} \times n_k \times r_k$ and each element is defined [197] as

$$\mathcal{V}(i_1, i_2, \ldots, i_d) = \sum_{\alpha_0, \alpha_1, \ldots, \alpha_d}^{r_0, r_1, \ldots, r_d} G_1(\alpha_0, i_1, \alpha_1)$$
$$G_2(\alpha_1, i_2, \alpha_2) \ldots G_d(\alpha_{d-1}, i_d, \alpha_d) \tag{4.23}$$

where α_k is the index of summation, which starts from 1 and stops at rank r_k. $r_0 = r_d = 1$ is for the boundary condition and $n_1, n_2, \ldots, n_d$ are known as mode size. Here, r_k is the core rank and G is the core for this tensor decomposition. By using the

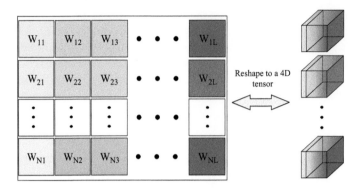

Figure 4.8   Block matrices and their representation by a 4D tensor

notation of $G_k(i_k) \in \mathbb{R}^{r_{k-1} \times r_k}$, we can rewrite the above equation in a more compact way:

$$\mathcal{V}(i_1, i_2, \ldots, i_d) = G_1(i_1)G_2(i_2) \ldots G_d(i_d) \qquad (4.24)$$

where $G_k(i_k)$ is an $r_{k-1} \times r_k$ matrix, a slice from the 3D matrix G_k.

Such a representation is memory-efficient to store high-dimensional data and hence with significant energy saving as well. For example, a d-dimensional tensor requires $N = n_1 \times n_2 \times \cdots \times n_d = n^d$ number of parameters. However, if it is represented using the tensor-train format, it takes only $\sum_{k=1}^{d} n_k r_{k-1} r_k$ parameters. Thus, if one can manage to reduce the rank of each core, one can efficiently represent data with high compression rate and store them distributively. By permuting neural network weight into high-dimensional data, one can compress the neural network. Here, let us define a TNN if the weight of the neural network can be represented in the tensor-train data format. For instance, a 2D weight $W \in \mathbb{R}^{L_0 \times L_1}$ can be reshaped to a $k_1 + k_2$-dimensional tensor $\mathcal{W} \in \mathbb{R}^{l_{0,1} \times l_{0,2} \times \cdots \times l_{0,k_1} \times l_{1,1} \times l_{1,2} \times \cdots \times l_{1,k_2}}$ by factorizing $L_0 = \prod_{m=1}^{k_1} l_{0,m}$ and $L_1 = \prod_{m=1}^{k_2} l_{1,m}$ and such tensor can be decomposed into the tensor-train data format to save storages[1].

4.4.2   Tensor-train-based neural network

To make TNN clear, this section starts with a general feedforward neural network and then extend it to the tensor-train-based neural network. For the ease of illustration, this section uses a single hidden-layer neural network as an example and the same principle can be applied to the multilayer neural network [199–201]. Generally, the training of a neural network is performed based on data features X and labels T with N_t number of training samples, N dimensional input features and M classes. During

---

[1]Interested readers can refer to [197,198] for more details on the tensor-train data format.

the training, one needs to minimize the error function with determined weights: W_1 (at input layer) and W_2 (at output layer) for a single hidden-layer neural network[2]:

$$E = ||T - f(W_1, W_2, X)||_2 \tag{4.25}$$

where $f(\cdot)$ is the trained model to perform the predictions from input.

This section mainly discusses the inference (testing) process and presents the training process later. The output of each layer is based on matrix multiplication and activation function. For instance, the output of the first layer H is mathematically defined as

$$preH = X_t W_1 + B_1, \ H = \frac{1}{1 + e^{-preH}} \tag{4.26}$$

where X_t is the testing data. $W_1 \in \mathbb{R}^{N \times L_1}$ and $B_1 \in \mathbb{R}^{N_t \times L_1}$ are the input weights and bias, respectively. Then, the neural network output for a single hidden-layer neural network is

$$Y = f(W_1, W_2, X_t)$$
$$p(i/y_i) \approx y_i, \ y_i \in Y \tag{4.27}$$

where i represents class index $i \in [1, \ M]$. We approximate the prediction probability for each class by the output of neural network.

For the tensor-train-based neural network, Figure 4.9 shows the general idea. A 2D weight is folded into a 3D tensor and then decomposed into tensor cores

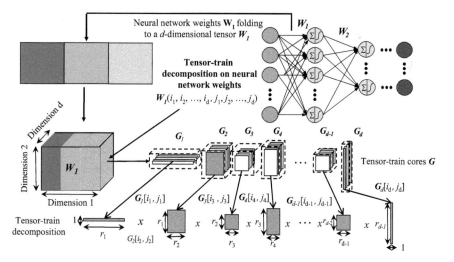

Figure 4.9   *Neural network weight tensorization and represented by tensor-train data format for parameter compression (from n^d to dnr^2)*

---

[2]We ignore bias for a better illustration.

$G_1, G_2, \ldots, G_d$. These tensor cores are relatively small matrices due to the small value of rank r leading to a high neural network compression rate. Then, the whole neural network will be trained in the tensor-train data format.

The TNN inference is a directly application of the tensor-train-matrix-by-vector operations [196,197]. We will use $W \in \mathbb{R}^{N \times L}$ to discuss the forward pass of neural network. First, we rearrange W to a d-dimensional tensor $\mathcal{W}$, whose kth dimension is a vector of length $n_k l_k$. Here, n_k and l_k are defined as $N = \prod_{k=1}^{d} n_k$ and $L = \prod_{k=1}^{d} l_k$. Without consideration of the bias B and activation function, the neural network forward pass $H = XW$ in the tensor-train data format is

$$\mathcal{H}(i) = \sum_{j=[j_1, j_2, \ldots, j_d]}^{l_1, l_2, l_3, \ldots, l_d} \mathcal{X}(j) G_1[i_1, j_1] G_2[i_2, j_2] \ldots G_d[i_d, j_d] \qquad (4.28)$$

where $i = i_1, i_2, \ldots, i_d, i_k \in [1, n_k]$, $j = j_1, j_2, \ldots, j_d, j_k \in [1, l_k]$ and $G_k[i_d, j_d] \in \mathbb{R}^{r_{k-1} \times r_k}$ is a slice of cores. We use a pair $[i_k, j_k]$ to refer an index of vector $[1 \, n_k l_k]$, where $G_k \in \mathbb{R}^{r_{k-1} \times n_k l_k \times r_k}$. Since the fully connected layer is a special case of convolutional layer with kernel size 1×1, such tensorized weights can also be applied to other convolutional layers.

This tensor-train-matrix-by-vector multiplication complexity is $O(dr^2 n_m \max(N, L))$ [196], where r is the maximum rank of cores G_i and n_m is the maximum mode size $m_k n_k$ of tensor $\mathcal{W}$. This can be very efficient if the rank r is very small compared to general matrix–vector multiplication. It is also favorable for distributed computation on ReRAM devices since each core is small and matrix multiplication is associative.

4.4.3 Training TNN

Tensor-train-based neural network is first proposed by [196] but its training complexity significantly increases due to the BP under the tensor-train data format. A layer-wise training provides good performance with reduced epoch number of backward propagation leading to a significant training time reduction [200–202]. Moreover, to perform a successful mapping of TNN, recursive training of TNN is required for the trade-off of accuracy and compression rate. Thereby, a fast layer-wise training method is developed in this chapter for TNN.

The training process of TNN is the same as general neural network layer-wise training but with the tensor-train data format. We first discuss the general training process following the training framework form [53] and then extend it to TNN. Given a single hidden layer with random generated input weight, the training process is to minimize:

$$\text{min. } ||HW_2 - T||_2 + \lambda ||W_2||_2 \qquad (4.29)$$

where H is the hidden-layer output matrix generated from the Sigmoid function for activation, and λ is a user-defined parameter that biases the training error and output weights [53]. The output weight W_2 is computed based on LS problem:

$$W_2 = (\tilde{H}^T \tilde{H})^{-1} \tilde{H}^T \tilde{T}, \ \tilde{H} \in \mathbb{R}^{N_t \times L}$$

$$\text{where } \tilde{H} = \begin{pmatrix} H \\ \sqrt{\lambda}I \end{pmatrix} \ \tilde{T} = \begin{pmatrix} T \\ 0 \end{pmatrix} \tag{4.30}$$

where $\tilde{T} \in \mathbb{R}^{(N_t+L_1) \times M}$ and M is the number of classes. $I \in \mathbb{R}^{L_1 \times L_1}$ and $\tilde{H} \in \mathbb{R}^{(N_t+L_1) \times L_1}$.

To build a multilayer neural network, backward propagation [199] or layer-wise training using the auto-encoder technique [200,201] can be applied. An auto-encoder layer is to set the single layer output T the same as input X and find an optimal weight to represent itself. By stacking auto-encoder layers on the final decision layer, we can build the multilayer neural network. Algorithm 4.3 summarizes the layer-wise training with MALS method.

TNN is to develop high-dimensional weights and use tensor-train decomposition method to compress it. For example, a $M \times N$ fully connected layer can be expressed as a 4D $m_1 \times m_2 \times n_1 \times n_2$ tensor. Therefore, instead of generating a random input weight A, we will generate a low rank tensor $\mathscr{A}$ by specifying the rank of each core $G_1, G_2, \ldots, G_i$. Then the input weight can be generated as (4.23) with each core G_i randomly generated.

Algorithm 4.3: Layer-wise training of neural network with modified LS solver

---

Input: Input set (X, T), X is the input data and T is the desired output depending on the layer architecture, activation function $G(a_i, b_i, x_j)$, number of hidden neuron node $L_0, L_1, \ldots, L_d$

Output: Neural network weight $W_1, W_2, \ldots, W_d$ for d-layer neural network

1: **for** $i = 1 : d$ **do**
2:     **if** $i == 1$ **then**
3:         Factorize L_0 and L_1 (e.g., $L_0 = l_{0,1} \times l_{0,2}$ and $L_1 = l_{1,1} \times l_{1,2}$).
4:         Randomly generate tensor cores $G_1 \in \mathbb{R}^{r_1 \times n_1 \times r_2}$, $G_2 \in \mathbb{R}^{r_2 \times l_1 \times r_3}$ and other tensor cores to represent a tensor $\mathscr{W}_1 \in \mathbb{R}^{n_1 \times n_2 \times l_1 \times l_2}$.
5:     **else**
6:         Random generated $\mathscr{W}_i$ following Steps 3, 4
7:         Perform tensor-train-matrix-by-vector multiplication based on (4.28), which equivalents to $preH_i = H_{i-1}W_{i-1}$.
8:         Perform activation function which equivalents to $H_i = 1/(1 + e_i^{-preH})$.
9:         Compute $\mathscr{W}_i$ using the MALS $||H_i \mathscr{W}_i - P||_2$.
10:        Note: For auto-encoder layers, P is the activation matrix H_{i-1} ($H_0 = X$). For the decision layer, P is the label matrix T.
11:     **end if**
12: **end for**

As discussed in the general neural network, the training of TNN requires to solve an LS problem in the tensor-train data format. For the output weight W_2 in (4.29), we propose a tensor-train-based LS training method using MALS algorithm (also known as density matrix renormalization group in quantum dynamics) [203,204]. The MALS for minimization of $||HW_2 - T||_2$ is working as follows.

For the output weight Γ, we have two potential solutions to achieve tensor-train data format. One straight way is to solve the general matrix LS problem and then reshape it to a high-dimensional tensor following iterative truncated support vector decomposition (SVD) algorithm [197]. This is similar to high-order SVD and performance degradation is significant with relatively small compression rate. Instead, we propose a tensor-train-based LS training method using MALS algorithm (also known as density matrix renormalization group in quantum dynamics) [203,204].

1. **Initialization**: Randomly initialized cores G and set $W_2 = G_1 \times G_2 \times \cdots \times G_d$. The process is the same as Steps 3, 4 in Algorithm 4.3.
2. **Sweep of cores**: Core G_k is optimized with other cores fixed. Left-to-right sweep from $k = 1$ to $k = d$.
3. **Supercore generated**: Create supercore $X(k, k + 1) = G_k \times G_{k+1}$ and find it by minimizing the LS problem $||H \times Q_{k-1} \times X_{k,k+1} \times R_{k+2} - T||_2$, reshape $Q_{k-1} = \prod_{i=1}^{k-1} G_i$ and $R_{k+2} = \prod_{i=k+2}^{d} G_i$ to fit matrix–matrix multiplication[3].
4. **Split supercore**: SVD $X(k, k + 1) = USV^T$, let $G_k = U$ and $G_{k+1} = SV^T \times G_{k+1}$. G_k is determined and G_{k+1} is updated. Truncated SVD can also be performed by removing smaller singular values to reduce ranks.
5. **Sweep termination**: Terminate if maximum sweep times reached or error is smaller than required.

The low-rank initialization is very important to have smaller rank r for each core. Each supercore generation is the process of solving LS problems. The complexity of LS for X are $O(n_m R r^3 + n_m^2 R^2 r^2)$ [204] and the SVD compression requires $O(n_m r^3)$, where R, r and n_m are the rank of activation matrix H_1, the maximum rank of core G and maximum mode size of W_2, respectively. By using truncated SVD, we can adaptively reduce the rank of each core to reduce the computation complexity and save memory storage.

Such tensorization can benefit from implementing large neural networks. First, by performing tensorization, the size of neural network can be compressed. Moreover, the computation load can also be reduced by adopting small tensor ranks. Second, a tensorization of weight matrix can decompose the big matrix into many small tensor-core matrices, which can effectively reduce the configuration time of ReRAM. Lastly, the multiplication of a small matrix can be performed in a highly parallel fashion on ReRAM to speed up the large neural network processing time.

---

[3]Details on Q_{k-1} and R_{k+2} can be found in [203,204]. Since each core is 3D tensors, permuting to 2D matrix is required. Without abuse of notations, we use G_k' to represent it.

Chapter 5

XIMA: the in-ReRAM machine learning architecture

5.1 ReRAM network-based ML operations

Among different hardware architectures, resistive random-access memory (ReRAM)-based architectures are seen to be one of the efficient architectures in terms of the area, power consumption and the computational latency. In this chapter, we will introduce two types of ReRAM neural networks with focus on intensive matrix multiplication operations. ReRAM-crossbar network can be used as matrix–vector multiplication accelerator and then to illustrate the detailed mapping. The coupled ReRAM oscillator network can be applied for low-power and high-throughput L2-norm calculation.

5.1.1 ReRAM-crossbar network

This section describes the matrix–vector multiplication on the binary ReRAM crossbar. It is the most popular operation in various data-analytic applications such as compressive sensing and machine learning (ML). For example, the feature extraction can be achieved by multiplying Bernoulli matrix in [205].

Matrix multiplication can be denoted as $Y = \Phi X$, where $X \in \{0, 1\}^{N \times P}$ and $\Phi \in \{0, 1\}^{M \times N}$ are the multiplicand matrices, and $Y \in \mathbb{Z}^{M \times P}$ is the result matrix.

5.1.1.1 Mapping of ReRAM crossbar for matrix–vector multiplication

In this section, hardware mapping of matrix multiplication on the ReRAM architecture is introduced. The logic required is a matrix–vector multiplier by the ReRAM crossbar. In general, one can utilize current merge on bitlines (BLs) to realize matrix–vector multiplication and then use an ReRAM-based flash analog–digital converter (ADC) for format conversion. Here, a three-step ReRAM-crossbar-based binary matrix–vector multiplier is presented, in which both the input and output of the ReRAM crossbar are binary data without the need of ADC. The three ReRAM-crossbar steps parallel digitizing, XOR and encoding are presented in details as follows. As the output of an ReRAM-crossbar array can be connected to the input of another ReRAM-crossbar array, one can utilize multiple ReRAM arrays in the logic block for the mappings. Here, the symbol s is used to denote the result of binary matrix–vector multiplication. As such, s follows

$$0 \leq s \leq N \tag{5.1}$$

where N is the maximum result. To illustrate the three-step procedure more clearly, let us consider the following matrix–vector multiplication as an illustrative example:

$$[00101011] \times [10111110]^{\mathrm{T}} = 3 \tag{5.2}$$

The output after the three-step procedure will be shown, here $s = 3$ and $N = 8$.

Parallel digitizing

The first step is called parallel digitizing, which requires $N \times N$ ReRAM crossbars. The idea is to split the matrix–vector multiplication to multiple inner-product operations of two vectors. Each inner product is computed by one ReRAM crossbar. For each crossbar, as shown in Figure 5.1, all columns are configured with same elements that correspond to one column in random Boolean matrix Φ, and the input voltages on wordlines (WLs) are determined by x. As the impedance of ReRAM $g_{on} \gg g_{off}$ (normally $\frac{g_{on}}{g_{off}} > 100$), current ReRAMs with high impedance are insignificant, so that the voltages on BLs approximately equal to $kV_r g_{on} R_s$ according to (3.9), where k is the number of ReRAMs in low-resistance state (g_{on}). The underlying assumption is that the number of columns is less than 100 because the ON/OFF ratio is finite.

It is obvious that voltages on BLs are all identical. Therefore, the key to obtain the inner product is to set a ladder-type sensing threshold voltages for each column:

$$V_{\mathrm{th},j} = \frac{(2j + 1)V_r g_{on} R_s}{2} \tag{5.3}$$

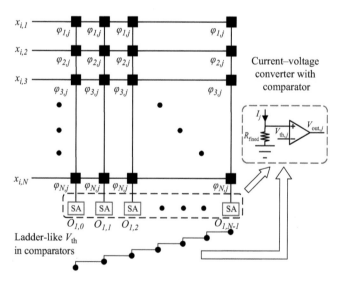

Figure 5.1   *Parallel digitizing step of ReRAM crossbar in matrix multiplication*

where $V_{th,j}$ is the threshold voltage for the jth column. The $O_{i,j}$ is used to denote the output of column j in ReRAM-crossbar step i after sensing. Therefore, the output of a column is given by

$$O_{1,j} = \begin{cases} 1, & j \leq s \\ 0, & j > s \end{cases}$$ (5.4)

where s is the inner-product result. In other words, the first $(N - s)$ output bits are 0 and the rest s bits are 1 ($s <= N$). In the presented example, $x_i = [00101011]$ and $\phi_i = [10111110]$; thus, the corresponding output $O_1 = [11100000]$.

XOR operation for ML

The inner-product output of parallel digitizing step is determined by the position where $O_{1,j}$ changes from 0 to 1. The XOR takes the output of the first step and performs XOR operation for every two adjacent bits in $O_{1,j}$, which gives the result index. For the same example of $s = 3$, one needs to convert the first-step output $O_1 = [11100000]$ to $O_2 = [001000000]$. The XOR operation based on ReRAM crossbar is shown in Figure 5.2. According to parallel digitizing step, $O_{1,j}$ must be 1 if $O_{1,j+1}$ is 1. Therefore, XOR operation is equivalent to the AND operation $O_{1,j} \oplus O_{1,j+1} = O_{1,j}\overline{O_{1,j+1}}$, and therefore, we have

$$\overline{O_{2,j}} = \begin{cases} \overline{O_{1,j} + O_{1,j+1}}, & j < N - 1 \\ \overline{O_{1,j}}, & j = N - 1 \end{cases}$$ (5.5)

In addition, the threshold voltages for the columns have to follow the following flow:

$$V_{th,j} = \frac{V_r g_{on} R_s}{2}$$ (5.6)

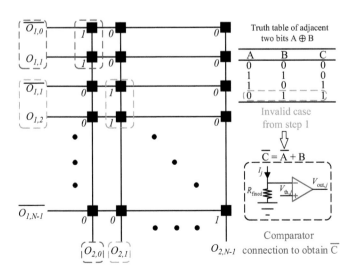

Figure 5.2   XOR step of ReRAM crossbar in matrix multiplication

Equations (5.5) and (5.6) show that only output of *s*th column is 1 on the second step, where *s* is the inner-product result. Each crossbar in XOR step has the size of $N \times (2N - 1)$.

Encoding

The third step is to consider the output of XOR step and produce *s* in binary format as an encoder. Therefore, O_3 should be in the binary format of *s*. In the considered example, $O_3 = [00000011]$ when $s = 3$. In the output of XOR step, as only one input will be 1 and others are 0, according binary information is stored in corresponding row, as shown in Figure 5.3. Encoding step needs $N \times n$ ReRAMs, where $n = \lceil \log_2 N \rceil$ is the number of bits in order to represent N in binary format. The thresholds for the encoding step are set following (5.6) as well.

Adding and shifting for inner-product result

The output of encoding step is in binary format, but some processes are needed to obtain the final inner-product result. As a result, adder and shifter are designed to complete this process as shown in Figure 5.4. We suppose the original data is 8-bit

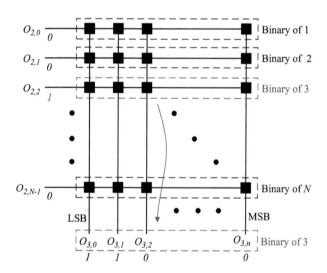

Figure 5.3   *Encoding step of ReRAM crossbar in matrix multiplication*

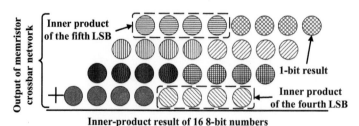

Figure 5.4   *ReRAM-based inner-product operation*

and data dimension is 512, the workload of adder is 512 without any acceleration. With the three-step ReRAM-crossbar accelerator as preprocessing, the workload of adder can be significantly reduced to 9 ($\log_2 512$). Detailed comparison results will be shown in Section 5.1.1.2.

5.1.1.2 Performance evaluation

Experimental application: feature extraction for fingerprint matching
Feature extraction or sparse representation is commonly applied such as in fingerprint image matching, which can be mapped with ($M \ll N$). This operation can minimize the volume of data to be stored in memory as well as minimize the complexity in data analytics applications. The following section shows how to map this operation on the digitalized ReRAM crossbar. In such a process, X is the original fingerprint image, which is of high dimension with ($N \times P$) pixels, Φ a random Bernoulli matrix with ($M \times N$) for feature extract and Y the features in low dimension with ($M \times P$) pixels. The according dimension reduction ratio γ is

$$\gamma = \frac{M}{N} \tag{5.7}$$

In the feature extraction phase of fingerprint image, the random Bernoulli matrix Φ is with fixed elements. Therefore, the elements of the Bernoulli matrix are stored in ReRAMs of logic block, and original image as the input of logic accelerator.

Experimental settings
The hardware evaluation platform is implemented on a computer server with 4.0 GHz core and 16.0 GB memory. Feature extraction is implemented by general processor, complimentary metal oxide semiconductor (CMOS)-based application specific integrated circuit (ASIC), non-distributed and distributed in-memory computing based on digitalized ReRAM crossbar, respectively. For the ReRAM-crossbar design evaluation, the resistance of ReRAM is set as 1 kΩ and 1 MΩ as on-state and off-state resistance, respectively, according to [206]. The general processor implementation is based on MATLAB® simulation on computer server. A CMOS-based feature extraction design is implemented by Verilog in distributed architecture and synthesized with CMOS 65-nm low-power process design kit (PDK). The working frequency of general processor implementation is 4.0 GHz while the CMOS-ASIC feature extraction design frequency is 1.0 GHz. For in-memory computing based on the proposed ReRAM crossbar, write voltage V_w is set as 0.8 V and read voltage V_r is set as 0.1 V as well as duration time of 5 ns. In addition, the analog computation on ReRAM crossbar is performed for comparison based on design in [207].

General performance comparison
In this section, 1,000 fingerprint images selected from [208] are processed as binarization images and stored in memory with 328 × 356 resolution. To agree with patch size, random Bernoulli $N \times M$ matrix is with fixed N and M of 356 and 64, respectively. The detailed comparison is shown in Table 5.1 with numerical results including energy consumption and delay obtained for one image on average of 1,000 images.

Table 5.1 *Performance comparison of matrix–vector multiplication under among software and hardware implementations.*

Implementation		Frequency	Area	Time	Power	Energy
CPU (MATLAB)		4.0 GHz	177 mm^2	1.78 ms	84 W	0.1424 J
CMOS-ASIC		1.0 GHz	5 mm^2	69.632 μs	34.938 W	2.4457 mJ
Digitized XIMA	ReRAM	200 MHz	3.28 mm^2	4.92 μs	4.096 W	20.15 μJ
	CMOS		128 μm^2	1.311 ms	100 μW	0.131 μJ
	Overall		3.28 mm^2	1.316 ms	4.096 W	20.16 μJ
Distributed digitized XIMA	ReRAM	200 MHz	0.05 mm^2	4.92 μs	4.096 W	20.15 μJ
	CMOS		8192 μm^2	20.48 μs	6.4 mW	0.131 μJ
	Overall		0.06 mm^2	25.40 μs	4.102 W	20.28 μJ
Distributed analog XIMA	ReRAM	200 MHz	0.05 mm^2	1.64 μs	1.28 W	2.1 μJ
	CMOS		8.27 mm^2	20.48 μs	6.4 mW	0.131 μJ
	Overall		8.32 mm^2	22.12 μs	1.29 W	2.13 μJ

Here the CMOS in crossbar in-memory computation accelerator (XIMA) refers to the memory controllers.

Among hardware implementations, in-memory computing based on the accelerated XIMA achieves better energy efficiency compared to CMOS-based ASIC. Non-distributed XIMA (only one data and logic block inside memory) needs fewer CMOS control buses, but large data communication overhead on a single-layer crossbar compared to distributed ReRAM crossbar. Although distributed analog ReRAM crossbar can achieve the best efficiency from energy perspective, it has larger area compared to its digital counterpart. As shown in Table 5.1, ReRAM crossbar in analog fashion only consumes 2.1 μJ for one vector multiplication while the proposed architecture requires 20.15 μJ because most of power consumption comes from ReRAM in computing instead of ADCs. However, ADCs need more area so that ReRAM crossbar with analog fashion is 8.32 mm^2 while the proposed one is only 0.05 mm^2 because of the high density of ReRAM crossbar.

Calculation error of analog and digitalized ReRAM crossbar are compared in Figure 5.6, where M and N are both set as 256. Here the calculation error is the result variation of two schemes: ADC with analog ReRAM and sense amplifier with digital ReRAM. The ReRAM error rate refers to the variation of write voltage applied on the device. Calculation error is very low when ReRAM error rate is smaller than 0.004 for both analog and digitalized fashion ReRAM. However, when ReRAM error rate is larger than 0.004, calculation error of analog fashion ReRAM crossbar increases rapidly, while digitalized fashion ReRAM increases slowly. However, when ReRAM error rate reaches 0.01, calculation error rate of analog ReRAM crossbar goes to 0.25, much higher than the other one with only 0.07. As such, computational error can be reduced in the described architecture compared to analog fashion ReRAM crossbar.

Scalability study

Hardware performance comparison among CMOS-based ASIC and non-distributed and distributed XIMA with varying *M* is shown in Figure 5.5. From area consumption perspective shown in Figure 5.5(a), distributed ReRAM crossbar is much better than

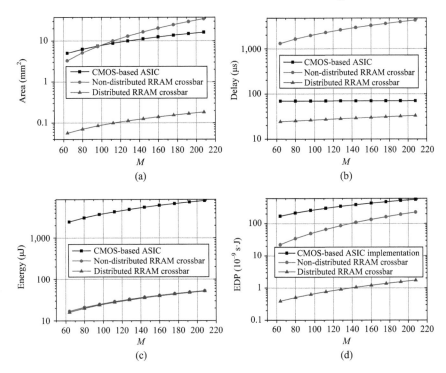

Figure 5.5   Hardware performance scalability under different reduced dimension for (a) area; (b) delay; (c) energy; (d) EDP

the other implementations. With increasing M from 64 to 208, its total area is from 0.057 mm^2 to 0.185 mm^2, approximately 100× smaller than the other two approaches. Non-distributed ReRAM crossbar becomes the worst one when $M > 96$. From the delay perspective, as shown in Figure 5.5(b), non-distributed ReRAM crossbar is the worst, as it has only one control bus and takes too much time on preparing of computing. Delay of non-distributed ReRAM crossbar grows rapidly while distributed ReRAM crossbar and CMOS-based ASIC implementation maintains on approximately 21 and 70 μs, respectively, as the parallel design. For the energy efficiency, as shown in Figure 5.5(c), both non-distributed and distributed ReRAM crossbars do better as logic accelerator is off at most of time. The discussed architecture also performs the best in energy-delay product (EDP) shown in Figure 5.5(d). Distributed XIMA performs the best among all implementation under different specifications. The EDP is from 0.3 × 10^{-9} to 2 × 10^{-9}s · J, which is 60× better than non-distributed ReRAM crossbar and 100× better than CMOS-based ASIC.

What is more, hardware performance comparison with varying N is shown in Figure 5.7. Area and energy consumption trend is similar to Figure 5.5. But for the computational delay, the discussed architecture cannot maintain constant delay as shown in Figure 5.5(b) due to larger time required to configure the input, but still the best among the three. Distributed XIMA still achieves better performance than the other two.

5.1.2   Coupled ReRAM oscillator network

5.1.2.1   Coupled-ReRAM-oscillator network for L2-norm calculation

In a coupled oscillator network, this chapter considers the ReRAM oscillator cell similar to the one shown in Figure 3.15(a) (R_s replaced with a PMOS). By altering the gate

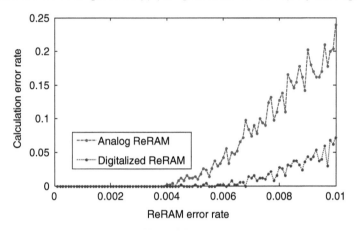

Figure 5.6   Calculation error comparison between multilevel and binary ReRAM

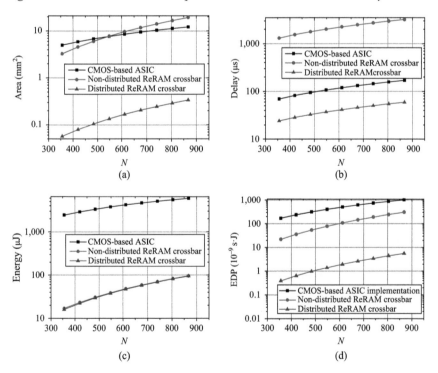

Figure 5.7   Hardware performance scalability under different original dimension for (a) area; (b) delay; (c) energy; (d) EDP

voltage of the PMOS, one can control the oscillatory frequency as in Figure 3.15(d). Referring to the previous works [209,210], the discussed coupled-ReRAM-oscillator network is shown in Figure 5.8(a). Here, the oscillators are directly coupled with ReRAMs. The oscillatory frequency of each oscillator is determined by multiple input voltages. As mentioned in Figure 3.15(d), the voltage-controlled P-channel metal–oxide–semiconductor (PMOS) can be viewed as a voltage-controlled resistor. Figure 5.8(b) and (c) is the schematic of the oscillators with one input and multiple inputs. After directly coupling, one can have an inverter and a feedback resistor with a diode-connected NMOS. Because of the rectifying property of diode-connected NMOS, these elements guarantee that the current will only pass from the oscillator network to V_{out}. An RC circuit is design at V_{out} so that one can measure the DC voltage of V_{out}. The output voltage indicates the relative synchronization of the coupled oscillators.

5.1.2.2 Performance evaluation

The detailed evaluation of ReRAM-based oscillator is shown in Table 5.2. Compared with the design in [209,210], it has power consumption and can be controlled by

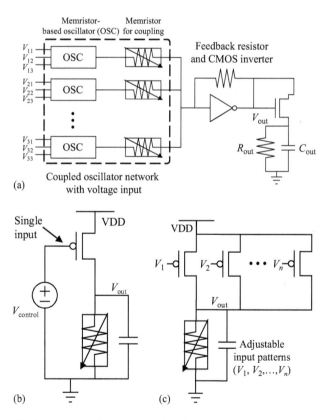

Figure 5.8 *(a) ReRAM oscillator network schematic. (b) Oscillator with single input. (c) Oscillator with multiple input*

multiple voltage inputs easily. As the current through ReRAM-based oscillator is low, the working frequency of the oscillator is lower in some of the compared existing works.

As discussed above, V_{out} is charged by the oscillator network. Therefore, the capacitance of C_{out} should be large enough to avoid the voltage drop at V_{out}. At the meantime, large capacitance leads to a large settling time. Figure 5.9 shows the transient response with $C_{out} = 1, 2, 5$ and 20 pF, respectively. Obviously $C_{out} = 5$ pF is the best configuration because we can capture a stable output at 7.5 μs. In this simulation, the R_{out} is set as 10 MΩ.

5.2   ReRAM network-based in-memory ML accelerator

This section introduces the different computing accelerators based on ReRAM devices. First, the distributed ReRAM-crossbar in-memory architecture (XIMA) will be illustrated in detail. The integration of ReRAM-crossbar-based storage and

Table 5.2   Detailed evaluation of ReRAM-based oscillator

Parameter	V_{DD}	I_{max}	I_{min}	Power	Frequency	Area
Value	1 V	9 μA	3 μA	5.87 μW	6 MHz	0.49 μm^2

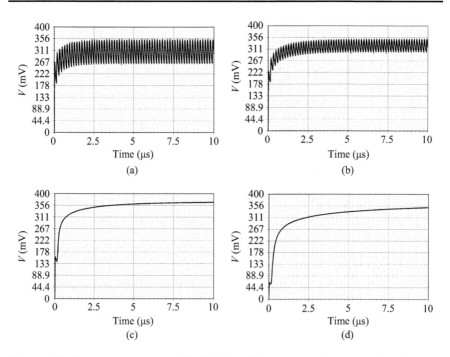

Figure 5.9   Transient response of ReRAM oscillator network output with (a) $C_{out} = 1$ pF; (b) $C_{out} = 2$ pF; (c) $C_{out} = 5$ pF; (d) $C_{out} = 20$ pF

computing brings advantages on throughput. After that, two types of 3D CMOS-ReRAM architectures will be introduced. The major merits of the 3D architecture are less area overhead as well as higher throughput by the 3D interconnection.

5.2.1 Distributed ReRAM-crossbar in-memory architecture

Conventionally, the processor and memory are separate components that are connected through I/Os. With limited width and considerable RC delay, the I/Os are considered the bottleneck of system overall throughput. As memory is typically organized in H-tree structure, where all leaves of the tree are data arrays, it is promising to impose in-memory computation with parallelism at this level. In the following section, a distributed ReRAM-crossbar in-memory architecture (XIMA) is discussed. Such an architecture can be used for several ML applications, as presented in Section 7.5.

5.2.1.1 Memory-computing integration

As both data and logic units have uniform structure when implemented on ReRAM crossbar, half of the leaves are exploited as logic elements and are paired with data arrays. The discussed architecture is illustrated in Figure 5.10. The distributed local data-logic pairs can form one local data path such that the data can be processed locally in parallel, without the need of being read out to the external processor.

Coordinated by the additional controlling unit called *in-pair control bus*, the in-memory computing is performed in following steps: (1) logic configuration: processor issues the command to configure logic by programming logic ReRAM crossbar into specific pattern according to the functionality required; (2) load operand: processor sends the data address and corresponding address of logic accelerator input; (3) execution: logic accelerator can perform computation based on the configured

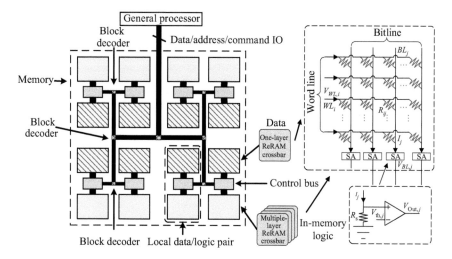

Figure 5.10   Overview of distributed in-memory computing architecture on ReRAM crossbar

logic and obtain results after several cycles; (4) write-back: computed results are written back to data array directly but not to the external processor.

With emphasis on different functionality, the ReRAM crossbars for data storage and logic unit have distinctive interfaces. The data ReRAM crossbar will have only one row activated at a time during read and write operations, and logic ReRAM crossbar; however, one can have all rows activated spontaneously as rows are used to take inputs. As such, the input and output interface of logic crossbar requires analog-to-digital (AD) or digital-to-analog (DA) conversions, which could outweigh the benefits gained. Therefore, in this chapter, a conversion-free digital-interfaced logic ReRAM-crossbar design is presented, which uses three layers of ReRAM crossbars to decompose a complex function into several simple operations that a digital crossbar can tackle.

5.2.1.2   Communication protocol and control bus

The conventional communication protocol between external processor and memory is composed of *store* and *load* action identifier, address that routes to different locations of data arrays and data to be operated. With additional in-memory computation capacity, the presented distributed in-memory computing architecture requires modifications on the current communication protocol. The new communication instructions are proposed in Table 5.3, which is called in-pair control.

In-pair control bus needs to execute instructions in Table 5.3. SW (store word) instruction is to write data into ReRAMs in data array or in-memory logic. If the target address is in a data array, it will be a conventional write or result write-back; otherwise it will be logic configuration. LW (load word) instruction performs similar to a conventional read operation. ST (start) instruction means to switch on the logic block for computing after the computation setup has been done. WT (wait) operation is to stop reading from instruction queue during computing.

Besides the communication instructions, memory address format is also different from that in the conventional architecture. To specify a byte in the proposed architecture, address includes the following identifier segments. First, the data-logic pair index segment is required, which is taken by block decoders to locate the target

Table 5.3   Protocols between external processor and control bus.

Instruction	Operation 1	Operation 2	Action	Function
SW	Address 1	Address 2	Address 1 data to Address 2	Store data, configure logic, in-memory results write-back
	Data	Address	Store data to address	
LW	Address	—	Read data from address	Standard read
ST	Block Index	—	Switch logic block on	Start in-memory computing
WT	—	—	Wait for logic block response	Halt while performing in-memory computing

data-logic pair. Second, one-bit flag is needed to clarify that whether the target address is in data array or in-memory logic crossbar. Third, if logic accelerator is the target, additional segment has to specify the layer index. Lastly, rest of address segment are row and column indexes in each ReRAM crossbar. An address example for data array and in-memory logic is shown in Figure 5.11.

To perform logic operation, the following instructions are required to performed. First, one can store the required input data and ReRAM values with SW operation. Second, an ST instruction will be issued to enable all the columns and rows to perform the logic computing. The WT instruction is also performed to wait for the completion of logic computing. At last, LW instruction is performed to load the data from the output of ReRAM crossbar.

Given the new communication protocol between general processor and memory is introduced, one can design the according control bus as shown in Figure 5.11. The control bus is composed of an instruction queue, an instruction decoder, an address decoder and an static random access memory (SRAM) array. As the operation frequency of ReRAM crossbar is slower than that of external processor, instructions issued by the external processor will be stored in the instruction queue first. They are then analyzed by instruction decoder on a first-come-first-serve (FCFS) basis. The address decoder obtains the row and column index from the instruction, and SRAM array is used to store temporary data such as computation results, which are later written back to data array.

5.2.2 3D XIMA

5.2.2.1 3D single-layer CMOS-ReRAM architecture

Recent works such as [211–216] have shown that the 3D integration supports heterogeneous stacking as different types of components can be fabricated separately,

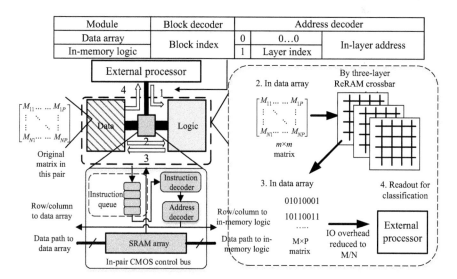

Figure 5.11   Detailed structure of control bus and communication protocol

and layers can be stacked and implemented with different technologies. Therefore, stacking nonvolatile memories on top of microprocessors enables cost-effective heterogeneous integration. Furthermore, works in [217–221] have also shown the feasibility to stack ReRAM on CMOS to achieve smaller area and lower energy consumption.

The discussed 3D CMOS-ReRAM accelerator is shown in Figure 5.12(a). This accelerator is composed of a top layer of WLs, a bottom layer of CMOS circuits and vertical connection between both layers by ReRAM. In this architecture, the ReRAM crossbar performs matrix–vector multiplication and also vector addition, as shown in Figure 5.12(b). Here, we use an example $Y = X \cdot W$ to show the mapping scheme of matrix–vector multiplication. The matrix W needs to be stored in ReRAM crossbar by writing the corresponding resistance. To perform the computations, X is converted to WL voltages and one can obtain the output current I denoting Y. One can simply convert the current to voltage and utilize the ADC for digital conversion [147]. The readout circuit of ReRAM crossbar is implemented by the bottom-layer CMOS. In addition, the control signals of the ReRAM crossbar and other operations (pooling, activation) are also realized by CMOS.

The 3D single-layer CMOS-ReRAM architecture will be used for tensorized neural network (TNN) in the following chapters. This book will further introduce the detailed mapping and results in Sections 6.2 and 6.2.3.

5.2.2.2   3D multilayer CMOS-ReRAM architecture

Besides the 3D single-layer CMOS-ReRAM architecture, this chapter also discusses the 3D multilayer CMOS-ReRAM architecture for online ML applications as well. This 3D multilayer CMOS-ReRAM accelerator with three layers is shown in Figure 5.13(a). This accelerator is composed of a two-layer ReRAM-crossbar and one-layer CMOS circuit. As Figure 5.13(a) shows, Layer 1 of ReRAM crossbar is implemented as a buffer to temporarily store input data to be processed. Layer 2 of ReRAM crossbar performs logic operations such as matrix–vector multiplication and

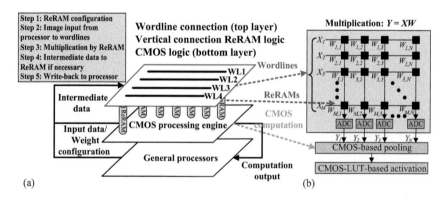

Figure 5.12   *(a) 3D CMOS-ReRAM accelerator architecture; (b) ReRAM-based matrix–vector multiplication engine*

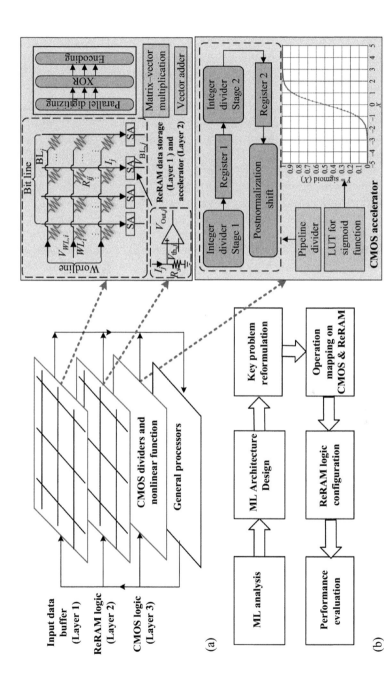

Figure 5.13 (a) 3D multilayer CMOS-ReRAM accelerator architecture; (b) incremental ML algorithm mapping flow on proposed accelerator

also vector addition, as discussed earlier. Note that buffers are designed to separate resistive networks between Layers 1 and 2. The last layer of CMOS contains read-out circuits for ReRAM crossbar and performs as logic accelerators designed for other operations besides matrix–vector multiplication, including pipelined divider, look-up table (LUT) designed for division operation and activation function in ML.

Moreover, Figure 5.13(b) shows the workflow for incremental ML based on the proposed architecture. First, the detailed architecture of ML (e.g., number of layers and activation function) is determined based on the accuracy requirements and data characteristics. Second, operations of this ML algorithm are analyzed and reformulated so that all the operations can be accelerated in 3D multilayer CMOS-ReRAM architecture as illustrated in Figure 5.13(a). Furthermore, the bit width operating on ReRAM crossbar is also determined by balancing the accuracy loss and energy saving. Finally, logic operations on ReRAM crossbar and CMOS are configured based on the reformulated operations, energy saving and speedup.

Such a 3D multilayer CMOS-ReRAM architecture has advantages in three manifold. First, by utilizing ReRAM crossbar for input data storage, leakage power of memory is largely removed. In a 3D architecture with TSV interconnection, the bandwidth from this layer to next layer is sufficiently large to perform parallel computation. Second, ReRAM crossbar can be configured as computational units for the matrix–vector multiplication with high parallelism and low power. Lastly, with an additional layer of CMOS-ASIC, more complicated tasks such as division and non-linear mapping can be performed. As a result, the whole training process of ML can be fully mapped to the proposed 3D multilayer CMOS-ReRAM accelerator architecture towards real-time training and testing.

The 3D multilayer CMOS-ReRAM architecture will be used for online ML (both learning and inference phases) in the following chapters. We will further introduce the detailed mapping and results in Sections 6.2 and 6.2.3.

Chapter 6
The mapping of machine learning algorithms on XIMA

This chapter presents the mapping of multiple machine learning applications on different resistive random-access memory (ReRAM)-based architectures discussed in Chapter 5. For each application, a detailed mapping strategy, experimental settings and evaluation results are presented here.

6.1 Machine learning algorithms on XIMA

First, this chapter presents a detailed mapping of several machine learning applications on distributed in-memory computing architecture (XIMA), including single-layer feedforward neural network (SLFN)-based learning, binary convolutional neural network (BCNN)-based inferences on passive array as well as One Selector One ReRAM (1s1R) array.

6.1.1 SLFN-based learning and inference acceleration

The details of SLFN-based learning are presented in [148]. In [148], one maps the SLFN-based learning and inference process according to the algorithm and network in Section 4.2. In this network, matrix–vector multiplication, the major operation in machine learning on ReRAM crossbar is implemented by three steps with detailed mapping strategy for each step. The process of mapping of $\mathbf{X}'\mathbf{A}$ to ReRAM is shown in Figure 4.3 as example.

In matrix–vector multiplication, let us assume the output matrix is $\mathbf{Y}$. For better understanding, we replace $\mathbf{X}'$ with $\mathbf{X}$ and $\mathbf{A}$ with Φ, and the equation becomes $\mathbf{Y} = \mathbf{X}\Phi$. For every element in $\mathbf{Y}$, it follows

$$y_{ij} = \sum_{k=1}^{N} x_{ik}\varphi_{kj} \tag{6.1}$$

where x and φ are the elements in $\mathbf{X}$ and Φ, respectively. The calculation of y_{ij} by four-step ReRAM crossbar is shown in the following subsections.

6.1.1.1 Step 1. Parallel digitizing

The first step parallel digitizing requires an $N \times N$ ReRAM crossbar. The idea is to split the matrix–vector multiplication to multiple inner-product operations of two vectors. Each inner product is produced ReRAM crossbar as shown in Figure 6.1(a). x is set as crossbar input and φ is written in ReRAM cells. In $N \times N$ ReRAM crossbar, resistance of ReRAMs in each column is the same, but Vth among columns are different. We have

$$V_{\text{th},j} = \frac{(2j+1)V_r R_{\text{fixed}}}{2R_{\text{on}}} \tag{6.2}$$

which are ladder-like threshold voltages to identify the result. If the inner-product result is s, the output of columns will be

$$O_{1,j} = \begin{cases} 1, & j \leq s \\ 0, & j > s \end{cases} \tag{6.3}$$

6.1.1.2   Step 2. XOR

The second step is exclusive OR (XOR) to identify the index of s where $O_{1,s} = 1$ and $O_{1,s+1} = 0$, so the operation is $O_{1,s} \oplus O_{1,s+1}$. According to (6.3), the case $O_{1,j} = 0$ and $O_{1,j+1} = 1$ is impossible, so the XOR operation can be converted to $O_{1,s}\overline{O_{1,s+1}}$ and $\overline{O_{1,s}} + O_{1,s+1}$. The mapping of ReRAM-crossbar input and resistance in this step is shown in Figure 6.1(b), and threshold voltage configuration is

$$V_{\text{th},j} = \frac{V_r R_{\text{fixed}}}{2R_{\text{on}}} \tag{6.4}$$

Therefore, only the output of sth column is 1 and the others are 0.

6.1.1.3   Step 3. Encoding

The third step takes the output of XOR step and produces s in binary format as an encoder. The input of ReRAM crossbar is from the second step and only one input is 1, so that according binary format is stored in corresponding row, as shown in

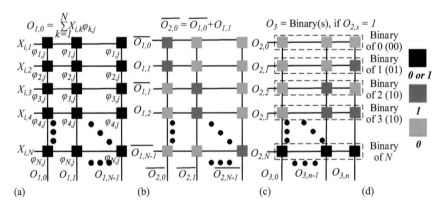

(a)   (b)   (c)   (d)

Figure 6.1   Detailed mapping for digitalized matrix–vector multiplication: (a) parallel digitizing; (b) XOR 2; (c) encoding; (d) legend of ReRAM mapping

Figure 6.1(c). Encoding step needs an $N \times n$ ReRAM crossbar, where $n = \lceil \log_2 N \rceil$ is the number of bits in order to represent N in binary format. The thresholds for the encoding step are set following (6.4) as well.

6.1.1.4 Step 4. Adding and shifting for inner-product result

The output of encoding step is in binary format, but some processes are needed to obtain the final inner-product result (Figure 6.2). Adder and shifter are designed to complete this process as shown in Figure 6.1(d). Let us consider the original data are 8-bit and data dimension is 512, the workload of adder is 512 without any acceleration for the purpose of illustration. With four-step ReRAM-crossbar accelerator as preprocessing, the workload of adder can be significantly reduced to 9 ($\log_2 512$).

6.1.2 BCNN-based inference acceleration on passive array

The details of this section have been presented in [222]. As indicated in previous works, ReRAM crossbar can be applied to perform logic operations, especially the dot-product-based convolutions. Previous mapping of convolutional neural network (CNN) are mainly based on the traditional analog ReRAM crossbar [145,150]. The main limitation is that there can exist a huge nonuniform analog resistance for undetermined states in the analog computation, which can result in convolution error.

Here, we will map the bitwise CNN-based inference process according to the algorithm and network in Section 4.3.3. This section focuses on the mapping of all the bitwise CNN operations on the passive array-based XIMA such as convolution, batch normalization, pooling and activation functions.

6.1.2.1 Mapping bitwise convolution

According to (6.5), the bitwise convolution can be split into several XNOR and bit-count results of two vectors. To implement (6.5), we can use two AND operations for a_{k-1}^b and w_k^b as well as their complements. Therefore, the bitwise convolution on ReRAM crossbar can be shown as follows:

$$s_k = \sum_{i=1}^{N} w_k^b \otimes a_{k-1}^b = \sum_{i=1}^{N} (w_k^b \cdot a_{k-1}^b + \overline{w_k^b} \cdot \overline{a_{k-1}^b}) \tag{6.5}$$

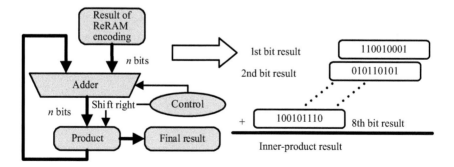

Figure 6.2   ReRAM-based inner-product operation

The mapping of the bitwise convolution is shown in Figure 6.3(a). It requires a $2N \times N$ ReRAM crossbar, where N is the number of element in the vector. All columns are configured with the same elements that correspond to one column in binary weight w_k^b of the neural network, and the wordline (WL) voltages are determined by the binary input a_{k-1}^b. Due to the large ratio between R_{off} and R_{on}, the current through the bitline (BL) is approximately equal to $\frac{s_k V_r R_s}{R_{on}}$, where s_k is the inner-product result in (6.6). Since the current of all BLs is identical, the ladder-like threshold voltages $V_{th,j}$ are set as follows:

$$V_{th,j} = \frac{(2j+1)V_r R_s}{2R_{on}} \tag{6.6}$$

where $V_{th,j}$ is the threshold voltage for the jth column. If one uses s' to denote the output array, and $s'(j)$ to denote the output of column j in ReRAM crossbar, we can have

$$s_k'(j) = \begin{cases} 1, & j < s_k \\ 0, & j \geq s_k \end{cases} \tag{6.7}$$

In this case, the inner-product results s_k can be recognized that the first $(N - s_k)$ output bits are 0 and the rest s_k bits are 1. The relation between s_k' and s_k can be expressed as $s_k' = g(s_k)$.

As described in (6.5), each binary weight vector w_k performs bitwise convolution with several input features. As a result, each logic block in Figure 6.2 stores a binary vector w_k, while the control bus transmits the input feature sequentially. In this case, bitwise convolution can be performed in parallel in separated logic blocks.

6.1.2.2   Mapping bitwise batch normalization

Bitwise batch normalization requires two digital ReRAM crossbars in the implementation. In the first ReRAM crossbar, it performs the XOR operation on adjacent bits of the output of bitwise convolution. It can be expressed as

$$s_k''(j) = \begin{cases} 1, & j = s_k \\ 0, & j \neq s_k \end{cases} \tag{6.8}$$

After that, the second ReRAM crossbar builds a look-up table (LUT). Since μ, σ^2, γ and β are all fixed in the inference stage, (6.8) can be rewritten as

$$a_k = f(s_k) \tag{6.9}$$

where $f(\cdot)$ represents the LUT. As a result, the LUT is stored in the second ReRAM crossbar according to the parameters μ, σ^2, γ and β. As described in (6.8), only the s_kth row of the LUT is selected, so the batch normalization result can be directly read out. The threshold voltage of both ReRAM crossbars is

$$V_{th} = \frac{V_r R_s}{2R_{on}} \tag{6.10}$$

To have a better illustration, Figure 6.3(b) shows the detailed mapping and Table 6.1 shows the values to store in the second ReRAM crossbar when $\mu = 2.5$, $\sigma^2 = 5$, $\gamma = 1$ and $\beta = 0$ referred to the IEEE-754 standard.

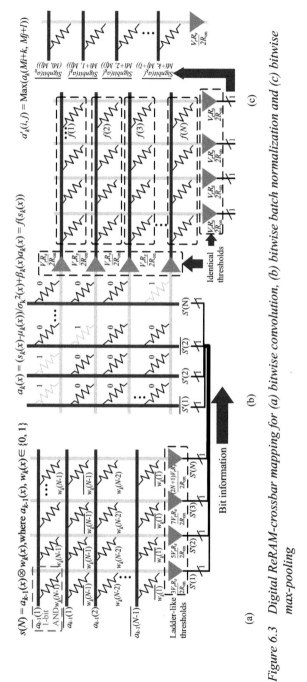

Figure 6.3 Digital ReRAM-crossbar mapping for (a) bitwise convolution, (b) bitwise batch normalization and (c) bitwise max-pooling

Table 6.1   Binary format stored in ReRAM crossbar

BinConv output	Batch normalization	Floating binary format
0	−0.5	10111111000000000000000000000000
1	−0.3	10111110100110011001100110011010
...	...	...
7	0.9	00111111011001100110011001100110

6.1.2.3   Mapping bitwise pooling and binarization

According to (6.9), one can perform the binarization first and then perform max-pooling. The bitwise activation in (6.8) can be achieved by selecting the sign-bit of the binary format output of Figure 6.3(b). In max-pooling, the output is 0 only when all the numbers in the pooling region are negative. As a result, one can add all the complementary sign-bit in the pooling region. If the result is not 0, it indicates that at least one positive number is available in the pooling region, resulting in the pooling result 1. In summary, the max-pooling in (6.5) can be rewritten as

$$a'_k(i,j) = \begin{cases} 1, \text{if} \sum \overline{\text{Sign}\{a_k(Mi + k, Mj + l)\}} > 0 \\ 0, \text{otherwise} \end{cases} \tag{6.11}$$

As a result, both of the bitwise max-pooling and binarization can be implemented by the addition operation performed on the digital ReRAM crossbar with 1 column, as shown in Figure 6.3(c).

6.1.2.4   Summary of mapping bitwise CNN

As a summary, the four operations of the bitwise CNN in Figure 4.7(b) can be fully mapped onto the digital ReRAM crossbar. All the threshold voltages are fixed even if the parameters of bitwise CNN are changed. Although these operations are implemented in different ReRAM-crossbar array, the input/output formats of them are compatible so that one can directly connect them as shown in the logic block in Figure 6.3 with pipeline used. The pipeline design is based on Table 6.2, so that each stage implements a layer. CONV-2, CONV-4 and CONV-6 are the stages which require the most ReRAM cells and computation time.

As a result, more logic blocks are assigned to these steps to relieve the critical path. In our simulation, half of the digitized ReRAM crossbars are used to perform these three layers. Moreover, since the output feature from Figure 6.3(c) is binary, the area overhead and energy consumption of the data storage can be significantly reduced. In addition, because layers in Table 6.2 are implemented in different data-logic pairs, the volume of data transmitted is also decreased.

Table 6.2   *Bitwise CNN configuration of CIFAR-10 data set*

Name	Filter/weight	Output size
CONV-1	$3 \times 3 \times 3 \times 128$	$128 \times 32 \times 32$
CONV-2	$3 \times 3 \times 128 \times 128$	$128 \times 32 \times 32$
MP-2	2×2	$128 \times 16 \times 16$
CONV-3	$3 \times 3 \times 128 \times 256$	$256 \times 16 \times 16$
CONV-4	$3 \times 3 \times 256 \times 256$	$256 \times 16 \times 16$
MP-4	2×2	$256 \times 8 \times 8$
CONV-5	$3 \times 3 \times 256 \times 512$	$512 \times 8 \times 8$
CONV-6	$3 \times 3 \times 512 \times 512$	$512 \times 8 \times 8$
MP-6	2×2	$512 \times 4 \times 4$
FC-1	$8,192 \times 1,024$	$1,024$
FC-2	$1,024 \times 1,024$	$1,024$
FC-3	$1,024 \times 10$	10

6.1.3   BCNN-based inference acceleration on 1S1R array

In this work, we will present mappings of bitwise CNN operations on the sneak-path-free digital 1S1R ReRAM crossbar. The mapping detail is a little different compared to the mapping on passive array. Different from the signed realization in previous works [149,223], we will use unsigned bitwise operation in the mapping.

6.1.3.1   Mapping unsigned bitwise convolution

As described in Section 6.1.2, dot-product operation is the majority in bitwise convolution. Suppose that a single dot-product operation has N numbers, the basic operation can be expressed as

$$s_{x,y} = \sum_{i=1}^{N} a_{x,i} \cdot w_{i,y} \tag{6.12}$$

where $a_x, i, w_{i,y} \in \{-1, +1\}$. To implement the negative weights, [149,223] use two ReRAM crossbars to represent positive and negative weights, respectively. However, this solution requires a subtraction operation for every complementary BL output. It is obvious that the subtraction implementation leads to extra CMOS circuit with more area and energy consumption. To avoid this problem, one can apply the conversion by XNOR operation ($\odot$) in $\{0, 1\}$ introduced in [189,224], as shown in Table 6.3.

Since $a' \odot w' = a' \cdot w' + \overline{a'} \cdot \overline{w'}$, one can directly map $a', \overline{a'}$ as WL inputs, and $w', \overline{w'}$ as ReRAM conductances. We can use s' to denote the new bitwise convolution result as

$$s'_{x,y} = \sum_{i=1}^{N} a'_{x,i} \odot w'_{i,y} = \sum_{i=1}^{N} (a'_{x,i} \cdot w'_{i,y} + \overline{a'_{x,i}} \cdot \overline{w'_{x,i}}) \tag{6.13}$$

Table 6.3   Conversion from signed bitwise convolution to unsigned bitwise XNOR

a	w	Multiplication	a'	w'	XNOR
+1	+1	+1	1	1	1
+1	−1	−1	1	0	0
−1	+1	−1	0	1	0
−1	−1	+1	0	0	1

Since s must be an even integer and $s \in [-N, N]$ while $s' \in [0, N]$, the relation can be summarized as $s = 2s' - N$. Although this mapping strategy requires the same number of ReRAM devices as the one in [149,223], it only needs an inverter for each input bit.

6.1.3.2   Mapping batch normalization, pooling and binarization

Section 4.3.3 has explained these three steps with detailed equations, but it is simpler to map them on ReRAM crossbar. We can notice that the order of binarization and pooling does not affect the final output. Therefore, by combining batch normalization and binarization, we can use $c = \mu - \beta\sqrt{\sigma^2}/\gamma$ from BatchNorm (parameters for the $\{0, 1\}$ convolution fashion) as the threshold to compare with the bitwise convolution result. Although the corresponding voltage of c is generated by limited-bit DAC, it is still more energy-efficient than the ADC for analog ReRAM crossbar. The comparison process is binarization with only 0 or 1 output. These two steps can be summarized as

$$Out = \begin{cases} 1, & \sum_{i=1}^{N} a_{x,i} \odot w_{i,y} \geq \mu - \beta\sqrt{\sigma^2}/\gamma \\ 0, & \sum_{i=1}^{N} a_{x,i} \odot w_{i,y} < \mu - \beta\sqrt{\sigma^2}/\gamma \end{cases} \tag{6.14}$$

As for pooling operation, we can put a single-output ReRAM crossbar and configure the comparator threshold as $\frac{V_r R_s}{2(R_s + R_{LRS})}$ to detect if any binarization result in the pooling region is 1.

Figure 6.4 shows the summary of bitwise CNN mapping on the proposed digital ReRAM crossbar. Since the output of each BL is also in $\{0, 1\}$ fashion, it can be directly used for the binary input feature of the next layer.

6.1.4   L2-norm gradient-based learning and inference acceleration

The details of this section have been presented in [225]. This section illustrates mapping of the multilayer feedforward neural network-based learning and inference processes according to the algorithm and network in Section 4.2.2. This section focuses on the mapping of all the matrix–vector multiplication operations and L2-norm calculation on the passive array and coupled oscillator-based XIMA.

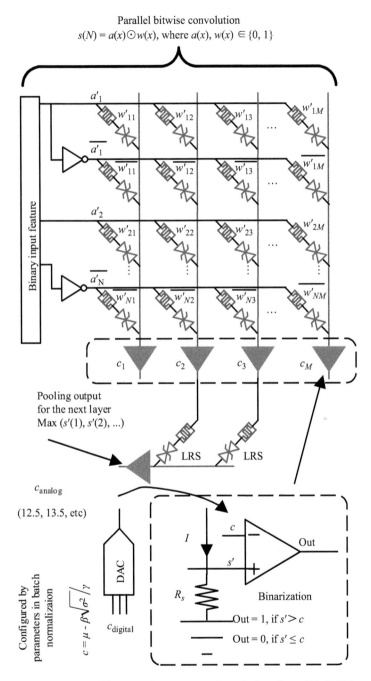

Figure 6.4   Mapping of bitwise CNN on sneak-path-free digital ReRAM crossbar

6.1.4.1   Mapping matrix–vector multiplication on ReRAM-crossbar network

With the introduction of binary-memristor-crossbar network, one can perform matrix–vector multiplication [147]. It has much better nonuniformity under process variation when compared to the multiple-level-valued analog memristor crossbar. As discussed in Section 6.1.2, the key operations in machine learning (feature extraction and convolution) requires a large number of matrix–vector multiplication.

As discussed earlier, the key operations (6.13) and (6.14) requires a large number of matrix–vector multiplication. For instance, consider $\mathbf{Y} = \mathbf{HW}$ as an example for mapping multiplication on crossbar. For every element in $\mathbf{Y}$, it follows, here, we take the operation of $\mathbf{Y} = \mathbf{HW}$ as an example for mapping the multiplication on the crossbar. For every element in $\mathbf{Y}$, it follows

$$y_{ij} = \sum_{k=1}^{N} h_{ik} w_{kj} \tag{6.15}$$

where h and w are the elements in $\mathbf{H}$ and $\mathbf{W}$, respectively.

For the crossbar structure in Figure 6.4, the current through each BL follows

$$I_j = \sum_{i=1}^{m} \frac{V_{wl,i} R_{\text{fixed}}}{R_{ij}} \tag{6.16}$$

As a result, we can map h_{ik} and w_{kj} on $V_{wl,i}$ and R_{ij}, respectively. By measuring the current through BL with binary digitization, one can derive the result y_{ij} in the digital domain. The detailed operation can be referred to the work in [147].

Note that for real numbers, one needs only a few more shifted additions to complete the final process of matrix–vector multiplication with memristor crossbar. Figure 6.5 shows that we only need four-shifted addition with 8-bit precision to calculate the final inner product. In addition, Sigmoid function can be implemented in memristor crossbar with LUT.

6.1.4.2   Mapping L2-norm calculation on coupled ReRAM oscillator network

In a coupled oscillator network, we use the memristor oscillator cell similar to that in Figure 3.15(a) (Rs replaced with a PMOS). By altering the gate voltage of the PMOS, we can control the oscillatory frequency as in Figure 3.15(d). Referring to previous works [209,210], the proposed coupled-memristor-oscillator network is shown in Figure 5.8(a). Here, oscillators are directly coupled with memristors. The oscillatory frequency of each oscillator is determined by multiple input voltages. As mentioned in Figure 3.15(d), the voltage-controlled PMOS can be viewed as a voltage-controlled resistor. Figures 5.8(b) and 5.8(c) are the schematic of oscillators with single input and multiple inputs. After directly coupling, one can have an inverter and a feedback resistor with a diode-connected NMOS. These elements guarantee that the current will only pass from the oscillator network to V_{out}. An RC circuit is designed at V_{out} so that we can measure the DC voltage of V_{out}. The output voltage indicates the relative synchronization of the coupled oscillators.

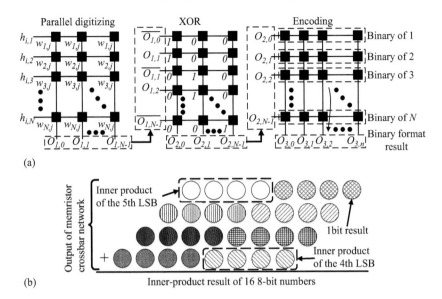

(a)

(b)

Figure 6.5   (a) Crossbar network for multiplication; (b) shifted additions

To perform (4.14) on oscillator network, we only need to use two inputs for each oscillator in Figure 5.8(c). To be more specific, one can have a mapping function as follows:

$$V_{ik1} = V_{\text{bias}} + \alpha t_{ik} \qquad\qquad V_{ik2} = V_{\text{bias}} - \alpha y_{ik} \qquad (6.17)$$

where α is a scale factor to link the oscillator input voltage, and t_{ik} and y_{ik} are the elements in matrices $\mathbf{T}$ and $\mathbf{Y}$, respectively.

As mentioned in [209,210], the coupled oscillator network can work as a degree-of-match (DOM) circuit to calculate L2-norm by fitting V_{out} to 2nd polynomial when there are two inputs for each oscillator in Figure 5.8(c). Therefore, the output voltage follows

$$V_{\text{out}} = V_{\text{min}} + \eta||\mathbf{T} - \mathbf{Y}||_2^2 = V_{\text{min}} + \eta \sum_{k=1}^{M} \sum_{i=1}^{N} (t_{ik} - y_{ik})^2 \qquad (6.18)$$

where η is a fitting parameter, and V_{min} is the output voltage when $||\mathbf{T} - \mathbf{Y}||_2^2 = 0$.

As such, one can use the coupled-memristor-oscillator network to the L2-norm error function in machine learning. The L2-norm result is obtained by curve fitting but not accurate computing. Compared to other implementations, such an oscillator network can complete the operation much faster because the square operation $(t_{ik} - y_{ik})^2$ can be performed simultaneously by the oscillator circuit. Moreover, the accumulation is also automatically achieved by the coupled network.

6.1.4.3 Mapping flow of multilayer neural network on ReRAM network

Based on the coupled-memristor-oscillator network and binary-memristor-crossbar network, we can accelerate direct-gradient-based L2-norm minimization for machine learning as shown in Figure 6.6. For the model part, we use two types: memristor oscillator and memristor crossbar. We find the parameter in oscillator network to calculate L2-norm, and map on crossbar network to calculate digitized matrix–vector multiplication. Afterwards, one can generate the initial weights of A and W to calculate the gradient δE. The best direction to minimize E can be derived. This process will be repeated several times till the minimization is reached only when $E^k - E^{k-1} <$ threshold.

6.1.5 Experimental evaluation of machine learning algorithms on XIMA architecture

We will show the detailed mapping of several machine learning applications on XIMA, including SLFN-based learning, BCNN-based inferences on passive array as well as 1S1R array.

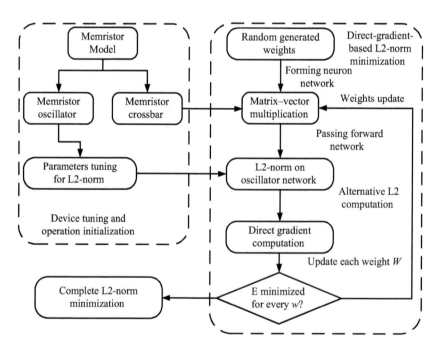

Figure 6.6 Mapping flow of machine learning on memristor network

6.1.5.1 SLFN-based learning and inference acceleration

Experiment settings

The hardware evaluation platform is implemented on a computer server with 4.0 GHz core and 16.0 GB memory. Feature extraction is implemented by general processor, CMOS-based application-specific integrated circuit (ASIC), non-distributed and distributed in-memory computing based on digitalized ReRAM crossbar, respectively. For the ReRAM-crossbar design evaluation, the resistance of ReRAM is set as 1 kΩ and 1 MΩ as on-state and off-state resistance, respectively, according to [206].

The general processor solution is performed by MATLAB® on a 4.0 GHz desktop. For CMOS-ASIC implementation, we implement it by Verilog and synthesize with CMOS 65-nm low-power process design kit (PDK). For ReRAM-crossbar-based solution, we verify the function in circuit level with SPICE tool NVM-SPICE [63]. By analyzing the machine learning algorithm, we obtain the basic operations and the number of ReRAM-crossbar logic units required.

The working frequency of general processor implementation is 4.0 GHz while the CMOS-ASIC feature extraction design frequency is 1.0 GHz. For in-memory computing based on the proposed ReRAM crossbar, write voltage V_w is set as 0.8 V and read voltage V_r is set as 0.1 V as well as duration time of 5 ns. In addition, the analog computation on ReRAM crossbar is performed for comparison based on design in [207].

In the following, we will show the performance of matrix–vector multiplication on ReRAM crossbar first. A scalability study is introduced to show the area, energy and computation delay with different matrix sizes. Afterwards, the evaluation of face recognition on in-memory architecture is presented. Finally, we will illustrate the object classification on three-dimensional (3D) CMOS-ReRAM architecture. Performance of different bid-width configurations will be also shown. In addition, the 3D CMOS-ReRAM solution will be compared with CMOS-ASIC as well as Graphics Processing Unit (GPU) implementation.

Performance evaluation

In this work, we implement the face recognition application on the in-memory architecture. We will analyze the computation complexity of face recognition first, and then evaluate the performance.

In the experiment, 200 face images of 13 people are selected from [226], with scaled image size 262 of each image **X**. In principal component analysis (PCA), feature size of image is further reduced to 128 by multiplying the matrix **R**. The number of hidden node L and classes m are 160 and 13, respectively. Based on the experimental settings, computation complexity is analyzed with results shown in Figure 6.7. Here 82% of computations are multiplication in output weight calculation, which is the most time-consuming procedure in neural network. Time consumption of each process in neural network is introduced in Figure 6.7(b). Since processes except activation function involve matrix–vector multiplication, we extracted this operation in the whole algorithm and found that 64.62% of time is consumed in matrix–vector multiplication, as shown in Figure 6.7(c).

We implement the face recognition applications by the SLFN on XIMA. In Table 6.4, general performance comparisons among MATLAB, CMOS-ASIC and ReRAM-crossbar accelerator are introduced, and the acceleration of each procedure as the formula described in Section 7.2 is also addressed. Among three implementations, ReRAM-crossbar architecture performs the best in area, energy and speed. Compared to MATLAB implementation, it achieves 32.84× speedup, 210.69× energy-saving and almost four-magnitude area-saving. We also design a CMOS-ASIC implementation with similar structure as ReRAM crossbar with better performance compared to

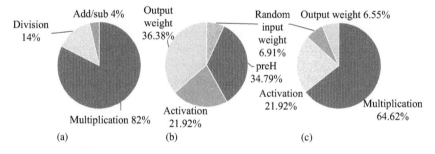

Figure 6.7   (a) Time-consumption breakdown for output weight calculation;
(b) neural network training computation effort analysis;
(c) multiplication analysis for neural network training (N = 200,
n = 128, L = 160 and m = 13)

Table 6.4   Face recognition performance comparison under different software and hardware implementations

Implementation	Frequency	Area	Power	Type	Time	Energy
CPU (MATLAB)	4.0 GHz	177 mm²	84 W	PCA	1.56 ms	131 mJ
				Input layer	0.98 ms	82 mJ
				L2-norm	92.5 ms	7.77 J
				Output layer	0.1 ms	8.40 mJ
				Overall	95.14 ms	7.99 J
CMOS-ASIC	1.0 GHz	5.64 mm²	39.41 W	PCA	195 μs	7.68 mJ
				Input layer	121.9 μs	4.80 mJ
				L2-norm	12.26 ms	483 mJ
				Output layer	12.4 μs	0.49 mJ
				Overall	12.59 ms	496 mJ
				Improvement	7.56×	16.11×
Distributed in-memory ReRAM-crossbar architecture	200 MHz	0.11 mm²	13.1 W	PCA	38.4 μs	0.5 mJ
				Input layer	24 μs	0.3 mJ
				L2-norm	2.83 ms	37.1 mJ
				Output layer	2.4 μs	30 μJ
				Overall	2.90 ms	37.93 mJ
				Improvement	32.84×	210.69×

MATLAB. ReRAM-crossbar architecture is 4.34× speedup, 13.08× energy-saving and 51.3× area-saving compared to CMOS-ASIC. The performance comparison is quite different from Table 5.1, because we applied different designs (ReRAM-crossbar size) is this two experiments according to the dimension of matrices.

The result of face recognition is shown in Figure 6.8. Five training classes are provided as an example with three test cases. Each test face will be recognized as the class with the largest score (prediction result as the index of *Max*(**Y**), marked in red color). In this example, Case 1 is identified as Class 1, while Cases 2 and 3 are classified into Classes 3 and 5, respectively.

6.1.5.2 L2-norm gradient-based learning and inference acceleration

Experiment settings

The hardware evaluation platform is implemented on a computer server with 4.0 GHz core and 16.0 GB RAM. For ReRAM-based oscillator network, we use the VerilogA model from [153] and device model from [151] as the ReRAM before forming process and simulate the network in Cadence Spectre. For ReRAM-based crossbar network, the resistance of ReRAM is set as 1 kΩ and 1 MΩ as on-state and off-state resistance, respectively, according to [206]. NVM-SPICE [63] is used for ReRAM-crossbar network verification. For comparison propose, we also implement the L2-norm gradient-based machine learning on general processor. The working frequency of general processor implementation is 3.46 GHz with 64.0 GB RAM. In addition, University of California Irvine (UCI) benchmark data are selected for comparisons [184]. Write voltage V_w is set as 0.8 V and read voltage V_r is set as 0.1 V as well as duration time of 5 ns.

Performance evaluation

To evaluate the proposed ReRAM network for machine learning, we use Iris in UCI data set as benchmark. First, we analyze the computation complexity in L2-norm-gradient-based machine learning. Figure 6.9(a) shows the time consumption of CMOS-CPU-based implementation. In simulation, we need to optimize the value

	Test case 1 (Y)	Test case 2 (Y)	Test case 3 (Y)
Test cases/ classes			
Class 1	1.518062	−0.79108	−0.58029
Class 2	−0.29803	−0.87155	−0.24397
Class 3	−0.95114	0.793256	−0.35867
Class 4	−0.65597	−0.44714	−0.70879
Class 5	−0.65955	0.262689	0.872497
⋮	⋮	⋮	⋮

Figure 6.8 Training samples and prediction value Y from (4.7) for face recognitions

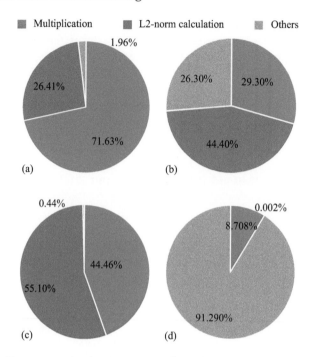

Figure 6.9 *Time-consumption proportion of Iris data set: (a) without ReRAM*
network; (b) with ReRAM network, and energy consumption proportion
of Mushroom data set; (c) without ReRAM network; (d) with ReRAM
network

of 32 weights to minimize the L2-norm. 71.63% computation time is consumed by
matrix–vector multiplication, and 26.41% time is consumed by L2-norm calculation.
Therefore, the total computation time can be significantly reduced by accelerating
these two operations.

To evaluate the ReRAM network performance in Iris data set, we use the proposed
ReRAM network to address matrix–vector multiplication and L2-norm calculation.
For the other operations (1.96% in Figure 6.9(a)), we still use CPU for calculation.
As there are 32 weights to be updated in the benchmark, we design 32 ReRAM-
oscillator networks to compute E for each w simultaneously. In the experiment, we
need to repeat this procedure for 7 times to derive the minimum of L2-norm. The
time consumption with ReRAM network is shown in Figure 6.9(b). We can see that
L2-norm becomes the dominant time-consuming operation. In addition, the matrix–
vector multiplication and L2-norm take only 3× as the other operations, which only
take little time in machine learning.

Figure 6.9(c) and (d) shows the energy efficiency achieved by the proposed
ReRAM network. The energy consumption of machine learning on ReRAM network
is significantly reduced. Note that each ReRAM-oscillator-network requires 7.5 μs
to perform the one-time L2-norm calculation with 5.87 μW according to Table 5.2.

Note that matrix–vector multiplication and L2-norm calculation are dominant in CMOS-CPU-based implementation. For Mushroom data set, they take over 99% of energy consumption. When we map these operations on the ReRAM network, their energy consumption is only 8.7%. We use four benchmarks in UCI data set [184] to measure the speedup and energy-saving, as shown in Table 6.5. Using the proposed ReRAM network, we can achieve 10× speedup and more than 50× energy-saving.

Table 6.5 Time and energy comparison on UCI data set

Benchmark	Training sample	Hidden nodes	Classes	Specifications	CPU	CPU with ReRAM
Iris	114	32	3	Time	0.0159 s	0.0012 s
				Multiplication	1.482 J	1.39 mJ
				L2-norm	0.546 J	0.1 µJ
				Total energy*	2.007 J	0.042 J
				Speedup	–	13.47×
				Energy-saving	–	49.21×
Mushroom	7333	40	2	Time	0.0574 s	0.005 s
				Multiplication	3.315 J	3.0 mJ
				L2-norm	4.108 J	7.584 µJ
				Total energy*	7.462 J	0.0357 J
				Speedup	–	11.48×
				Energy-saving	–	209.02×
Wine	160	40	3	Time	0.0409 s	0.0029 s
				Multiplication	3.562 J	3.3 mJ
				L2-norm	1.69 J	0.3 µJ
				Total energy*	5.317 J	0.0639 J
				Speedup	–	13.96×
				Energy-saving	–	83.21×
Liver	317	232	2	Time	0.521 s	0.0558 s
				Multiplication	13.77 J	12.9 mJ
				L2-norm	0.546 J	0.1 µJ
				Total energy*	53.86 J	0.12 J
				Speedup	–	9.34×
				Energy-saving	–	564.42×
Shuttle	14,500	170	7	Time	3.35 s	0.411 s
				Multiplication	11.27 J	10.56 mJ
				L2-norm	0.546 J	0.1 µJ
				Total energy*	424.27 J	0.0608 J
				Speedup	–	8.15×
				Energy-saving	–	7162.83×
Glass	192	105	7	Time	0.4 s	0.0304 s
				Multiplication	27.64 J	25.90 mJ
				L2-norm	24.22 J	4.47 µJ
				Total energy*	52 J	0.109 J
				Speedup	–	13.16×
				Energy-saving	–	477.06×

* The total energy includes multiplication, L2-norm and other operations (e.g., gradient calculation) performed in CPU.

Note that the improvement depends on the training size of benchmark. For example, the L2-norm calculation is the dominant operation in Mushroom and Liver so that we can save over 99.5% energy consumption when using the proposed ReRAM network. For Iris and Wine, matrix–vector multiplication is dominant so that the energy-saving is below 99%.

6.1.5.3   BCNN-based inference acceleration on passive array

Experimental settings

Baselines In the simulation, we have implemented different baselines for comparison using both MNIST and CIFAR-10 benchmarks. The detail of each baseline is listed as follows:

CPU: The BNN simulation is run in Matconvnet [227] on a computer server with 3.46 GHz core and 64.0 GB RAM. The BNN network is referred to Table 6.2.

Design of digital ReRAM: The ReRAM device model for BNN is based on [63,64,139] with the resistance of ReRAM set as 0.5M and 5M as on-state and off-state, respectively, with working frequency of 200 MHz. Sense amplifier is based on the design of [228]. The BNN network is also referred to Table 6.2.

Others: GPU-based [188] bitwise CNN implementations and field programmable gate array (FPGA)-based [229], CMOS-ASIC-based [230] and analog-ReRAM-based [146] conventional CNN implementations are selected for performance comparisons as well.

Network The overall network architecture of the bitwise CNN (called BNN) is shown in Table 6.2. It has six binary convolutional (BinConv) layers, three max-pooling (MP) layers and three fully connected (FC) layers.

It takes a 32×32 RGB image as the input of the first layer. We use 128 sets of binary filters, and each set contains three binary filters to process the data from R, G and B channels, receptively. The width and height of each BinConv layer is fixed to 3×3 with stride of 1 and zero padding of 1. The BinConv layer performs the bitwise convolution between input feature maps and weights followed by the bitwise batch normalization and the binary activation. Note that the computation for FC layers can be treated as a convolution with stride of 0 and zero padding of 0. Thus, we refer the matrix multiplication in FC layers to convolution as well.

As shown in Table 6.2, two cascaded convolutional layers form a convolutional block with equivalent 5×5 convolution window. This configuration provides more powerful representation capacity with less amount of weights compared with the direct 5×5 implementation. Meanwhile, binary batch normalization is applied after the convolution to accelerate and stabilize the training. We adopt the binary activation to each BinConv layer and FC layer with the exception for the last FC layer. The output of the last FC layer is fed into the softmax layer [231] without binarization to generate a probabilistic distribution of ten classes.

Besides CIFAR-10, we also show the experiment on MNIST data set [232], with detailed parameters in Table 6.6, which is pretrained on a server. Compared to parameters of CIFAR-10, we use conventional 5×5 convolutional cores in MNIST.

Performance evaluation

We first show accuracy comparison between the analog ReRAM and the digitized ReRAM under device variation. We then show accuracy comparison between the conventional CNN with direct-truncated prevision and the proposed bitwise CNN. Various benchmarks such as CIFAR-10 [233] and MNIST [232] are used here.

Error under device variation In the previous discussion, the digitized ReRAM crossbar has better programming accuracy than the analog ReRAM crossbar. Figure 6.10 shows a 200-time Monte-Carlo simulation of a single ReRAM device programming process with different write voltage V_w, where the voltage amplitude is under Gaussian distribution on the $(3\sigma = 3\%V_w)$, and each column denotes a region of 5 kΩ. It is clear that the digital ReRAM crossbar (only 500 kΩ and 5MΩ) can achieve a

Table 6.6   Bitwise CNN configuration of MNIST data set

Name	Filter/weight	Output size
CONV-1	$5 \times 5 \times 1 \times 20$	$20 \times 28 \times 28$
MP-1	2×2	$20 \times 14 \times 14$
CONV-2	$5 \times 5 \times 20 \times 50$	$50 \times 14 \times 14$
MP-2	2×2	$50 \times 7 \times 7$
FC-1	$2,450 \times 500$	500
FC-2	500×10	10

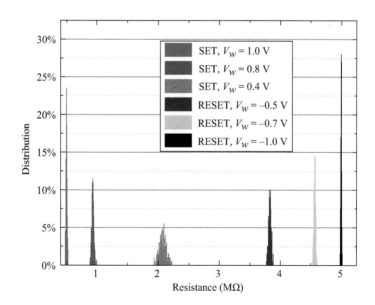

Figure 6.10   ReRAM configuration with voltage amplitude variation following Gaussian distribution

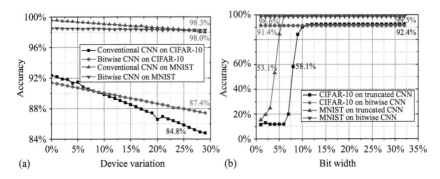

Figure 6.11   (a) Accuracy comparison with analog ReRAM under device variation;
(b) accuracy comparison with truncated CNN with approximation

better uniformity than the analog ReRAM crossbar. The accuracy comparison against device variation on ReRAM is shown in Figure 6.11(b). The percentage of device variation defines the maximum resistance offset, and each ReRAM device follows standard deviation. Monte-Carlo is applied in the generation of device variation. In CIFAR-10, one can observe that when the device variation (ReRAM resistance value) is more than 8%, there is a large output current error reported. For example, when the device variation reaches 29%, the digital ReRAM can have an accuracy of 87.4% with only 4% decreased compared to no variations, better than the analog one with an accuracy of 84.8% with 7.6% decreased. In MNIST, the digital ReRAM is always better even when the device variation is larger than 27%.

Error under approximation For a precision-bit direct-truncated CNN, we use the conventional approach to train the full-precision (32-bit) CNN first, and then decrease the precision of all the weights in the network. The numerical experiment results of weights with different bit-widths are shown in Figure 6.11(b). Here, the weights in the bitwise CNN is 1 bit, whose accuracy of is not changed. In CIFAR-10, although the accuracy of the full precision (32-bit) can reach 92.4% in the direct-truncated CNN, the bit-width influences the accuracy a lot especially when the bit-width is smaller than 10. For example, when the precision decreases to 6-bit, the accuracy drops down to only about 11.8%. In MNIST, the accuracy of the direct-truncated CNN drops significantly when the bit-width is smaller than 6-bit. The results show that the proposed bitwise CNN can perform much better than the direct-truncated CNN.

Scalability study To achieve a better energy efficiency of BNN, we do the scalability study to find out the BNN parameters for both good testing accuracy and energy efficiency. We use a four-layer BNN on MNIST benchmark as a baseline (100% energy efficiency, as shown in Table 6.6), and change the number of output maps of Layer 2 (CONV-2, 50) and hidden nodes of Layer 3 (FC-1, 500), as shown in Figure 6.12(a) and (b). For each energy-efficiency configuration, we do a 20-epoch

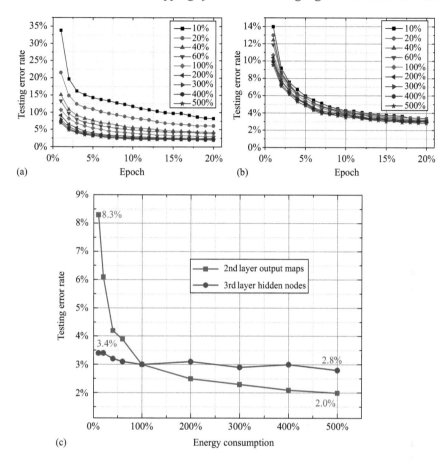

Figure 6.12   Scalability study of testing error rate under different energy consumption with (a) Layer 2 output maps and (b) Layer 3 hidden nodes; (c) comparison with Layer 2 output maps and Layer 3 hidden nodes

training to make a fair comparison. When the number of hidden nodes or output maps decreases, the energy efficiency is better but it will cause higher testing error rate. To summarize the scalability study, Figure 6.12(c) shows that the hidden nodes of Layer 2 is more sensitive to testing accuracy. As a result, increasing the hidden nodes of Layer 2 is better for higher accuracy while decreasing the hidden nodes of Layer 3 is better for energy efficiency.

Performance comparison In this section, $1,000$ images with 32×32 resolution in CIFAR-10 are selected to evaluate the performance among all implementations. Parameters including binary weights, and LUT for batch normalization have been configured by the training process. The detailed comparison is shown in Table 6.7 with numerical results including area, system throughput, computation time and energy consumption. Figure 6.13 shows a recognition example of CIFAR-10 data set. In the numerical experiment, every batch comprises ten images and the results are calculated in parallel. The detailed result figure is included in the supplementary file. The black square represents to the class that each image belongs.

The overall power comparison among all the implementations is shown in Table 6.7 under the similar accuracy of 91.4% in CIFAR-10. Compared to CPU-based and GPU-based bitwise CNN, the proposed digital ReRAM-based implementation can achieve up to four-magnitude smaller power. Moreover, compared to FPGA-based and CMOS-ASIC-based conventional CNN, the digital ReRAM-based implementation is 4, 155× and 62× smaller power.

Table 6.7   Performance comparison among different software and hardware implementations on CIFAR-10 BCNN

Implementations	CPU (Mat-convnet)	GPU [188]	FPGA [229]	CMOS-ASIC [230]	Analog ReRAM [146]	Digital passive ReRAM
Network category	Bitwise CNN	Bitwise CNN	CNN	CNN	CNN	Bitwise CNN
Frequency	3.46 GHz	1.05 GHz	100 MHz	250 MHz	–	100 MHz
Power	130 W	170 W	18.7 W	278 mW	–	4.5 mW
Area (mm^2)	240	601	–	12.25	–	0.78
System throughput	1.48 GOPS	493 GOPS	62 GOPS	42 GOPS	-	792 GOPS
Frame per second	1.2 FPS	400 FPS	46 FPS	35 FPS	-	643 FPS
Energy efficiency (GOPS/W)	0.011	2.9	3.32	151	2,000	176,000
Area efficiency (GOPS/mm^2)	0.006	0.82	–	3.43	–	1,015

– refers to the data not reported.

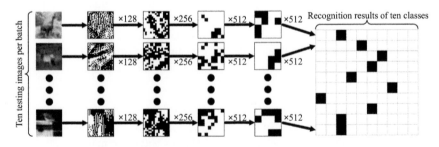

Figure 6.13   Image recognition example of CIFAR-10 data set

In addition, we analyze the detailed power characteristics of the proposed digital ReRAM design in Figure 6.14. First, we analyze the power distribution on convolution, batch normalization, pooling and activation, respectively. Figure 6.14(a) shows that 89.05% of power is consumed by convolution, while 9.17% of power is for batch normalization, and the rest only takes 1.78%. Second, we analyze the power distribution on different bitwise CNN layers in Table 6.2. Results in Figure 6.14(b) show that CONV-6 consumes the most power 25.92%, while CONV-4 and CONV-2 also consume more than 23% of the total power. In general, there is over 98% of power consumed by CONV-2 to CONV-6 layers.

For the throughput performance, we use GOPS (giga operations per second) to evaluate all the implementations. The proposed digital ReRAM can achieve 792 GOPS, which is 535× and 1.61× better than CPU-based and GPU-based implementations, respectively. It is also 12.78× and 18.86× better than FPGA-based and CMOS-ASIC. For energy efficiency, the digital ReRAM achieves 176 TOPS/W, three-magnitude better than the CMOS-ASIC-based CNN. In area-efficiency comparison, the digital ReRAM is 296× better than CMOS-ASIC. The digital ReRAM is the best among all the implementations on both throughput and efficiency.

The design exploration of CIFAR-10 is shown in Figure 6.15. We change the number of CONV-4 output maps to find out the optimized parameter. The normalized energy consumption is referred to the configuration in Table 6.7. The result shows that the accuracy will not increase when the number is larger than 256. When it is lower than 256, the accuracy drops down even though it has better energy consumption and throughput. As a result, the parameters in Table 6.2 are optimal with specifications in Table 6.7.

6.1.5.4   BCNN-based inference acceleration on 1S1R array

Baselines and networks For this experiment, different baselines are implemented for comparison using both CIFAR-10 and MNIST [232] benchmarks, as in Section 6.1.5.3. The detail of each baseline is listed as follows:

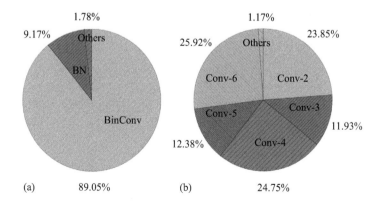

Figure 6.14   Power consumption of bitwise CNN for (a) different operations and (b) different layers

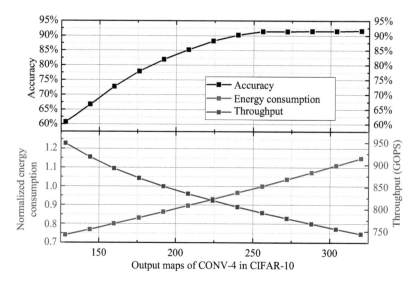

Figure 6.15   Performance with different number of CONV-4 output maps in CIFAR-10

Bitwise CNN: We implement bitwise CNN on digital ReRAM crossbar with working frequency of 100 MHz. Comparator on each BL is based on the design of [228]. In the 1S1R array, the drift-type ReRAM in [139] is applied with $R_{LRS} = 500$ kΩ and $R_{HRS} = 5$ MΩ . Meanwhile, the diffusive-type ReRAM is taken from [137,138] with $R_{on} = 9$ kΩ and $R_{off} = 9$ kΩ. For performance comparison, CPU implementation is run in Matconvnet on a computer server with 3.46 GHz core and 64.0 GB RAM. The GPU-based design is referred to [188], and a CMOS-ASIC design in 40-nm technology is also realized.

Conventional CNN: FPGA-based [229] and CMOS-ASIC-based [234] implementations are compared. Moreover, an analog ReRAM-crossbar-based realization are simulated.

ReRAM device simulation

To illustrate the sneak-path-free effect of the 1S1R implementation, we use SPICE simulation with the same input voltages for Figure 3.14(a) and (c). In the write operation, we set the target $R_{i,j}$ as high resistance state (HRS) and the sneak-path ReRAMs, $R_{i,j-1}, R_{i+1,j-1}, R_{i+1,j}$ are HRS, low resistance state (LRS) and LRS, respectively. By applying $V_{WL,i} = 1$ and $V_{BL,j} = 0$ with other nets floating, the sneak-path ReRAM $R_{i,j-1}$ in direct connection is changed from 5 to 1.4 MΩ, while the one in the 1S1R implementation remains the original resistance shown in Figure 6.16. In the read operation, we set $R_{i,j}$ as HRS and the sneak-path ReRAMs are all LRS. According to the results in Figure 6.17, the direct connection implementation will read $3R_{LRS}//R_{HRS}$ due to the sneak-path effect. Though it takes 500 ns to turn on the selector with read voltage, the target ReRAM can be precisely read out.

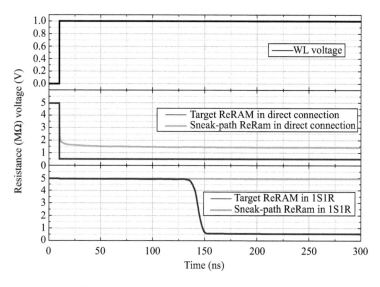

Figure 6.16 Sneak-path-free effect in 1S1R implementation for write operation

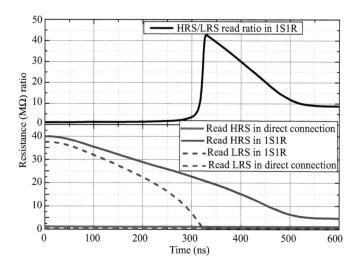

Figure 6.17 Sneak-path-free effect in 1S1R implementation for read operation

Although the 500 ns read time of the proposed 1S1R is much longer than 10 ns of direct connection, the total read energy will not increase much. As shown in Figure 6.17, because the selector in LRS branch can be turned on faster than the one in RHS branch, the RHS/LRS ratio in the read operation can reach 44 instead of the ideal value 10 (5M/500k). As a result, using selector can achieve a larger difference between LRS and RHS readings.

In addition, we show the ReRAM resistance variation with different write voltage V_w in Figure 6.18. We use five sets of ideal V_w from 0.6 to 1.0 V following Gaussian distribution ($3\sigma = 5\%V_w$), and 2,000 data points are simulated to show the distribution of configured ReRAM resistance value in each set. Each column in Figure 6.18 represents a resistance range of 10 kΩ. The results show that the digital ReRAM (LRS with 1.0 V here) has a much better uniformity with input variation compared to analog ReRAM like [150], leading a better programming accuracy.

Performance comparison

We select CIFAR-10 as the benchmark to evaluate all the implementations. Table 6.8 summarizes the performance under similar classification accuracy of 91.4%.

Power consumption Compared to CPU-based and GPU-based bitwise CNN, the proposed digital ReRAM-based implementation can achieve up to 4× smaller power. Compared to simulation result of CMOS-ASIC bitwise CNN, it has 3.17× smaller power. Moreover, compared to FPGA-based and CMOS-ASIC-based conventional CNN, the digital ReRAM-based implementation is 2,968× and 44.1× smaller power, respectively.

In addition, we analyze the detailed power characteristics of the proposed digital ReRAM design in Figure 6.14. First, we analyze the power distribution on convolution, batch normalization, pooling and activation, respectively. Figure 6.14(a) shows that 89.05% of power is consumed by convolution, while 9.17% of power is for batch normalization, and the rest only takes 1.78%. Second, we analyze the power distribution on different bitwise CNN layers in Table 6.2. Results in Figure 6.14(b) show that CONV-6 consumes the most power 25.92%, while CONV-4 and CONV-2 also

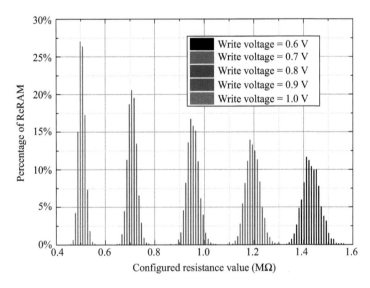

Figure 6.18   Programming inaccuracy for different target resistances with voltage amplitude variation following Gaussian distribution

Table 6.8   *Performance comparison under different software and hardware implementations*

Implementations	CPU (Mat- convnet)	GPU [188]	FPGA [229]	CMOS- ASIC [230]	CMOS- ASIC simulation	Digital 1S1R ReRAM
Network category	Bitwise CNN	Bitwise CNN	CNN	CNN	Bitwise CNN	Bitwise CNN
Frequency	3.46 GHz	1.05 GHz	100 MHz	250 MHz	30 MHz	100 MHz
Power	130 W	170 W	18.7 W	278 mW	20 mW	6.3 mW
Area (mm^2)	240	601	–	12.25	10	1.02
System throughput	1.48 GOPS	493 GOPS	62 GOPS	42 GOPS	621 GOPS	792 GOPS
Energy efficiency (GOPS/W)	0.011	2.9	3.32	151	31,000	126,000
Area efficiency (GOPS/mm^2)	0.006	0.82	–	3.43	62.1	776

– refers to the data not reported.

consume more than 23% of the total power. In general, there is over 98% of power consumed by CONV-2 to CONV-6 layers.

Throughput and energy efficiency For the throughput performance, we use GOPS to evaluate all the implementations. The proposed digital ReRAM can achieve 792 GOPS, which is 535×, 1.61× and 1.28× better than CPU-based, GPU-based and CMOS-ASIC-based bitwise CNN, respectively. It is also 12.78× and 18.86× better than FPGA-based and CMOS-ASIC-based CNN. For energy efficiency, the digital ReRAM achieves 126 TOPS/W, three-magnitude better than the CMOS-ASIC-based CNN. In area-efficiency comparison, the digital ReRAM is 296× better than CMOS-ASIC-based CNN as well. The digital ReRAM is the best among all the implementations on both throughput and efficiency.

6.2   Machine learning algorithms on 3D XIMA

In addition, this chapter presents a detailed mapping of machine learning applications on 3D CMOS-ReRAM architecture, including SLFN-based learning and tensorized neural network (TNN) inference.

6.2.1   On-chip design for SLFN

The details of this section are obtained from [235]. This work presents mapping the SLFN-based learning and inference processes according to the algorithm and network in Section 4.2. This section will focus on the mapping of all the matrix–vector multiplication operations on ReRAM crossbar and other operations in CMOS. Multilayer 3D CMOS-ReRAM architecture in Figure 5.13 is used for the acceleration.

This section will first discuss the data quantization on the proposed architecture. Then this section illustrates how to map matrix–vector multiplication on ReRAM-crossbar layer. Finally, CMOS-ASIC accelerator is also designed in Layer 3 for remaining operations in pipelined and parallel fashion.

6.2.1.1 Data quantization

To implement the whole training algorithm on the proposed 3D multilayer CMOS-ReRAM accelerator, the precision of the real values requires a careful evaluation. Compared to the software double precision floating point format (64-bit), the values in the training algorithm are truncated into finite precision. By cross-validation from software, a balanced point between hardware resource and testing accuracy can be achieved. A general N_b bit fixed point representation with m_b bit integer and n_b bit fraction point is shown as follows:

$$y = -b_{N_b-1}2^{m_b} + \sum_{l=0}^{N_b-2} b_l 2^{l-n_b} \tag{6.19}$$

In the described accelerator, one needs to first assign a fixed 16 bit-width for normalized input data such as $\mathbf{X}, \mathbf{Y}$ and $\mathbf{D}$ with scale factor $m_b = 0$ and $n_b = 16$. For weights such as $\mathbf{A}$ and $\mathbf{B}$ in SLFN, one can determine m_b by finding the logarithm of dynamic range (i.e., $\log_2(Max - Min)$) and n_b is set as $16 - m_b$. Furthermore, one needs to apply greedy search method based on the testing accuracy to find the optimal bit-width. The bit-width is reduced with cross-validation applied to evaluate the effect. By dynamic tuning the bit-width, our objective is to find the minimum bit-width with acceptable testing accuracy loss.

6.2.1.2 ReRAM layer implementation for digitized matrix–vector multiplication

The matrix–vector multiplication is illustrated with the example of output layer (4.7) calculation, where each element in $\mathbf{Y}$ is calculated using $y_{ij} = \sum_{k=1}^L h_{ik}\gamma_{kj}$. Such a multiplication can be expressed in terms of binary multiplication [147].

$$y_{ij} = \sum_{k=1}^L \left(\sum_{e=0}^{E-1} B_e^{h_{ik}} 2^e\right)\left(\sum_{g=0}^{G-1} B_g^{\gamma_{kj}} 2^g\right)$$

$$= \sum_{e=0}^{E-1}\sum_{g=0}^{G-1}\left(\sum_{k=1}^L B_e^{h_{ik}} B_g^{\gamma_{kj}} 2^{e+g}\right) = \sum_{e=0}^{E-1}\sum_{g=0}^{G-1} s_{eg} 2^{e+g} \tag{6.20}$$

where s_{eg} is the accelerated result from ReRAM crossbar. $B^{h_{ik}}$ is the binary bit of h_{ik} with E bit-width and $B^{\gamma_{kj}}$ is the binary bit of γ_{kj} with G bit-width. As mentioned above, bit-width E and G are decided using cross-validation in design to achieve balanced accuracy and hardware usage [236].

Step 1: Parallel digitizing: It requires an $L \times L$ ReRAM crossbar. Each inner product is produced ReRAM crossbar as shown in Figure 6.19(a). h_i is set as crossbar input and γ is written in ReRAM cells. In the $L \times L$ ReRAM crossbar, resistance of ReRAMs in each column is the same, but V_{th} among columns is different. As a result, the output of each column mainly depends on ladder-like threshold voltages $V_{th,j}$. If the inner-product result is s, the output of Step 1 is like $(1 \cdots 1, 0 \cdots 0)$, where $O_{1,s} = 1$ and $O_{1,s+1} = 0$.

Step 2: XOR: It is to identify the index of s with the operation $O_{1,s} \oplus O_{1,s+1}$. Note that $O_{1,s} \oplus O_{1,s+1} = 1$ only when $O_{1,j} = 1$ and $O_{1,j+1} = 0$ from Step 1. The mapping of ReRAM-crossbar input and resistance is shown in Figure 6.19(b), and threshold voltage configuration is $V_{th,j} = \frac{V_r R_s}{2 R_{on}}$. Therefore, the index of s is identified by XOR operation.

Step 3: Encoding: The third step produces s in binary format as an encoder with the thresholds as Step 2. The input from the second step produces $(0 \cdots 1, 0 \cdots 0)$ like result where only the sth input is 1. As a result, only the sth row is read out and no current merge occurs in this step. The according binary format $binary(s)$ is an intermediate result and stored in the sth row, as shown in Figure 6.19(c). Encoding step needs an $L \times n$ ReRAM crossbar, where $n = \lceil \log_2 L \rceil$ is the number of bits in order to represent 1 to L in binary format.

6.2.1.3   CMOS layer implementation for decoding and incremental least-squares

In the CMOS layer, decoding and more complex operations for incremental least-squares solution are designed. Since the output from ReRAM layer is in binary format, decoding is required to obtain the real values. Adder and shifter are designed in Layer 3 with CMOS to complete this process as shown in Figure 6.20.

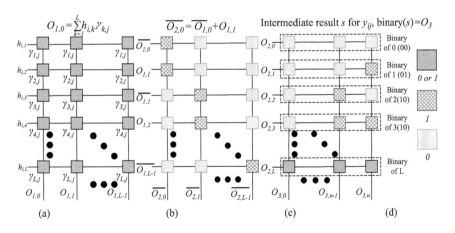

(a)   (b)   (c)   (d)

Figure 6.19   Detailed mapping for digitalized matrix–vector multiplication on ReRAM crossbar: (a) parallel digitizing; (b) XOR; (c) encoding; (d) legend of mapping

To fully map the incremental machine learning on the proposed 3D multilayer CMOS-ReRAM accelerator, there are following operations needed in CMOS-ASIC including sorting in (4.3), nonlinear mapping in (4.4) and division. Figure 6.21 shows the detailed mapping of the supervised classification on the proposed 3D multilayer CMOS-ReRAM accelerator. The ReRAM logic layer (Layer 2) will work as vector core with parallel process elements for multiplication and summation. The scalar core is implemented to perform scalar operation including division. A sequential divider is implemented with five-stage pipelines to reduce critical path latency. Nonlinear mapping such as Sigmoid function for activation is also implemented in LUT (4.4). As a result, the whole training process including both feature extraction and classifier

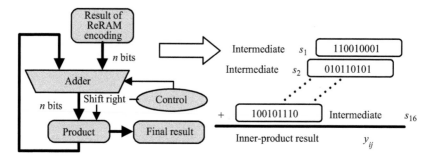

Figure 6.20   Inner-product operation on ReRAM crossbar

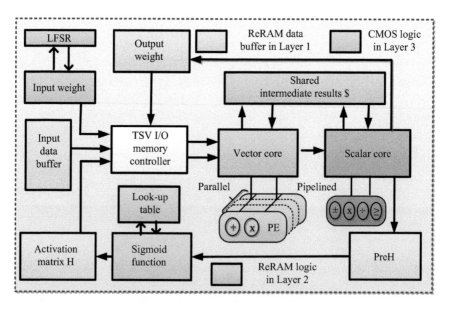

Figure 6.21   Detailed pipelined and parallel mapping of CMOS-ASIC accelerator

learning can be mapped to the proposed 3D multilayer CMOS-ReRAM accelerator with small accuracy loss accelerator with small accuracy loss.

6.2.2   On-chip design for TNNs

TNNs are another prominent class of machine learning architectures in the present time. In this section, we will map a two-layer TNN-based inference processes according to the algorithm and network in Section 4.4. This section also discusses how to utilize the proposed 3D multilayer CMOS-ReRAM architecture to design the TNN accelerator.

6.2.2.1   Mapping on multilayer architecture

Let us first discuss the CMOS layer design, which performs the high-level control of TNN computation. Then a highly parallel ReRAM-based accelerator is introduced with the TNN architecture and dot-product engine.

CMOS layer accelerator

To fully map TNN on the 3D multilayer CMOS-ReRAM accelerator, the CMOS logic needs to be designed mainly for logic control and synchronization using top-level state machine. It prepares the input data for computing cores, monitors the states of ReRAM logic computation and determines the computation layer of neural network. Figure 6.22 shows the detailed mapping of the TNN on the proposed 3D multilayer CMOS-ReRAM accelerator. This is a folded architecture by utilizing the sequential operation of each layer on the neural network. The testing data will be collected from ReRAM memory through-silicon via (TSV) and then sent into vector core to perform vector–matrix multiplication through highly parallel processing elements in the ReRAM layer. The ReRAM layer has many distributed ReRAM-crossbar structures to perform multiplication in parallel. Then the computed output from ReRAM will be transferred to scalar score to perform accumulations. The scaler core can perform addition, subtraction and comparisons. Then the output from the scalar core will be sent to the sigmoid function model for activation matrix in a pipelined fashion, which performs the computation of (4.4). The activation matrix H will be used for the next layer computation. As a result, the whole TNN inference process can be mapped to the 3D multilayer CMOS-ReRAM accelerator.

In addition, to support TNN on ReRAM computation, a dedicated index LUT is needed. Since the weight matrix is actually folded into a high-dimensional tensor as shown in Figure 4.8, a correct index selection function called bijective function is designed. The bijective function for weight matrix index is also performed by the CMOS layer. Based on the top state diagram, it will choose the correct slice of tensor core $G_i[i, j]$ by determining the i, j index. Then the correct ReRAM-crossbar area will be activated to perform vector–matrix multiplication.

ReRAM layer accelerator

In the ReRAM layer, this section presents the design of ReRAM layer accelerator for highly parallel computation using single instruction multiple data method to support data parallelism.

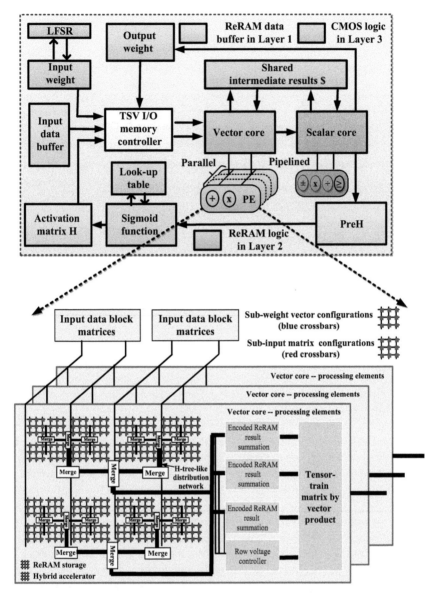

Figure 6.22   Data control and synchronization on the layer of CMOS with highly parallel ReRAM-based processing elements

Highly parallel TNN accelerator on the ReRAM layer The TNN accelerator has to be designed to support highly parallel tensor-train-matrix-by-vector multiplication by utilizing the associative principle of matrix product. According to (4.28), $\mathcal{X}(\mathbf{i})$ needs to be multiplied by d matrices unlike the general neural network. As a result, if traditional matrix–vector multiplication in serial is applied, data need to be stored in the ReRAM array for d times, which is time-consuming. Since the size of tensor cores in the TNN is much smaller than the weights in the general neural network, multiple matrix–vector multiplication engines can be placed in the ReRAM logic layer. When then input data are loaded, the index of G_i can be known. For instance, one needs to compute $X(j)G_1[i_1,j_1]G_2[i_2,j_1]G_3[i_3,j_1]G_i[i_4,j_1]$ given $d = 4$ for the summation in (4.28). $G_1[i_1,j_1]G_2[i_2,j_1]$ and $G_3[i_3,j_1]G_i[i_4,j_1]$ in (4.28) can be precomputed in a parallel fashion before the input data $\mathcal{X}(i)$ are loaded.

As shown in Figure 6.23, the tensor cores (TC1-6) are stored in the ReRAM logic layer. When the input data $\mathcal{X}(j)$ come, the index of each tensor core is loaded by the logic layer controllers first. The controller will write the according data from the tensor cores to ReRAM cells. As a result, the matrix–vector multiplication of G_i can

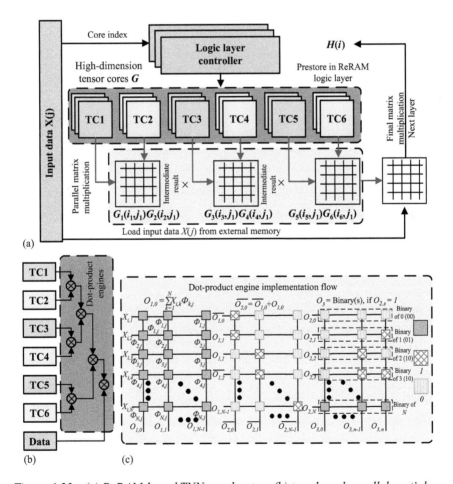

Figure 6.23   (a) ReRAM-based TNN accelerator; (b) tree-based parallel partial result multiplication; (c) ReRAM-based dot-product engine

be performed in parallel to calculate the intermediate matrices while $\mathcal{X}(\mathbf{i})$ is in the loading process. After all the intermediate matrices are obtain, they can be multiplied by $\mathcal{X}(\mathbf{i})$ so that the operations in ReRAM logic layer can be efficient.

Highly parallel dot-product engine on the ReRAM layer We further develop the digitalized ReRAM based dot-product engine on the ReRAM layer. The tensor-train-matrix-by-vector operation can be efficiently accelerated by the fast dot-product engine on the ReRAM layer, as shown in Figure 6.23(b). By taking correct index of cores, each operation can be divided into a vector-vector dot product operation. Here, we design the dot-product engine based on [237]. The output matrix is Y, with input matrices X and Φ for better understanding. The overall equation is $Y = X\Phi$ with $Y \in \mathbb{R}^{M \times m}$, $X \in \mathbb{R}^{M \times N}$ and $\Phi \in \mathbb{R}^{N \times m}$. For every element in Y, it follows

$$y_{ij} = \sum_{k=1}^{N} x_{ik}\varphi_{kj} \tag{6.21}$$

where x and φ are the elements in X and Φ, respectively. The basic idea of implementation is to split the matrix–vector multiplication to multiple inner-product operations of two vectors x_i and φ_j. Such multiplication can be expressed in binary multiplication by adopting fixed-point representation of x_{ik} and φ_{kj}:

$$y_{ij} = \sum_{k=1}^{N} \left(\sum_{e=0}^{E-1} B_e^{h_{ik}} 2^e \right) \left(\sum_{g=0}^{G-1} B_g^{\gamma_{kj}} 2^g \right)$$

$$= \sum_{e=0}^{E-1} \sum_{g=0}^{G-1} \left(\sum_{k=1}^{N} B_e^{h_{ik}} B_g^{\gamma_{kj}} 2^{e+g} \right) = \sum_{e=0}^{E-1} \sum_{g=0}^{G-1} s_{eg} 2^{e+g} \tag{6.22}$$

where s_{eg} is the accelerated result from ReRAM crossbar. $B^{h_{ik}}$ is the binary bit of h_{ik} with E bit-width and $B^{\gamma_{kj}}$ is the binary bit of γ_{kj} with G bit-width. As mentioned above, bit-width E and G are decided during the algorithm level optimization. The matrix–vector multiplication based on (6.22) can be summarized in four steps on the ReRAM layer.

   Step 1: Index bijection: Select the correct slice of tensor cores $G_d[i_d, j_d] \in \mathbb{R}^{r_d \times r_{d+1}}$, where a pair of $[i_d, j_d]$ determines a slice from $G_d \in \mathbb{R}^{r_d \times n_d \times r_{d+1}}$. In the current example, the X and Φ to represent two selected slices from cores G_1 and G_2.

   Step 2: Parallel digitizing: It requires an $N \times N$ ReRAM crossbar. Each inner product is produced ReRAM crossbar as shown in Figure 6.23(c). h_i is set as crossbar input and γ is written in ReRAM cells. In the $N \times N$ ReRAM crossbar, resistance of ReRAMs in each column are the same, but Vth among columns are different. As a result, the output of each column mainly depends on ladder-like threshold voltages $V_{th,j}$. If the inner-product result is s, the output of step 1 is like $(1 \cdots 1, 0 \cdots 0)$, where $O_{1,s} = 1$ and $O_{1,s+1} = 0$.

   Step 3: XOR: It is to identify the index of s with the operation $O_{1,s} \oplus O_{1,s+1}$. Note that $O_{1,s} \oplus O_{1,s+1} = 1$ only when $O_{1,j} = 1$ and $O_{1,j+1} = 0$ from Step 1. The mapping of ReRAM-crossbar input and resistance is also shown in 6.23(c), and threshold voltage configuration is $V_{\text{th},j} = \frac{V_r R_s}{2R_{\text{on}}}$. Therefore, the index of s is identified by XOR operation.

Step 4: Encoding: The third step produces s in binary format as an encoder with the thresholds as Step 2. The input from the second step produces $(0 \cdots 1, 0 \cdots 0)$ like result where only the sth input is 1. As a result, only the sth row is read out and no current merge occurs in this step. The according binary format $binary(s)$ is an intermediate result and stored in the sth row, as shown in Figure 6.23(c). Encoding step needs an $N \times n$ ReRAM crossbar, where $n = \lceil \log_2 N \rceil$ is the number of bits in order to represent 1 to N in binary format.

By applying these four steps, one can map different tensor cores on ReRAM crossbars to perform the matrix–vector multiplication in parallel. Compared to the state-of-the-art realizations, this approach can perform the matrix–vector multiplication faster and more energy-efficient.

6.2.2.2 Mapping TNN on single-layer architecture

Further, this section shows how to map a two-layer TNN-based inference processes according to the algorithm and network in Section 4.4. This section further discusses how to utilize the 3D single-layer CMOS-ReRAM architecture to design the TNN accelerator. Compared to the mapping in Section 6.2.2, a higher parallelism can be achieved with a distributed mapping.

TNN accelerator design

According to (4.28), $\mathcal{X}(\mathbf{i})$ needs to be multiplied by d matrices unlike the general neural network. In this equation, it is only needed to take a slice of 3D matrix (i.e., a 2-D matrix) from each tensor core to perform the matrix–vector multiplication. Therefore, the computation complexity can be significantly reduced. We show the detailed accelerator design between two hidden layers of TNN in Figure 6.24. Since the parameters of the neural network are compressed, one can store all the weights of TNN in ReRAM crossbar, following Figure 5.12(b). The input data $\boldsymbol{H}_1$ is processed by several tensor cores, CMOS pooling and activation serially.

The detailed design of a tensor core is also shown in Figure 6.24. In each tensor core, one has to store different slices of the 3D matrix into different ReRAM crossbars. Since only one 2D matrix is used at a time, two tensor-core Multiplexers (MUX) are used so that only one matrix is connected to the input voltage as well as the output ADC. The TC selection module controls the input and output MUX according to i and j. For the tensor cores in the middle, the ADC/DAC pair can be removed since one does not need a digital representation for ReRAM-crossbar inputs.

Benefits summary of TNN on 3D CMOS-ReRAM architecture

From the algorithm optimization perspective, such tensorization can benefit of implementing large neural networks. First, by performing tensorization, the size of neural network can be compressed. Moreover, the computation load can also be reduced by adopting small tensor ranks. Second, a tensorization of weight matrix can decompose the big matrix into many small tensor-core matrices, which can effectively reduce the

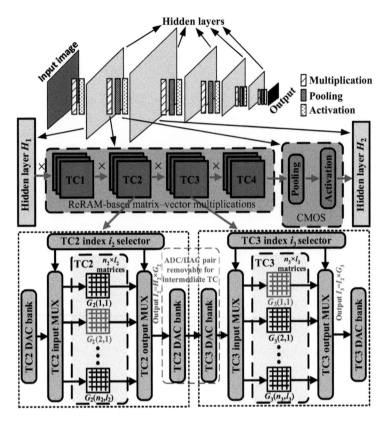

Figure 6.24   Mapping details of highly parallel 3D single-layer CMOS-ReRAM accelerator for TNN

configuration time of ReRAM. Lastly, the multiplication of small matrix can be performed in a highly parallel fashion on ReRAM to speed up the large neural network processing time.

From the hardware computing architecture perspective, the proposed 3D CMOS-ReRAM accelerator can greatly improve the energy efficiency and neural network processing speed. The matrix–vector multiplication can be intrinsically implemented by ReRAM crossbar. Compared to CMOS, a multibit tensor-core weight can be represented by a single ReRAM, and the addition can be realized by current merging. Moreover, as all the tensor cores for the neural network weights are stored in the ReRAM devices, better area efficiency can be achieved. The power consumption of the proposed CMOS-ReRAM is much smaller than the CMOS implementation due to nonvolatile property of ReRAM. In the TNN accelerator design shown in Figure 6.24, only a slice of the 3D matrix is active while most of the matrices are inactive. For traditional CMOS realization, it costs huge static power for the inactive tensor-core weights. But in the discussed architecture, the inactive matrices do not consume power so that the energy utilization is high, resulting a better energy efficiency.

6.2.3 Experimental evaluation of machine learning algorithms on 3D CMOS-ReRAM

6.2.3.1 On-chip design for SLFN-based face recognition

Experimental settings

In the experiment, different baselines are implemented for performance comparisons. The detail of each baseline is listed as follows:

Baseline 1: General processor. The general process implementation is based on MATLAB on a computer server with 3.46 GHz core and 64.0 GB RAM.

Baseline 2: GPU. The GPU implementation is performed by MATLAB GPU parallel toolbox on the same server. An Nvidia GeForce GTX 970 is used for the acceleration of matrix–vector multiplication operations for learning on neuron network.

Baseline 3: 3D-CMOS-ASIC. The 3D-CMOS-ASIC implementation with proposed architecture is done by Verilog with 1 GHz working frequency based on CMOS 65nm low power PDK. Power, area and frequency are evaluated through Synopsys DC compiler (D-2010.03-SP2). TSV model in [238] is included for area and power evaluation. 512 vertical TSVs are assumed between layers to support communication and parallel computations [239].

Proposed 3D-ReRAM-CMOS: The settings of CMOS evaluation and TSV model are the same as Baseline 3. For the ReRAM-crossbar design evaluation, the resistance of ReRAM is set as $1k\Omega$ and 1 MΩ as on-state and off-state resistance respectively according to [206] with working frequency of 200 MHz.

Performance evaluation

Scalability analysis To evaluate the proposed 3D multilayer CMOS-ReRAM architecture, we performed the scalability analysis of energy, delay and area on glass UCI data set [184]. In SLFN, the number of hidden nodes may change depending on the accuracy requirement. As a result, the improvement of proposed accelerator with different L from 64 to 256 is evaluated as shown in Figure 6.25. With the increasing L, more computing units are designed in 3D-CMOS-ASIC and ReRAM crossbar to evaluate the performance. When L reaches 256, ReRAM crossbar can achieve $2.1\times$ area-saving and $10.02\times$ energy-saving compared to 3D-CMOS-ASIC. In Figure 6.25(d), energy-delay-product (EDP) of ReRAM crossbar increases faster than 3D-CMOS-ASIC. As the size of ReRAM crossbar is proportional to square of L, the EDP improvement of ReRAM crossbar is less with larger L. However, it still shows great advantage in EDP with $51\times$ better than 3D-CMOS-ASIC when $L = 500$, which is large number of hidden node for glass benchmark of nine features.

Bit-width configuration analysis Table 6.9 shows the testing accuracy under different data sets [184,240], and configurations for machine learning of support vector machine (SVM) and SLFN. It shows that the accuracy of classification is not very sensitive to the ReRAM configuration bits. For example, the accuracy of Iris data set is working with negligible accuracy at 5 ReRAM bit-width. When the ReRAM bit-width increased to 6, it performs the same as 32 bit-width configurations. Similar observation is found in [236] by truncating algorithms with limited precision for better

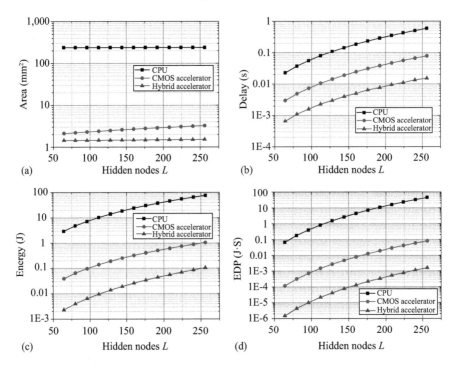

Figure 6.25   Scalability study of hardware performance with different hidden node numbers for (a) area, (b) delay, (c) energy and (d) EDP

energy efficiency. Please note that training data and weight-related parameters are quantized to perform matrix–vector multiplication on ReRAM-crossbar accelerator. Figure 6.26 shows the energy comparisons under different bit-width configurations for CMOS and ReRAM under the same accuracy requirements. An average of 4.5× energy saving can be achieved for the same number of bit-width configurations. The energy consumption is normalized by the CMOS 4 bit-width configuration. Furthermore, we can observe that not always smaller number of bits achieves better energy saving. Fewer number of bit-width may require much larger neuron network to perform required classification accuracy. As a result, its energy consumption increases.

Performance analysis Figure 6.27 shows the classification values on image data [240] with an example of five classes. As mentioned before, the index with maximum values (highlighted in red) is selected to indicate the class of test case. A few sample images are selected. Please note that 50, 000 and 10, 000 images are used for training and testing with ten classes. In Table 6.10, performance comparisons among MATLAB, 3D-CMOS-ASIC and 3D multilayer CMOS-ReRAM accelerator are presented, and the acceleration of each procedure based on the formula described is also addressed.

Table 6.9 *Testing accuracy of machine learning techniques under different data set and configurations (normalized to all 32 bits)*

Data sets	Size	Features	Classes	Bit-width	Accuracy (%) SVM[‡]	SLFN
Glass	214	9	6	4	100.07	100.00
				5	93.88	99.30
				6	99.82	99.30
Iris	150	4	3	4	98.44	94.12
				5	100.00	94.18
				6	100.00	100.00
Seeds	210	7	3	4	97.98	82.59
				5	99.00	91.05
				6	99.00	98.51
Arrhythmia	179	13	3	4	96.77	97.67
				5	99.18	98.83
				6	99.24	100.00
Letter	20,000	16	7	4	97.26	53.28
				5	98.29	89.73
				6	99.55	96.13
CIFAR-10	60,000	1,600[†]	10	4	98.75	95.71
				5	99.31	97.06
				6	99.31	99.33

[†] 1,600 features extracted from 60,000 32×32 color images with ten classes.
[‡] Least-squares SVM is used for comparison.

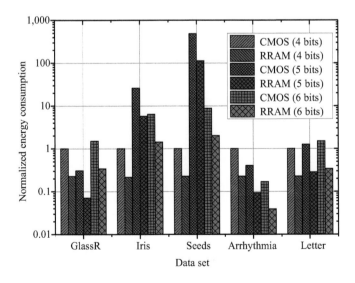

Figure 6.26 *Energy-saving comparison under different bit-width of CMOS and ReRAM with the same accuracy requirement*

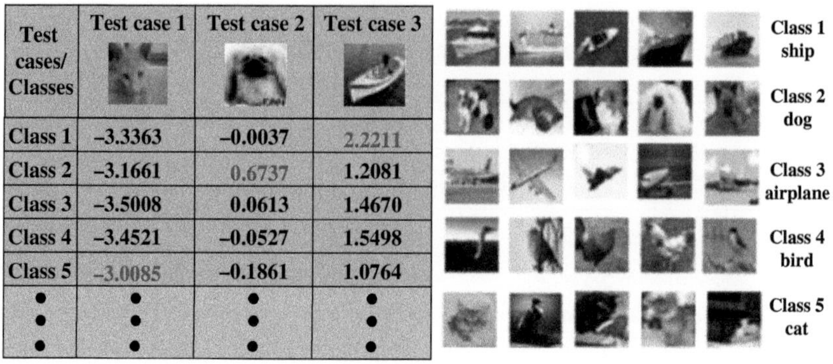

Test cases/Classes	Test case 1	Test case 2	Test case 3
Class 1	–3.3363	–0.0037	2.2211
Class 2	–3.1661	0.6737	1.2081
Class 3	–3.5008	0.0613	1.4670
Class 4	–3.4521	–0.0527	1.5498
Class 5	–3.0085	–0.1861	1.0764
• • •	• • •	• • •	• • •

Class 1 ship

Class 2 dog

Class 3 airplane

Class 4 bird

Class 5 cat

Figure 6.27   Online machine learning for image recognition on the proposed 3D multilayer CMOS-ReRAM accelerator using benchmark CIFAR-10

Table 6.10   Performance comparison under different software and hardware implementations

Implementation	Hardware specifications	Computation	Operations	Time	Energy
CPU (MATLAB)	3.46 GHz 240 mm^2 130 W	Feature extraction	Sort	1473.2 s	191.52 kJ
			Multiplication	736.6 s	95.76 kJ
		Input layer	Multiplication	729.79 s	94.87 kJ
		L2-norm	Division	294.34 s	38.26 kJ
			Multiplication	1667.95 s	216.83 kJ
		Output layer	Multiplication	750.3 s	97.54 kJ
		Overall	–	5651.88 s	734.78 kJ
3D-CMOS-ASIC[†]	1.0 GHz 1.86 mm^2 39.41 W	Feature extraction	Sort	216.65 s	78 J
			Multiplication	97.43 s	3,840 J
		Input layer	Multiplication	96.53 s	3,800 J
		L2-norm	Division	43.29 s	15 J
			Multiplication	220.62 s	8,690 J
		Output layer	Multiplication	99.25 s	3,910 J
		Overall	–	773.77 s	20.34 kJ
		Improvement	–	7.3×	36.12×
3D-CMOS-ReRAM[†]	1.0 GHz 1.86 mm^2 39.41 W	Feature extraction	Sort	216.65 s	78 J
			Multiplication	22.43 s	293 J
		Input layer	Multiplication	22.22 s	291 J
		L2-norm	Division	43.29 s	15 J
			Multiplication	50.79 s	670 J
		Output layer	Multiplication	22.85 s	300 J
		Overall	–	378.22 s	1,643 J
		Improvement	–	14.94×	447.17×

[†]6 bit-width configuration is implemented for both CMOS and ReRAM.

Among the three implementations, 3D multilayer CMOS-ReRAM accelerator performs the best in area, energy and speed. Compared to MATLAB implementation, it achieves 14.94× speedup, 447.17× energy-saving and 164.38× area-saving. We also design a 3D-CMOS-ASIC implementation with similar structure as 3D multilayer CMOS-ReRAM accelerator with better performance compared to MATLAB. The proposed 3D multilayer CMOS-ReRAM 3D accelerator is 2.05× speedup, 12.38× energy-saving and 1.28× area-saving compared to 3D CMOS-ASIC. To compare the performance with GPU, we also implemented the same code using MATLAB GPU parallel toolbox. It takes 1163.42*s* for training benchmark CIFAR-10, which is 4.858× faster than CPU. Comparing to our proposed 3D multilayer CMOS-ReRAM architecture, our work is 3.07× speedup and 162.86× energy saving. Detailed comparisons of each step are not shown due to the limited space of table.

6.2.3.2   Results of TNN-based on-chip design with 3D multilayer architecture

Experimental settings

In the experiment, we have implemented different baselines for performance comparisons. The detail of each baseline is listed as follows:

Baseline 1: General CPU processor. The general process implementation is based on MATLAB with optimized C-program. The computer server is with 6 cores of 3.46 GHz and 64.0 GB RAM.

Baseline 2: General GPU processor. The general-purpose GPU implementation is based on the optimized C-program and MATLAB parallel computing toolbox with CUDA-enabled Quadro 5000 GPU [241].

Baseline 3: 3D CMOS-ASIC. The 3D CMOS-ASIC implementation with proposed architecture is done by Verilog with 1 GHz working frequency based on CMOS 65nm low power PDK. Power, area and frequency are evaluated through Synopsys DC compiler (D-2010.03-SP2). TSV area, power and delay are evaluated based on Simulator DESTINY [218] and fine-grained TSV model CACTI-3DD [242]. The buffer size of the top layer is set 128 MB to store tensor cores with 256 bits data width. The TSV area is estimated to be 25.0 μm^2 with capacitance of 21 fF.

Proposed 3D CMOS-ReRAM: The settings of CMOS evaluation and TSV model are the same as Baseline 2. For the ReRAM-crossbar design evaluation, the resistance of ReRAM is set as 500 kΩ and 5 MΩ as on-state and off-state resistance and 2V SET/RESET voltage according to [139] with working frequency of 200 MHz. The CMOS and ReRAM integration is evaluated based on [64].

To evaluate the proposed architecture, we apply UCI [184] and MNIST [232] data set to analyze the accelerator scalability, model configuration analysis and performance analysis (Table 6.11). The model configuration is performed on MATLAB first using tensor-train toolbox [204] before mapping on the 3D CMOS-ReRAM architecture. To evaluate the model compression, we compare our method with support vector decomposition (SVD)-based node-pruned method [243] and general neural network [53]. The energy consumption and speedup are also evaluated. Note that the code for performance comparisons is based on optimized C-Program and deployed as the mex-file in the MATLAB environment.

Table 6.11   Bandwidth improvement under different number of hidden nodes for MNIST data set

Hidden node[†] (L)	256	512	1,024	2,048	4,096
Memory required (MB)	1.025	2.55	7.10	22.20	76.41
Memory set (MB)	2M	4M	8M	32M	128M
Write bandwidth imp.	1.14%	0.35%	0.60%	3.12%	6.51%
Read bandwidth imp.	5.02%	6.07%	9.34%	20.65%	51.53%

[†]Four-layer neural network with three FC layers $784 \times L, L \times L$ and $L \times 10$.

Performance evaluation

3D Multilayer CMOS-ReRAM accelerator scalability analysis Since neural network process requires frequent network weights reading, memory read latency optimization configuration is set to generate ReRAM memory architecture. By adopting 3D implementation, simulation results show that memory read and write bandwidth can be significantly improved by 51.53% and 6.51%, respectively, comparing to 2D implementation. For smaller number of hidden nodes, read/write bandwidth is still improved but the bottleneck shifts to the latency of memory logic control.

To evaluate the proposed 3D multilayer CMOS-ReRAM architecture, we perform the scalability analysis of energy, delay and area on MNIST data set [232]. This data set is applied to multilayer neural network and the number of hidden nodes may change depending on the accuracy requirement. As a result, the improvement of proposed accelerator with different L from 32 to 2,048 is evaluated as shown in Figure 6.28. With the increasing L, more computing units are designed in 3D CMOS-ASIC and ReRAM crossbar to evaluate the performance. The neural network is defined as a four-layer network with weights $784 \times L, L \times L$ and $L \times 10$. For computation delay, GPU, 3D CMOS-ASIC and 3D CMOS-ReRAM are close when $L = 2,048$ according to Figure 6.28(b). When L reaches 256, 3D CMOS-ReRAM can achieve $7.56\times$ area-saving and $3.21\times$ energy-saving compared to 3D CMOS-ASIC. Although the computational complexity is not linearly related to the number of hidden node numbers, both energy consumption and EDP of ReRAM crossbar increase with the rising number of hidden node. According to Figure 6.28(d), the advantage of the hybrid accelerator becomes smaller when the hidden node increases, but it can still have a $5.49\times$ better EDP compared to the 3D CMOS-ASIC when the hidden node number is 2,048.

Model configuration analysis Figure 6.29 shows the testing accuracy and running time comparisons for MNIST data set. It shows a clear trend of accuracy improvement with increasing number of hidden nodes. The running time between TNN and general neural network is almost the same. This is due to the relative large rank $r = 50$ and computation cost of $O(dr^2 n \max(N, L))$. Such tensor-train-based neural network achieve $4\times$ and $8.18\times$ model compression within 2% accuracy loss under 10,24 and 20,48 number of hidden nodes, respectively. Details on model compression are shown in Table 6.12. From Table 6.12, we can observe that the compression rate is directly

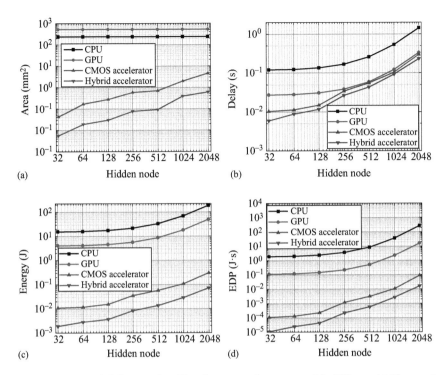

Figure 6.28   Scalability study of hardware performance with different hidden node numbers for (a) area, (b) delay, (c) energy and (d) EDP

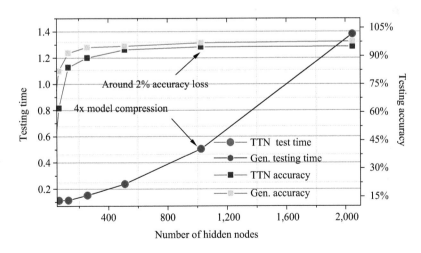

Figure 6.29   Testing time and accuracy comparison between TTN and general neural network (Gen.) with varying number of hidden nodes

Table 6.12   Model compression under different number of hidden nodes and tensor ranks on MNIST data set

Number of hidden nodes[†]	32	64	128	256	512	1,024	2,048
Compression	5.50	4.76	3.74	3.23	3.01	4.00	8.18
Rank[‡]	15	20	25	30	35	40	45
Compression	25.19	22.51	20.34	17.59	14.85	12.86	8.63
Accuracy (%)	90.42	90.56	91.41	91.67	93.47	93.32	93.86

[‡]Number of hidden nodes are all fixed to 2,048 with four FC layers.
[†]All tensor rank is initialized to 50.

Table 6.13   Testing accuracy of learning techniques under different data set and bit-width configuration

Data sets	32-bit acc. (%) & compr.		4-bit acc. (%) & compr.		5 bit acc. (%) & compr.		6 bit acc. (%) & compr.	
Glass	88.6	1.32	89.22	10.56	83.18	8.45	88.44	7.04
Iris	96.8	1.12	95.29	8.96	96.8	7.17	96.8	5.97
Diabetes	71	3.14	69.55	25.12	69.4	20.10	71.00	16.75
Adult	78.8	1.87	75.46	14.96	78.15	11.97	78.20	9.97
Leuke	88.9	1.82	85.57	14.56	87.38	11.65	88.50	9.71
MNIST	94.38	4.18	91.28	33.44	92.79	26.75	94.08	22.29

connected with the rank r, where the memory storage can be simplified as dnr^2 from $\sum_{k=1}^{d} n_k r_{k-1} r_k$ but not directly linked to the number of hidden nodes. One can also observe that by setting tensor-core rank to 35, $14.85\times$ model compression can be achieved with acceptable accuracy loss. Therefore, initialization of a low-rank core and the SVD split of supercore in MALS algorithm are important steps to reduce the core rank and increase compression rate.

Bit-width configuration analysis To implement the whole neural network on the proposed 3D multilayer CMOS-ReRAM accelerator, the precision of real values requires a careful evaluation. Compared to the software double-precision floating point format (64-bit), values are truncated into finite precision. By using the greedy search method, an optimal point for hardware resource (small bit-width) and testing accuracy can be achieved.

Our tensor-train-based neural network compression techniques can work with low-precision value techniques to further reduce the data storage. Table 6.13 shows the testing accuracy by adopting different bit-width on UCI data sets [184] and MNIST [232]. It shows that accuracy of classification is not very sensitive to the ReRAM configuration bits for UCI data set. For example, the accuracy of Iris data set is working well with negligible accuracy at 5 ReRAM bit-width. When the ReRAM bit-width increased to 6, it performs the same as 32 bit-width configurations. Please note that the best configuration of quantized model weights varies for different data sets and requires careful evaluation.

Performance analysis In Table 6.14, performance comparisons among C-Program-optimized CPU performance, GPU performance, 3D CMOS-ASIC and 3D multilayer CMOS-ReRAM accelerator are presented for 10, 000 testing images. The acceleration of each layer is also presented for three layers (784 × 2,048, 2,048 × 2,048 and 2,048 × 10). Please note that the dimension of weight matrices are decomposed into [4 4 7 7] and [4 4 8 8] with 6 bit-width and maximum rank 6. The compression rate is 22.29× and 4.18× with and without bit truncation. Here, the compression rate is the ratio of volume of weights before and after compression. Among the four implementations, 3D multilayer CMOS-ReRAM accelerator performs the best in area, energy and speed. Compared to CPU, it achieves 6.37× speedup, 2,612× energy-saving and 233.92× area-saving. For GPU-based implementation, our proposed 3D CMOS-ReRAM architecture achieves 1.43× speedup and 694.68× energy-saving. We also design a 3D CMOS-ASIC implementation with similar structure as 3D multilayer CMOS-ReRAM accelerator with better performance compared to CPU- and GPU-based implementations. The proposed 3D multilayer CMOS-ReRAM 3D accelerator is 1.283× speedup, 4.276× energy-saving and 9.339× area-saving compared to 3D CMOS-ASIC.

The throughput and energy efficiency for these four cases are also summarized in Table 6.14. For energy efficiency, the discussed accelerator can achieve 1,499.83 GOPS/W, which has 4.30× better energy efficiency comparing to 3D the CMOS-ASIC result (347.29 GOPS/W). In comparison to our GPU baseline, it has 694.37× better energy efficiency comparing to NVIDIA Quadro 5000. For a newer

Table 6.14 Performance comparison under different hardware implementations on MNIST data set with 10,000 testing images

Implementation	Hardware specifications	Computations	Time	Speedup	Energy	Energy-saving
CPU [244]	3.46 GHz	Layer 1	0.44 s	–	57.23 J	–
	240 mm^2	Layer 2	0.97 s	–	125.74 J	–
	130W	Layer 3	0.045 s	–	5.82 J	–
	74.64GOPS	Overall	1.45 s	–	188.8 J	–
GPU [241]	513 MHz	Layer 1	0.04 s	11.06×	4.05 J	9.46×
	529 mm^2	Layer 2	0.289 s	3.36×	43.78 J	2.87×
	152 W	Layer 3	2.4 ms	18.67×	0.3648 J	15.96×
	328.41 GOPS	Overall	0.33 s	4.40×	50.19 J	3.76×
3D CMOS-ASIC architecture	1.0 GHz	Layer 1	0.032 s	13.9×	33.3 mJ	1, 711.8×
	9.582 mm^2	Layer 2	0.26 s	3.71×	0.276 J	455.4×
	1.037 W	Layer 3	2.4 ms	18.4×	2.6 mJ	2, 262×
	367.43 GOPS	Overall	0.295 s	4.92×	0.312 J	604.9×
3D CMOS-ReRAM architecture	100 MHz	Layer 1	0.025 s	17.77×	7.9 mJ	7, 286×
	1.026 mm^2	Layer 2	0.20 s	4.80×	0.64 J	25.86×
	0.317 W	Layer 3	1.7 ms	25.86×	0.5 mJ	11, 000×
	475.45 GOPS	Overall	0.23 s	6.37×	0.072 J	2, 612×

†Four-layer neural network with weights 784 × 2,048, 2,048 × 2,048 and 2,048 × 10.

GPU device (NVIDIA Tesla K40), which can achieve 1,092 GFLOPS and consume 235 W [241], our proposed accelerator has 347.49× energy-efficiency improvement.

6.2.3.3   TNN-based distributed on-chip design on 3D single-layer architecture

Experiment settings

In the experiment, we have implemented different baselines for performance comparisons. The detail of each baseline is listed as follows:

Baseline 1: General processor (CPU/GPU). The general processor implementation is based on optimized C-program on a computer server with 6 cores of 3.46 GHz and 64.0 GB RAM. A Nvidia GeForce GTX 970 is used as reference for the GPU performance comparison.

Baseline 2: 2D CMOS-ASIC. The 2D CMOS-ASIC implementation with proposed architecture is done by Verilog with 1 GHz working frequency based on CMOS 65-nm low-power PDK. Power, area and frequency are evaluated through Synopsys DC compiler (D-2010.03-SP2).

Baseline 3: 3D CMOS-ASIC. The 3D CMOS-ASIC implementation is the same as 2D version but features with TSV communication. TSV area, power and delay are evaluated based on Simulator DESTINY [218] and fine-grained TSV model CACTI-3DD [242]. The buffer size of the top layer is SRAM based and set 128 MB to store tensor cores. The TSV area is estimated to be 25.0 μm^2 with capacitance of 21 fF. TSV model in [238] is included for area and power evaluation; 512 vertical TSVs are assumed between layers to support communication and parallel computations [239].

Proposed 3D CMOS-ReRAM: The settings of CMOS evaluation and TSV model are the same as Baseline 3. For the ReRAM-crossbar design evaluation, the resistance of ReRAM is set as 1 kΩ and 1 MΩ as on-state and off-state resistance and 2V SET/RESET voltage according to [206] with working frequency of 200 MHz. The CMOS and ReRAM integration is evaluated based on [64].

To evaluate the proposed architecture, we apply CIFAR-10 [233] and MNIST [232] data set to analyze the neural network compression and architecture performance analysis. The energy-efficient neural network is designed on MATLAB first using Tensor-train toolbox [204] and tensor network [196]. After determining the network configuration and compression rate, it is then fully optimized using C-program as CPU-based result. Then we apply nonuniform quantization to perform tensor-core quantization before mapping on the 3D CMOS-ReRAM architecture. To evaluate the model compression, we compare our method with SVD-based node-pruned method [243] and general neural network [53]. The energy efficiency and speedup are also evaluated.

Energy-efficient tensor-compressed neural network

To achieve high compression rate, we first apply nonuniform quantization for tensor-core weights. As shown in Figure 6.30, the probability density function of tensor-core weights can be modeled as Gaussian distribution. For such known pdf, we can effectively find the optimal level representative values with minimized mean square error. Figure 6.31 shows the trade-off between accuracy, bit-width and compression

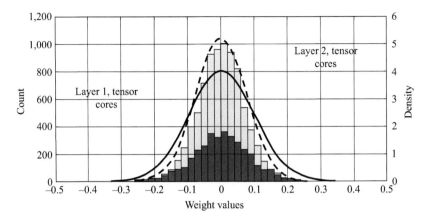

Figure 6.30   TNN Layer 1 weight and Layer 2 weight histogram with approximate Gaussian distribution

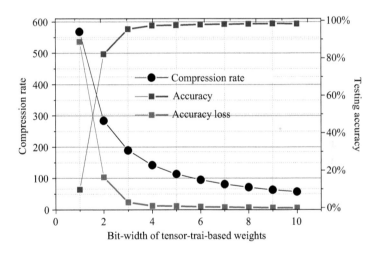

Figure 6.31   Compression rate and accuracy with increasing bit-width

rate on MNIST data set with three-layer neural network. Table 6.15 shows the clear effect of quantization on the compression rate. In general, bit-width quantization can help improve 3× more compression rate on neural network.

To have a fair comparison with [245], we also adopted LeNet-300-100 network [232], which is a two hidden FC layer network (784×300, 300×100, 100×10). Under such configuration, [245] can achieve 40× compression with error rate 1.58% using quantization (6-bit precision), pruning and Huffman coding techniques. By adopting

Table 6.15   Model compression under different numbers of hidden nodes and tensor ranks on MNIST data set

Rank[‡]	2	4	6	8	10	12
Compression ($\times$)	69.73	61.70	52.53	43.54	35.71	29.30
Q-Compression ($\times$)	223.4	179.49	152.81	139.33	114.23	93.76
Error rate (%)	4.28	4.14	4.03	4.08	3.97	3.79

[‡]Number of hidden nodes are all fixed to 1,024 with 1 hidden layer.

Table 6.16   Bandwidth improvement under different number of hidden nodes for MNIST data set

Hidden node[†] (L)	256	512	1,024	2,048	4,096
Memory required (MB)	1.025	2.55	7.10	22.20	76.41
Memory set (MB)	2M	4	8	32	128
Write bandwidth improvement	1.14%	0.35%	0.60%	3.12%	6.51%
Read bandwidth improvement	5.02%	6.07%	9.34%	20.65%	51.53%

[†] Four-layer neural network with three FC layers $784 \times L$, $L \times L$ and $L \times 10$.

9 bit-width configuration on tensorized layer, we can achieve even more compression rate ($142\times$) with maintained accuracy (1.63%).

We also apply the proposed TNN to CIFAR-10 data set. CIFAR-10 data set consists of 60,000 images with size of $32 \times 32 \times 3$ under ten different classes. We adopt LeNet-alike neural network [232] and we use a two-layer FC TNN to replace the last two FC layers, which is 512×64 and 64×10. By adopting nonuniform tensor-core bit quantization (8 bit-width), we can achieve $17.6\times$ compression on FC layers and $2\times$ on the whole network, respectively, with the same accuracy loss (2%).

Energy-efficient 3D CMOS-ReRAM architecture

Since neural network process requires frequent network weights reading, memory read latency optimization configuration is set to generate ReRAM memory architecture. By adopting 3D implementation, simulation results show that memory read and write bandwidth can be improved by 51.53% and 6.51%, respectively, comparing to 2D implementation as shown in Table 6.16. For smaller number of hidden nodes, read/write bandwidth is still improved but the bottleneck shifts to the latency of memory logic control.

In Table 6.17, performance comparisons among general processors, 2D CMOS-ASIC, 3D CMOS-ASIC and 3D CMOS-ReRAM accelerator are presented, and the acceleration of each layer is also presented for two layers ($784 \times 10, 24$ and $10, 24 \times 10$). Please note that input weight is decomposed into [4 4 7 7] and [4 4 8 8] with maximum rank 6 and 6 bit-width. Among the four implementations, 3D CMOS-ReRAM accelerator performs the best in area, energy and speed. Compared to 2D CMOS implementation, it achieves $1.515\times$ speedup, $3.362\times$ energy-saving and

Table 6.17   Performance comparison under different hardware implementations on MNIST data set (10k test images)

Implementations	CPU	GPU	2D CMOS-ASIC	3D CMOS-ASIC	3D CMOS-ReRAM	
Frequency	3.46 GHz	200 MHz	1.0 GHz	1.0 GHz	100 MHz	
Power	130 W	152 W	779 mW	649 mW	351 mW	
Area (mm^2)	240	529	12.69	4.63	0.61	
System throughput	73.63 GOPS	256.32 GOPS	244.53 GOPS	286.44 GOPS	370.64 GOPS	
Energy-efficiency	0.57 GOPS/W	1.69 GOPS/W	313.98 GOPS/W	441.36 GOPS/W	1,055.95 W GOPS/W	
Network compressed	Yes	Yes	Yes	Yes	No	Yes
Time	1.452 s	0.213 s	0.223 s	0.191 s	0.747 s	0.1473 s
Energy	188.79 J	32.376 J	0.1738 J	0.1237 J	0.2621 J	0.0517 J

[†] 10k test images on three-layer neural network with two FC layers $784 \times 1,024$ and $1,024 \times 10$; 6 bit-width is adopted for tensor-core weights with maximum rank 6.

20.80× area-saving. We also design a 3D CMOS-ASIC implementation with similar structure as 3D CMOS-ReRAM accelerator with better performance compared to 2D CMOS-ASIC. The proposed 3D CMOS-ReRAM accelerator is 1.294× speedup, 2.393× energy-saving and 7.59× area-saving compared to 3D CMOS-ASIC. We also performed the mapping of uncompressed neural network on 3D CMOS-ReRAM architecture. In addition, for CIFAR-10 data set, we estimate 2.79× and 2.23× energy-saving comparing to 2D CMOS-ASIC and 3D CMOS-ASIC architecture, respectively.

For energy efficiency, our proposed accelerator can achieve 1,055.95 GOPS/W, which is equivalent to 7.661 TOPS/W for uncompressed neural network. Our proposed TNN accelerator can also achieve 2.39× better energy efficiency comparing to 3D CMOS-ASIC result (441.36 GOPS/W), and 227.24× better energy efficiency comparing to Nvidia Tesla K40, which can achieve 1,092 GFLOPS and consume 235 W.

Part III

Case studies

Chapter 7
Large-scale case study: accelerator for ResNet

7.1 Introduction

A residual network (ResNet) is a convolutional neural network (CNN)-based network with much deeper hierarchical architecture using the residual connection [246,247], which has become the common network model for deep learning. It is, however, quite challenging to realize the ResNet into terminal hardware with efficient interference [248–251] such as high throughput (TOPs) yet low power (mW). It requires a completed re-examination from both machine learning algorithm as well as underneath hardware.

First from machine learning algorithm perspective, to achieve a deep learning at terminal hardware, the network needs to be simplified. For example, a ResNet-50 network contains almost 50 convolution layers, which dominate the network complexity. As most convolution filter now is a small-sized (3×3, 5×5, etc.) operator. A direct-truncated quantization method has been reported in recent work [252]. Lately, some approaches [253–255] demonstrate their quantization feasibility of using low-bitwidth weights and activations, thus considerably reducing the memory requirement and computation complexity. Low-bitwidth gradients [256] are further generalized to train CNNs. Other works perform the quantization after network training or apply the straight-through estimator on CNNs [257]. Moreover, binarized neural networks (BNNs) are introduced [222,224] and further implemented on a digital resistive random-access memory (ReRAM)-based accelerator. While some of these methods have shown good performances with small-scale network models [258–260], however, none has applied a trained quantization strategy to large-scale networks (e.g., ResNet-50) on large-scale classification tasks (e.g., ImageNet) with certain accuracy.

Next, from hardware and device perspective, traditional computing architecture needs significant data migration between memory and processor. It leads to low efficiency for both bandwidth and energy for machine learning, especially the deeper ResNet. The recent emerging nonvolatile memory (NVM) technologies have shown significantly reduced standby power as well as the possibility for in/near-memory computing [225,261–263]. For example, the ReRAM device [57,62,264] in crossbar can be used to store the weights and also to perform the convolution.

For this case study, we have developed a quantized large-scale ResNet-50 network using ImageNet [265] benchmark with high accuracy. We further show that the quantized ResNet-50 network can be realized on ReRAM crossbar with significantly improved throughput and energy efficiency. The findings in this chapter can be outlined as follows:

1. We adopt a trained quantization strategy with *all-integer computations* of the *large-scale* deep ResNet, for the first time, to such low-bitwidth subject to an accuracy control.
2. We propose an algorithm-hardware codesign of the complimentary metal oxide semiconductor (CMOS)-ReRAM accelerator with novel digital-to-analog converter (DAC)/analog-to-digital converter (ADC) circuits developed.

Experiment results show that the proposed accelerator can achieve $432\times$ speedup and six-magnitude more energy efficiency than a central processing unit (CPU)-based implementation; $1.30\times$ speedup and four-magnitude more energy efficiency compared to a graphics processing unit (GPU)-based implementation; and $15.21\times$ faster and $498\times$ more energy efficiency than a CMOS-application specific integrated circuit (ASIC)-based implementation.

7.2   Deep neural network with quantization

The traditional direct implementation of the CNN-based network would require unnecessary software and hardware resources with poor parallelism. Previous work in [256,266] suggests a neural network using quantized constraints during training. In this section, we propose a hardware-friendly algorithm design of the large-scale ResNet model with quantized parallelism for convolution, residual block, batch normalization (BN), max-pooling and activation function. Instead of traditional quantization methods carrying out original 32-bit floating-point arithmetic with additional weight/activation quantization process, we present the all-integer arithmetic with quantized variables and computations only during both training and inference. Due to the remarkable compression on computational complexity and storage size, it becomes feasible to further implement the quantized network on ReRAM crossbar, which will be discussed in Section 7.4.

7.2.1   Basics of ResNet

The deep ResNet has achieved outstanding performance in many applications due to its effectiveness. Different from the traditional CNN-based network structure, ResNet utilizes a residual connection to address the degradation problem by training a very deep network.

A ResNet is composed of a series of residual blocks, and each residual block contains several stacked convolutional layers. The rectified linear unit (ReLU) layers [267] and the BN layers [190] are also regarded as the component of convolutional layers in a ResNet. Specifically, we adopt a ResNet with 50 layers (ResNet-50) [246] that is substantially deep to extract rich and discriminative features. The specific structure of ResNet-50 is shown in Figure 7.1, including 16 residual blocks and each contains three convolution layers. There is an add-residual operation at the end of each residual block, which can be represented by

$$A_{k+2} = F(A_{k-1}, W_k, W_{k+1}, W_{k+2}) + A_{k-1} \tag{7.1}$$

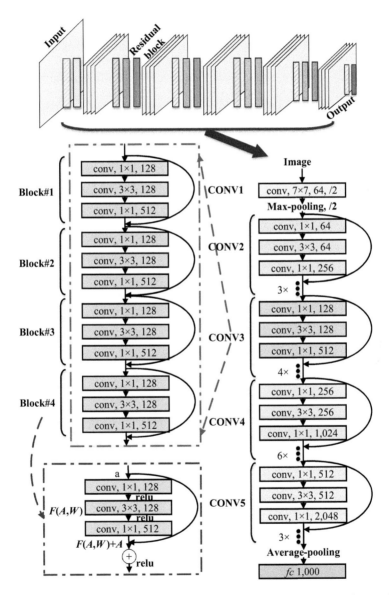

Figure 7.1   Detailed structure of ResNet-50: 49 convolution layers and 1 FC layer

where A_{k-1} and A_{k+2} denote the input and output feature matrices of the residual block, meanwhile A_{k+2} can be considered as the input of the next residual block, and the function $F(\circ)$ denotes the residual mapping to be learned.

7.2.2   Quantized convolution and residual block

The convolution is the most expensive computation of ResNet and any other CNN-based network. Recently, the low-bitwidth convolution in [188,256] has shown the promising performance, which quantizes the convolution with low-bitwidth parameters to reduce the hardware resource with considerable accuracy.

First, we present the low-bitwidth convolution with 4-bit quantized values as $\{-4, -2, -1, 0, 1, 2, 4\}$ for weight matrices. It should be noted that we quantize weights to the powers of 2. In this way, the quantization algorithm can strike a balance between model compactness and capacity, which has been experimentally verified by testing several realizations from the state-of-the-arts (reported in Section 7.5.3.1). Furthermore, half voltage operating scheme [268] is applied to overcome the sneak-path problem, and the large intervals of weights will help to maintain high robustness under device variation (reported in Section 7.5.3.2). As shown in Figure 7.2(a), assuming w_k is the full-precision element and w_k^q is the quantized-valued element of weight matrix W_k in the kth layer, they have the approximation as $w_k \approx \alpha w_k^q$ with a nonnegative scaling factor α. Each weight element in convolution layers can be 4-bit quantized as follows:

$$
w_k^q = \text{quantize}(w_k) = \begin{cases} +4, & w_k > 1.5\Delta \\ +2, & 1.5\Delta \geq w_k > \Delta \\ +1, & \Delta \geq w_k > 0.5\Delta \\ 0, & |w_k| \leq 0.5\Delta \\ -1, & -\Delta \leq w_k < -0.5\Delta \\ -2, & -1.5\Delta \leq w_k < -\Delta \\ -4, & w_k < -1.5\Delta \end{cases} \tag{7.2}
$$

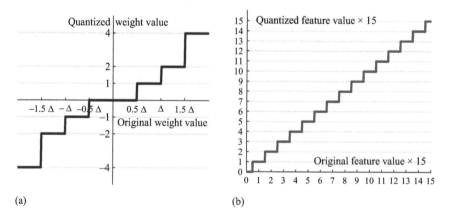

(a)   (b)

Figure 7.2   *4-bit quantization strategy of (a) weight and (b) feature*

where quantize($\circ$) represents the proposed 4-bit quantization strategy, and Δ is a nonnegative threshold parameter, which can be calculated as

$$\Delta \approx \frac{0.7}{n} \sum_{i=1}^{n} |w_k| \tag{7.3}$$

where n is the number of elements in weight matrix. Also we develop a 4-bit quantization strategy for the features based on [256], which quantizes a real-number feature element a_{k-1} to a 4-bit feature element a_{k-1}^q of feature matrix A_{k-1} in kth layer. This strategy is defined as follows:

$$a_{k-1}^q = \frac{1}{2^4 - 1} \text{quantize}(a_{k-1}) = \text{round}[(2^4 - 1)a_{k-1}] \tag{7.4}$$

where the round($\circ$) function takes the nearest integer (takes the bigger integer if the decimal part is exactly 0.50). Therefore, the 4-bit quantized feature a_{k-1}^q has the value range as $\frac{1}{15} \times \{0, 1, 2, \ldots, 15\}$, which is shown in Figure 7.2(b).

Having both 4-bit features and weights, we perform the 4-bit quantized convolution as

$$s_k^q(x, y, z) = \sum_{i=1}^{D_k} \sum_{j=1}^{H_k} \sum_{l=1}^{V_k} w_k^q(i, j, l, z)$$
$$\times a_{k-1}^q(i + x - 1, j + y - 1, l) \tag{7.5}$$

where $a_{k-1}^q \in \mathbb{R}^{D_{k-1} \times H_{k-1} \times V_{k-1}}$ and $w_k^q \in \mathbb{R}^{d_k \times h_k \times v_k}$ are the 4-bit quantized feature and weight element, and s_k^q is the computation result. Here, D_k, H_k and V_k are mode sizes of the features and d_k, h_k and v_k are those of the weight kernels, which can be seen in Figure 7.3. Compared with a real-valued CNN-based network in the full-precision data format, since the weights and features can be stored in 4-bit, both software and hardware resources required for the quantized convolutional layer, called the QConv, can be significantly reduced. Meanwhile, the QConv with 4-bit parameters leads to a higher energy efficiency and parallelism when implemented on the in-memory computing devices.

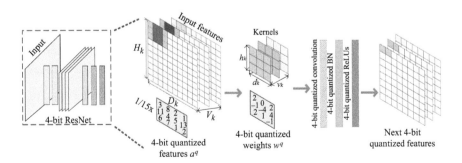

Figure 7.3   Computation flow of deep residual network ResNet-50 with 4-bit quantization

For residual block described in (7.1), we perform the proposed optimizations by straightforwardly replacing the elements in A_{k+2}, A_{k-1}^q, W_k, W_{k+1} and W_{k+2}, as shown in Figure 7.3. Therefore, the add-residual operation at the end of each residual block is also quantized as 4-bit.

7.2.3   Quantized BN

BN accelerates the training process and reduces the overall impact of the weight scale [190]. The normalization procedure is required to stabilize the deep ResNet. However, in the original CNN-based network, BN requires many multiplications (calculating the full-precision deviation and dividing by it). In this section, the 4-bit quantized BN, called the quantized batch normalization (QBN), is proposed to significantly compress the computation. The quantized computation in QBN can be represented by

$$a_k^{qbn}(x,y,z) = 2^{\text{round}(\log_2^{|s_k^q(x,y,z)|})}$$

$$\times \left[\frac{s_k^q(x,y,z) - \mu(x,y,z)}{\sqrt{\sigma^2(x,y,z)}} \gamma(x,y,z) + \beta(x,y,z) \right] \qquad (7.6)$$

where μ and $\sigma^2 \in \mathbb{R}^{D_k \times H_k \times V_k}$ are the expectation and variance over the batch, while $\gamma \in \mathbb{R}$ and $\beta \in \mathbb{R}^{D_k \times H_k \times V_k}$ are learnable parameters that scale the normalized value [190], and $2^{\text{round}(\log_2^{|s_k^q(x,y,z)|})}$ are quantized items which shift the normalized value. In the inference stage, μ, σ^2, γ and β are fixed to normalize the convolution output.

7.2.4   Quantized activation function and pooling

The activation function produces a nonlinear decision boundary via nonlinear combinations of the outputs of BN. In the deep ResNet, the ReLU is commonly used which is defined as $f(x) = \max(0, x)$ [267]. And the quantized ReLU layers, called the QReLUs, can be optimized as

$$a_k^{qrelu}(i,j) = \begin{cases} 0, & a_k^{qbn}(i,j) \leq 0 \\ \text{round}(a_k^{qbn}(i,j)), & \text{otherwise} \end{cases} \qquad (7.7)$$

where a_k^{qbn} is the output of the QBN and a_k^{qrelu} is the quantized activation generated in the kth layer.

We can take the QReLUs function for all real-number matrixes using the following example for a 2×2 region:

$$\begin{bmatrix} -7.63 & +3.11 \\ +12.46 & -5.89 \end{bmatrix} \Longrightarrow \begin{bmatrix} 0 & 3 \\ 12 & 0 \end{bmatrix} \qquad (7.8)$$

where the 2×2 real-value matrix denotes the output of QBN. The QReLUs filter out all the negative values to make the calculation more efficient and more feasible for hardware implementation.

Moreover, the pooling operation is optionally applied to select the most significant information from the features, which performs a downsampling across an $M \times M$

contiguous region on the feature. There are two kinds of pooling schemes commonly used in CNN-based network: max-pooling and average-pooling. The max-pooling takes the maximum value of the pooling region while the average-pooling takes the mean value of the pooling region. The deep ResNet begins with a max pooling and ends with a global average pooling layer and a $1,000$-way fully connected (FC) layer with a softmax layer. To save runtime memory and storage usage in inference, we can do the fusion as quantize($\circ$) function commutes with the max-pooling function:

$$\text{quantize}(\max(x, y)) = \max(\text{quantize}(x), \text{quantize}(y)) \tag{7.9}$$

and the quantized max-pooling, called the QPooling, is applied with the following equation:

$$a_k^{qp}(i, j) = \max[a_k^{qbn}(Mi + k, Mj + l)], (k, l \in (0, M)) \tag{7.10}$$

where a_k^{qbn} and a_k^{qp} are the features before and after pooling, respectively.

7.2.5 Quantized deep neural network overview

The overall working flow of the deep ResNet model with quantization and parallelization is presented in Figure 7.3. After the first layer, the QPooling will primarily work and feed the downsampled features into 4-bit QConv. Then each 4-bit QConv layer conducts a quantized convolution between 4-bit quantized features and weights. Then the feature output of QConv will be further processed by the QBN and QReLUs function. After every three convolution layers, the add-residual operation will be performed with 4-bit quantized parameters at the end of residual block.

As all the major parameters and expensive computation are performed with 4-bit quantization, the proposed 4-bit ResNet will get much less storage cost, faster speed as well as higher energy efficiency.

7.2.6 Training strategy

The detailed training strategy is presented in Algorithm 7.1. The network is assumed to have a feedforward linear topology, and the computation is performed with 4-bit quantization with high parallelism and efficiency. Note that the quantize($\circ$) and compute($\circ$) functions represent the corresponding quantization and computation methods mentioned above, the backward($\circ$) function specifies how to calculate parameter gradients in the backward propagation [254], and the update($\circ$) function presents how to update the parameters when their gradients are known [269].

After training, the proposed 4-bit ResNet model can be obtained, which is highly compressed through quantization. Compared to the original ResNet, the quantized ResNet benefits a lot from the large compression and high parallelization. It will reduce the complexity and enlarge the throughput of networks with low-bitwidth parameters, so that the implementation on the in-memory device also becomes more realizable.

Algorithm 7.1: Training quantized ResNet with 4-bit weights, features. L is the number of layers and g is the parameter gradient.

Require: previous inputs a_{k-1} and previous weights w_k.
Ensure: updated weights w_k^*.

    1. Computing the forward flow:

1: **for** $k = 1 : L$ **do**
2:     $w_k^q \leftarrow$ quantize(w_k)
3:     $a_{k-1}^q \leftarrow$ quantize(a_{k-1})
4:     $s_k^q \leftarrow$ compute(w_k^b, a_{k-1}^q)
5:     $a_k^{qbn} \leftarrow$ compute$(s_k^q, \mu, \sigma^2, \gamma, \beta)$
6:     **if** max-pooling layer **then**
7:         $a_k^{qp} \leftarrow$ compute(a_k^{qbn})
8:         $a_k^{qrelu} \leftarrow$ compute(a_k^{qp})
9:     **else**
10:        $a_k^{qrelu} \leftarrow$ compute(a_k^{qbn})
11:     **end if**
12:     $a_k^q \leftarrow a_k^{qrelu}$
13: **end for**

    2. Computing the backward gradients:

14: **for** $k = L : 1$ **do**
15:     $g_{a_{k-1}^q} \leftarrow$ backward$(g_{a_k^q}, w_k^q)$
16:     $g_{w_k^q} \leftarrow$ backward$(g_{a_k^q}, a_{k-1}^q)$
17: **end for**

    3. Accumulating the parameters gradients:

18: **for** $k = 1 : L$ **do**
19:     $w_k^* \leftarrow$ update$(w_k^q, g_{w_k^q})$
20: **end for**

7.3   Device for in-memory computing

In this section, the ReRAM-crossbar device will be presented which can be used for both storage and computation. And it will be employed to support a CMOS-ReRAM in-memory computing accelerator. The large-scale deep ResNet with quantization which has been discussed in Section 7.2 will be mapped.

7.3.1   ReRAM crossbar

ReRAM [62] is an in-memory computing device facing the future. The different resistance states of ReRAM can represent different parameters while computing. Besides working as storage memory, a ReRAM crossbar can be applied to perform logic operations [263], especially the dot-product-based convolutions.

    Previous works in [258,259] usually choose the two-terminal ReRAM device which only has two nonvolatile states: high-resistance state (HRS) and low-resistance state (LRS) to build an in-memory architecture, as shown in Figure 7.4(a). However, when the applied network becomes deeper and more complex, the two-terminal computing results in limitation on the performance of ReRAM crossbar while sacrifices the accuracy of network. For the implementation of proposed 4-bit ResNet-50, we apply the ReRAM model in [270], which has multibit resistance states. The states of proposed ReRAM device are determined by the distribution of set voltage V_{set}.

In one ReRAM crossbar, given the input probing voltage V_W on each writeline (WL), the current I_B on each bitline (BL) becomes the natural multiplication–accumulation of current through each ReRAM device. Therefore, the ReRAM-crossbar array can intrinsically perform the matrix–vector multiplication. Given an input voltage vector $V_W \in \mathbb{R}^{N \times 1}$, the output vector $I_B \in \mathbb{R}^{N \times 1}$ can be expressed as

$$\begin{bmatrix} I_{B,1} \\ \vdots \\ I_{B,M} \end{bmatrix} = \begin{bmatrix} c_{1,1} & \cdots & c_{1,M} \\ \vdots & \ddots & \vdots \\ c_{N,1} & \cdots & c_{N,M} \end{bmatrix} \begin{bmatrix} V_{W,1} \\ \vdots \\ V_{W,N} \end{bmatrix} \tag{7.11}$$

where $c_{i,j}$ is configurable conductance of the ReRAM resistance $R_{i,j}$, which can represent real value of weights. Compared to the traditional CMOS implementation, the ReRAM device can achieve a higher level of parallelism and consumes less power including standby power.

Different from the traditional non-quantized two-terminal ReRAM crossbar, the proposed 4-bit quantized ReRAM crossbar is shown in Figure 7.4(b), and the 4-bit resistance is configured for each ReRAM device. Moreover, the novel designed 4-bit DACs are applied on WL to transfer the digital input, and the 4-bit ADCs are applied on BL to identify the analog output. Therefore, the sensed analog output can be encoded in quantized digital signal to produce the multiplied result [237].

Compared to the two-terminal ReRAM crossbar, the 4-bit ReRAM crossbar has a better robustness on the IR-drop in the large-size implementation, so that the wire resistance affects little on IR-drop. In addition, since only 4-bit inputs are configured

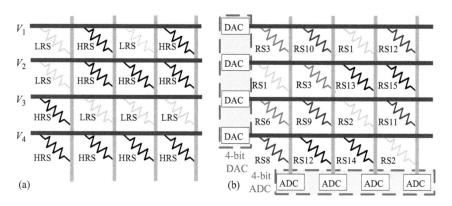

Figure 7.4 (a) Traditional two-terminal ReRAM crossbar; (b) 4-bit ReRAM crossbar with 4-bit DAC/ADC circuits

in quantized ReRAM crossbar, it has a better programming accuracy and can provide a better strategy for mapping deeper and large-scale networks.

7.3.2   Customized DAC and ADC circuits

To accommodate the multibit network on the ReRAM crossbar, we customize the designs of the 4-bit DAC and ADC, respectively, as shown in Figure 7.5(a) and (b). To save area, the DAC is implemented with the resistance to resistance (R2R) structure with a compact Opamp buffer. Compared with the traditional resistor ladder, the R2R uses uniform resistor values that favor better matching. The Opamp buffer uses feedforward structure to minimize current consumption and achieves fast settling. Biased by a g_m/I_d around 15, the current consumption of the whole Opamp is less than $13\,\mu\text{A}$ and achieves a $100\,\text{MHz}$ unity gain bandwidth. Meanwhile, an ADC scheme similar to that in [271] is employed to reduce the switching power, which uses asynchronous SAR to minimize the area and energy.

7.3.3   In-memory computing architecture

Based on the developed 4-bit ReRAM-crossbar device and novel DAC/ADC circuits, we present the CMOS-ReRAM in-memory computing accelerator with both memory storage and computation implemented as shown in Figure 7.6.

In this architecture, data–logic pairs are located in a distributed fashion, where data transmission among data block, logic block and external scheduler are maintained by a control bus. Therefore, logic block can read data locally and write back to the same data block after the logic computation is done [237]. As a result, the huge communication load between memory and general processor can be relieved because most of the data transmission is done inside data–logic pairs. Based on this in-memory computing architecture using the 4-bit CMOS-ReRAM accelerator, we will further introduce the strategy to map the proposed 4-bit quantized ResNet-50.

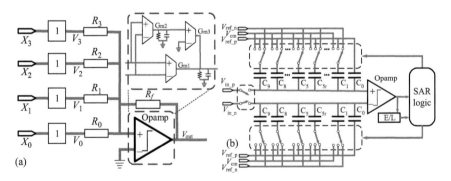

Figure 7.5   Simplified 4-bit (a) DAC and (b) ADC circuits

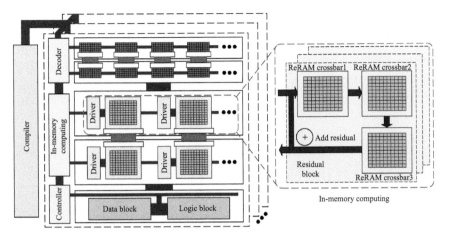

Figure 7.6   In-memory accelerator architecture based on 4-bit ReRAM crossbar for 4-bit quantized ResNet-50

7.4   Quantized ResNet on ReRAM crossbar

In this section, we present the detailed strategy to map the proposed large-scale ResNet with 4-bit quantization on the 4-bit CMOS-ReRAM, including quantized convolution and add-residual operations.

7.4.1   Mapping strategy

In order to avoid mapping negative weights on ReRAM-crossbar device, the 4-bit weights shown in Figure 7.2(a) are departed into positive weights w_{kp}^q and negative weights w_{kn}^q. Therefore, the quantized convolution can be presented by two separated multiplication operations, which are shown as

$$s_k^q = \sum_{i=1}^{N} w_k^q \cdot a_{k-1}^q = \sum_{i=1}^{N} (w_{kp}^q \cdot a_{k-1}^q + w_{kn}^q \cdot \overline{a_{k-1}^q})$$

(7.12)

$$a_{k-1}^q \in \frac{1}{15}\{0, 1, 2, \ldots, 15\}, w_k^q \in \{0, \pm1, \pm2, \pm4\}$$

to get the expected calculation result (keep weights positive), and the values of w_{kp}^q and w_{kn}^q will satisfy the following conditions:

$$w_{kp}^q = \begin{cases} w_k^q, & w_k^q \geq 0 \\ 0, & w_k^q < 0 \end{cases}$$

(7.13)

$$w_{kn}^q = \begin{cases} 0, & w_k^q \geq 0 \\ -w_k^q, & w_k^q \leq 0 \end{cases}$$

(7.14)

Table 7.1   Network model of quantized ResNet-50

Layer/residual block	Output size	Parameters (kernels, channels)
CONV1	112×112	$7 \times 7, 64$ 3×3 max pool
CONV2	56×56	$\begin{bmatrix} 1 \times 1, 64 \\ 3 \times 3, 64 \\ 1 \times 1, 256 \end{bmatrix} \times 3$
CONV3	28×28	$\begin{bmatrix} 1 \times 1, 128 \\ 3 \times 3, 128 \\ 1 \times 1, 512 \end{bmatrix} \times 4$
CONV4	14×14	$\begin{bmatrix} 1 \times 1, 256 \\ 3 \times 3, 256 \\ 1 \times 1, 1024 \end{bmatrix} \times 6$
CONV5	56×56	$\begin{bmatrix} 1 \times 1, 512 \\ 3 \times 3, 512 \\ 1 \times 1, 2048 \end{bmatrix} \times 3$
FC	1×1	7×7 average pool softmax output

Such all-positive trick makes it more feasible to implement a large-scale network on ReRAM crossbar. Specifically, the architecture of quantized ResNet-50 is shown in Table 7.1, which will be further mapped on the previously discussed 4-bit ReRAM crossbar.

7.4.2   Overall architecture

The whole mapping of residual block of proposed 4-bit ResNet-50 is shown in Figure 7.7. Since there are positive and negative lines for WL, the 4-bit ResNet-50 requires a $2N \times N$ ReRAM crossbar, where N is the number of elements in the feature matrices. The 4-bit DAC and the 4-bit ADC are applied to take input and output features. All columns are configured with the same elements that correspond to the quantized weight columns w_k^q of the neural network, and the WL voltages are determined by the analog input a_{k-1}^q transferred by the 4-bit DAC. Meanwhile, the output from every BL will be transferred to the digital signal by a 4-bit ADC. The s_k^q represents the convolution result, which can be seen in (7.5).

As described in (7.5), each quantized weight vector w_k^q performs quantized convolution with several input features. As a result, each logic block in Figure 7.6 stores a quantized vector w_k^q, while the control bus transmits the input feature sequentially. In this case, quantized convolution can be performed in parallel in separated logic blocks.

Although these operations are implemented on different ReRAM-crossbar arrays, the input/output formats of them are compatible so that one can directly connect them as shown in the logic block in Figure 7.6. As discussed in the in-memory computing

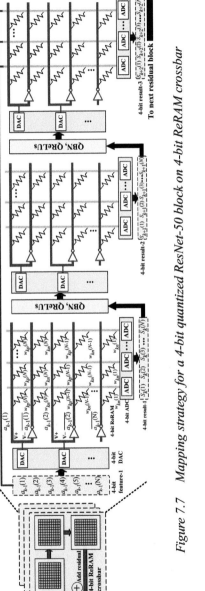

Figure 7.7 Mapping strategy for a 4-bit quantized ResNet-50 block on 4-bit ReRAM crossbar

architecture, one ResNet-50 residual block contains three convolution layers, and the add-residual operation is applied at the end of residual block to straightforwardly add the input of Layer 1 and the output of Layer 3.

As a summary, the 4-bit quantized convolution, BN, ReLUs and add-residual operations in Figure 7.1 can be mapped onto the proposed 4-bit CMOS-ReRAM accelerator and the max-pooling operations are performed in the additional processor. The pipeline design is based on Table 7.1. We observe that CONV2, CONV3, CONV4 and CONV5 are the stages which require the most ReRAM cells and computation time. As a result, more logic blocks are assigned to these steps to relieve the critical path. Since the output features from Figure 7.7 are 4-bit quantized, the area overhead and energy consumption of the data storage can be significantly reduced. In addition, as the layers in Table 7.1 are implemented with different data–logic pairs, the volume of data transmitted is also decreased.

7.5   Experiment result

7.5.1   *Experiment settings*

In the experiment, we have implemented different baselines for accuracy and performance comparison. Detailed setting of each baseline is listed as follows:

1.   Proposed 4-bit CMOS-ReRAM: We use the ReRAM model of [272] with uniformly separated resistance values in [1 kΩ, 5 kΩ] and a working frequency of 100 MHz.
2.   CPU: The general processor implementation is using Matconvnet [227] on a computer server with 6 cores of 3.46 GHz and 64.0 GB RAM.
3.   GPU: The general-purpose GPU implementation is based on a CUDA-enabled video card [188] with 1.05 GHz.
4.   State-of-the-art ReRAM-based architectures: Two existing ReRAM-based architectures [146,222].
5.   Others: The field programmable gate array (FPGA) [273], CMOS-ASIC [230] and micron automata processor [274] implementations of the conventional CNN networks.

To present the power of proposed architecture, we apply the large-scale ImageNet [265] data set to analyze the accuracy and performance of proposed 4-bit hardware accelerator. First, the model takes a $224 \times 224 \times 3$ RGB image as the input of the first convolution layer with 64 sets of quantized filters. After that, QPooling is applied to prepare data for the following layers. Next, the QConv layer of the first residual block performs the quantized convolution between input features and weights followed by the QPooling. Then the QBN is employed after the QConv to accelerate the training. Meanwhile, we adopt the QReLUs to each QConv layer to stabilize the process. For every layer stack, three cascaded convolution layers make up a residual block with an add-residual operation. In the end, the output of the last FC layer is fed into a softmax layer to generate a probabilistic distribution of 1,000 classes.

7.5.2   Device simulations

According to the sizes of feature matrix in ResNet-50, we employ a 128×64 ReRAM crossbar where the number of input features is set as 128 and the number of output channels is 64. We adopted the read/write latency and read/write energy from [275] as 29.31 ns/50.88 ns per spike, 1.08 pJ/3.91 nJ per spike. The final layouts of the proposed 4-bit DAC and ADC circuits are shown in Figure 7.8. We further report simulation results of the proposed CMOS-ReRAM accelerator. In Figure 7.9(a), 4-bit digital waveforms are converted into analog signals by the 4-bit DAC. Then in Figure 7.9(b), output waveforms are obtained by the 4-bit ADC for various ReRAM resistive states representing all possible w_{kp}^q. A high accuracy can be observed in the DAC/ADC circuits, and the whole CMOS-ReRAM accelerator permits a high performance and efficiency, as shown in Table 7.4.

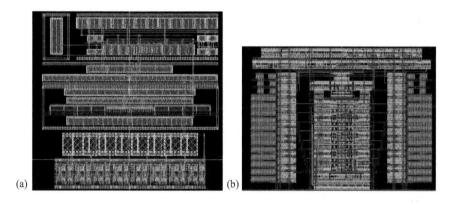

Figure 7.8   Layouts of the proposed 4-bit (a) DAC and (b) ADC

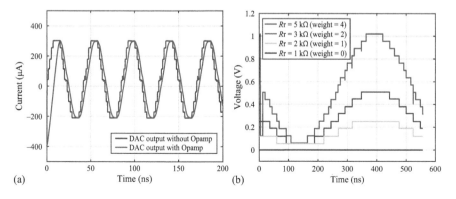

Figure 7.9   (a) Waveforms of the 4-bit DAC inputs; (b) 4-bit ADC outputs with different ReRAM resistances

7.5.3 Accuracy analysis

First, we report both the top-1 and top-5 accuracy comparison between the proposed 4-bit ResNet-50 and the full-precision ResNet-50 on ImageNet. It should be noted that in case of top-1 rate, we check if the top class having the highest probability is the same as the target label, and in case of top-5 rate, we check if the target label is one of the top five predictions with the highest probabilities. And then, the accuracy comparison under device variation is presented. At last, we report the accuracy comparison between the proposed quantized ResNet-50 and the direct-truncated ResNet-50 under bitwidth approximation.

7.5.3.1   Peak accuracy comparison

Figure 7.10 shows the evolution of top-1 and top-5 accuracy vs. epoch curves of the 4-bit ResNet-50 compared with the full-precision ResNet-50. It can be seen that quantizing the ResNet-50 to be 4-bit does not cause the training curve to be significantly different from the full-precision one. Only 3.3% prediction accuracy decreases for top-1 while only 2.5% accuracy losses for top-5 compared with the full-precision ResNet-50. Moreover, we report the top-5 accuracy comparison among different state-of-the-art quantization approaches in Table 7.2. It is observed that the proposed 4-bit trained quantization outperforms other realizations, which is 3.5% higher than the 4-bit fine-grained quantization [276] and 1.5% higher than the 5-bit incremental network quantization [277]. Therefore, we can conclude that the ResNet-50 with the proposed 4-bit trained quantization obtains a remarkable balance between large compression and high accuracy.

7.5.3.2   Accuracy under device variation

In the previous discussion, the 4-bit ReRAM crossbar has better programming accuracy than the traditional ReRAM crossbar so that it achieves a better uniformity. For

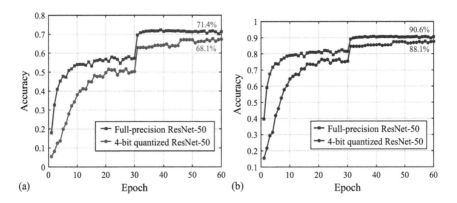

Figure 7.10   (a) Top-1 validation accuracy curves of quantized ResNet-50.
(b) Top-5 validation accuracy curves of quantized ResNet-50

Table 7.2   The top-5 accuracy comparison between
            the proposed network and state-of-the-art
            approaches on the ImageNet data set

Original ResNet-50 (32-bit) [246]	90.6%
Truncation-based quantization (4-bit) [252]	12.3%
Binary weight quantization (1-bit) [254]	78.7%
Ternary weight quantization (2-bit) [278]	81.2%
Fine-grained quantization (4-bit) [276]	84.6%
Incremental quantization (5-bit) [277]	86.8%
Discussed trained quantization (4-bit)	88.1%

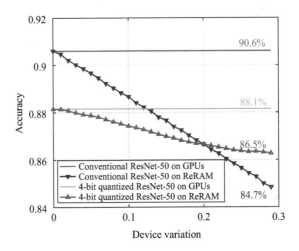

*Figure 7.11   Accuracy validation of quantized ResNet-50 under ReRAM-crossbar
               device variation*

further evaluation, we build a device variation model by using the Monte-Carlo simulation technique under different writing voltages V_w where the voltage amplitude
meets the Gaussian distribution ($\sigma = 1\% V_w$). Based on the variation model, we sys-
tematically set the parameter variation during the network training and can achieve
better accuracy under device variation. The accuracy comparison against device variation on ReRAM is shown in Figure 7.11. It can be observed that when the device
variation of ReRAM increases, there are output current errors. For example, when
the device variation reaches 29%, the 4-bit ReRAM crossbar has an accuracy of
86.5% with only 1.6% decreases compared with GPUs, better than the non-quantized
one with an accuracy of 84.7% with 5.9% decreased. The proposed CMOS-ReRAM
delivers higher robustness when the device variation is larger than 20%.

7.5.3.3 Accuracy under approximation

To evaluate the accuracy under bitwidth approximation, we choose the precision-bit direct-truncated method for comparison. For the proposed trained quantized ResNet-50 and direct-truncated ResNet-50, we first train the full-precision (32-bit) network, and then decrease the precision of all the weights and features in the network. The numerical results with different bitwidths are shown in Figure 7.12. In our model, the weights and features in the quantized ResNet-50 are 4-bit, whose accuracy has no significant loss compared with the full-precision ResNet-50. Although the accuracy of the 32-bit model reaches 90.6% in the direct-truncated ResNet-50, the bitwidth influences the accuracy a lot especially when the bitwidth is smaller than 10. For example, when the precision decreases to 6-bit, the accuracy drops down to only about 11.3%. The results show that the proposed quantized ResNet-50 can perform much better than the direct-truncated one.

Moreover, we further report the evaluation on accuracy and storage compression among different bitwidths. As shown in Table 7.3, the 4-bit ResNet-50 causes only

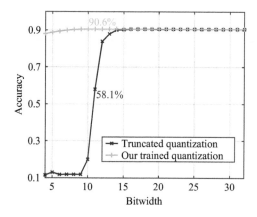

Figure 7.12 *Accuracy comparison with direct truncation-based quantization based on ResNet-50*

Table 7.3 *Accuracy validation of quantized ResNet-50 under bitwidth approximation*

Bitwidth	Accuracy	Storage compression
2-bit	32.9%	15.86
3-bit	71.5%	10.85
4-bit	88.1%	8.02
6-bit	88.7%	5.76
8-bit	89.8%	3.94
16-bit	90.5%	1.98
Full precision	90.6%	N/A

0.025 decrease on accuracy with 8.02 storage compression. It can be seen that accuracy decreases a lot when the bitwidth is smaller than 4, but not much improvement when bitwidth is larger than 4. There are some recent works to perform quantization on 8-bit and binary quantization [188]. However, 8-bit quantization results in higher accuracy still have significant hardware cost, while binary quantization cannot achieve a reasonable accuracy on a large-scale neural network. Therefore, we conclude that the 4-bit quantization can have good balance between accuracy and storage compression on the large-scale ResNet-50 network. It is the reason why 4-bit is determined to be the best quantization bitwidth for the large-scale ReRAM implementation.

7.5.4 Performance analysis

In the experiments, parameters with quantization have been configured by the training process, meanwhile every batch of inputs and results are calculated in parallel. In Table 7.4, performance comparison among CPU, GPU and other baselines is presented, which is evaluated on 100 testing images with 224×224 resolution.

7.5.4.1 Energy and area

Using the ReRAM model in [270], the current consumption of each ReRAM cell is less than $1\,\mu A$, where the voltage is set to be $5\,mV$ and the area consumption of each ReRAM cell is less than $4 \times 4\,\mu m^2$. Moreover, the current consumption of the proposed novel DAC/ADC is less than $13\,\mu A$ and the total area of DAC/ADC is less than $26 \times 27\,\mu m^2$. Having both settings of ReRAM and DAC/ADC models, the numerical results of energy consumption can be simulated as follows: $5\,mV \times 0.001\,mA \times 128 + 5\,mV \times 0.0122\,mA \times (128 + 1) = 8.509\,mW$. It should be noted that we load power on a single BL for each convolution operation, the value 128 denotes the amount of ReRAM cells and $(128 + 1)$ denotes the number of DACs/ADCs in one BL. The energy distribution is shown in Figure 7.13(a) and the convolution is the major operation that dominates 87.4% of the total energy. Also, we calculate the area consumption by $4\,\mu m \times 4\,\mu m \times 128 \times 64 + 26\,\mu m \times 27\,\mu m \times (128 + 64) = 265,856\,\mu m^2$. Based on the area model in [279], we present the area overhead of the proposed CMOS-ReRAM architecture in Figure 7.13(b). The area overhead of DAC/ADC is the largest part which occupies 32%, and the total area consumption is simulated as $830,800\,\mu m^2$. The energy and area consumption comparison among all the implementations are shown in Table 7.4. It can be seen that the implementation on the proposed 4-bit CMOS-ReRAM accelerator can achieve at least four-magnitude smaller energy consumption compared to GPU and CPU.

7.5.4.2 Throughput and efficiency

For the throughput performance, we use GOPS (giga operations per second) to evaluate all the implementations as shown in Tables 7.4 and 7.5. In the throughput comparison, the proposed 4-bit ReRAM crossbar is $432\times$ faster than CPU-based implementation, $10.31\times$ faster than FPGA-based implementation and $15.21\times$ faster than CMOS-ASIC-based implementation. As for energy efficiency, it can be four-magnitude better than GPU-based implementation and $498\times$ better than CMOS-ASIC-based implementation. And in area-efficiency comparison, it is $224\times$ better

Table 7.4 Performance comparison under different hardware implementations

Implementation	CPU [227]	GPU [188]	FPGA [273]	CMOS-ASIC [230]	Micron automata processor [274]	4-bit CMOS-ReRAM
Network	4-bit ResNet-50	4-bit ResNet-50	ResNet-50	Small-scale CNN	Small-scale CNN	4-bit ResNet-50
Frequency	3.46 GHz	1.05 GHz	240 MHz	250 MHz	300 MHz	100 MHz
Area	240 mm^2	601 mm^2	N/A	12.25 mm^2	N/A	0.83 mm^2
Average power	130 W	170 W	25 W	278 mW	0.5 W	8.5 mW
System throughput	1.48 GOPS	49 GOPS	560 GOPS	42 GOPS	251 GOPS	639 GOPS
Energy efficiency	0.011 GOP/J	2.9 GOP/J	22.4 GOP/J	151 GOP/J	502 GOP/J	75.2 TOP/J
Area efficiency	0.006 GOP/s/mm^2	0.82 GOP/s/mm^2	N/A	3.43 GOP/s/mm^2	N/A	770 GOP/s/mm^2

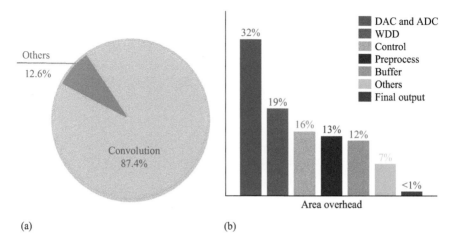

Figure 7.13 *(a) Divided energy profile and (b) divided area profile when implementing 4-bit ResNet-50 on 4-bit ReRAM crossbar*

Table 7.5 *Efficiency comparison among three ReRAM-based implementations*

	Throughput	Energy efficiency	Area efficiency
Two-terminal ReRAM [146]	N/A	2 TOP/J	N/A
Digital ReRAM [222]	563 GOPS	65.4 TOP/J	696 GOP/s/mm^2
Discussed 4-bit ReRAM	639 GOPS	75.2 TOP/J	770 GOP/s/mm^2

than the CMOS-ASIC-based implementation. As a conclusion, the proposed 4-bit ReRAM crossbar outperforms all the implementations on throughput, energy efficiency and area efficiency. There are still some challenges in accommodating the multibit network on the real-fabricated ReRAM such as the circuit designs of the DACs/ADCs and the robustness of the large-scale ReRAM crossbar. Nonetheless, since the proposed CMOS-ReRAM has provided an efficient and robust architecture with real circuit designs and simulations, it is more feasible to implement a large-scale neural network (e.g., VGG-16, SSD-50 and ResNet-101) on the real-fabricated ReRAM-based accelerator.

Chapter 8

Large-scale case study: accelerator for compressive sensing

8.1 Introduction

Biomedical wireless circuits for applications such as health telemonitoring [280,281] and implantable biosensors [282,283] are energy sensitive. To prolong the lifetime of their services, it is essential to perform the dimension reduction while acquiring original data. The compressive sensing [284] is a signal processing technique that exploits signal sparsity so that signal can be reconstructed under lower sampling rate than that of Nyquist sampling theorem. The existing works that apply compressive sensing technique on biomedical hardware focus on the efficient signal reconstruction by either dictionary learning [283,285] or more efficient algorithms of finding the sparsest coefficients [280,281,286]. However, these works, by improving the reconstruction on mobile/server nodes instead of data acquisition on sensor nodes, can only indirectly reduce the number of samples for wireless transmission with lower energy. In this work, we aim to achieve both high-performance signal acquisition and low sampling hardware cost at sensor nodes directly.

In compressive sensing, the sampling is performed by multiplying the original signal vector with a linear embedding matrix, which projects the high-dimensional data vector into a low-dimensional subspace with preserved intrinsic information. The concise representation is called a low-dimensional embedding. The sampling matrix can be either random, generally optimized or optimized towards specific data set. The random sampling matrices, Bernoulli or Gaussian, though easier to construct, have two major limitations. First, its guarantee on recoverability is only probabilistic and therefore large recovery error may be incurred. Second, its construction is independent on the data under investigation, and therefore the geometric information of data set cannot be exploited. The generally optimized sampling matrices, such as Reed–Muller code [287,288] or Puffer transformation [283], have deterministic recoverability by constructing matrices with minimized mutual coherence. However, they are still independent on data type of interest so that the performance cannot be maximized. The data-driven optimized embedding, on the other hand, can leverage geometric structure of data set in particular application with additional learning phase, which is especially beneficial for biomedical sampling hardware where target data type is predetermined. Signal acquisition by a data-driven optimized sampling matrix can preserve more intrinsic information of original signal, and therefore ensure more accurate signal reconstruction and/or higher compression ratio.

Most existing data-driven optimization methods only produce real-valued embedding matrices [289]. However, the hardware mapping of real-valued sampling matrix is much more power consuming than that of Boolean matrix. The reason is that for real-valued embedding operation, the required hardware resources, primarily full adders, are quadratically depending on the precision required, while only linearly for Boolean embedding mapping. Therefore, a Boolean sampling matrix is preferred as the significantly reduced hardware resources can contribute to higher energy efficiency and area efficiency. In fact, the random Bernoulli matrix is the most widely used sampling matrix in existing CMOS-based implementations for low power consumption [283,286,290]. In addition, the recent emerging resistive random-access memory (ReRAM) [62,291] in crossbar (or cross-point) structure [62] can provide intrinsic fabric for matrix–vector multiplication, which potentially enables both energy- and area-efficient hardware implementation of linear embedding. However, the limited ReRAM programming resolution also favors only Boolean embedding matrices to be mapped to ReRAM crossbar structure.

Therefore, the hardware realization of sampling matrix faces a dilemma. On the one hand, if data-driven optimized real-valued embedding, such as NuMax [289], is mapped for better recovery quality, large power overhead will be expected. On the other hand, if non-data-driven random Boolean embedding or Boolean Reed–Muller [287,288] embedding is mapped for better hardware energy efficiency, high signal recovery accuracy cannot be accomplished. Such trade-off is illustrated in Figure 8.1. Figure 8.1 also reveals that quantization of NuMax by straightforward truncation works only above precision of 16 bits, below which it will incur significant performance degradation. Therefore, without data-driven optimized Boolean

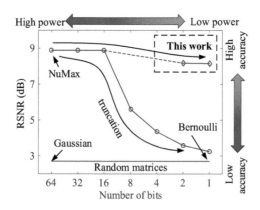

Figure 8.1   The comparison of information loss of NuMax through truncation quantization vs. proposed quantization. This work achieves both high signal recovery performance as well as low sampling hardware cost by proposed quantization algorithm

embedding, the advantages of both sides cannot be achieved simultaneously. The challenge to perform data-driven Boolean embedding optimization is that, with large amount of data set involved in the sampling matrix optimization, only convex methods with real-valued optimized matrices are feasible.

In this chapter, towards high-performance (data-driven) and low-power (Boolean) sampling, instead of optimizing Boolean embedding on original data set, we propose an optimizing algorithm that transforms a data-driven optimized real-valued sampling matrix to a Boolean sampling matrix. The proposed optimization flow is illustrated in Figure 8.2. As the input optimized real-valued embedding matrix is optimized towards the specific data set, and the proposed algorithm seeks least intrinsic information loss, so the resulted Boolean embedding matrix is still optimized towards the same training data set. In addition, we have discussed the corresponding hardware implementations based on both CMOS technology and emerging nonvolatile ReRAM technology for obtained optimized Boolean embedding. Such capability was first exploited in our preliminary work [249]. The numerical experiments demonstrate that the proposed data-driven Boolean embedding can combine both high signal quality and also low sampling power. Specifically, it can improve image recovery quality (reconstructed signal-to-noise ratio (RSNR)) by 9 dB compared to the non-data-driven Bernoulli embedding, and improve energy efficiency by 4.6× than that of data-driven real-valued sampling circuit.

The contributions of this chapter are summarized as follows:

- To our best knowledge, the data-driven optimized Boolean sampling matrix is constructed for the first time. Being Boolean and optimized towards data set, we achieve both the highest signal recovery quality and the best hardware energy efficiency among all existing schemes.
- We formulate the problem of finding the best transformation that quantizes real-valued sampling matrix into Boolean matrix with minimal information loss.

The rest of this chapter is organized as follows. Section 8.2 introduces the background of compressive sensing and near-isometric embedding. Section 8.3 presents

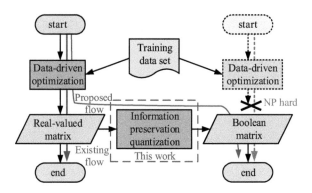

Figure 8.2 The proposed flow for data-driven Boolean sampling matrix optimization

the sampling hardware for Boolean embedding with the corresponding optimization problem formulated. Sections 8.4 and 8.5 detail two Boolean embedding optimization algorithms. Numerical results are presented in Section 8.6.

8.2   Background

8.2.1   Compressive sensing and isometric distortion

Recently, the emerging theory of compressive sensing has enabled the recovery of undersampled signal, if the signal is sparse or has sparse representation on certain basis, such as wavelet transformation and Fourier transformation. And the recovery can be achieved by solving

$$\underset{x \in \mathbb{R}^N}{\text{minimize}} \quad \|x\|_1$$

$$\text{subject to} \quad y = \Psi \Omega x \tag{8.1}$$

where $x \in \mathbb{R}^N$ is the sparse coefficients vector and $\Omega \in \mathbb{R}^{N \times N}$ is the basis on which the original signal is sparse; $\Psi \in \mathbb{R}^{M \times N}$ is the sensing matrix and $y \in \mathbb{R}^M$ ($M \ll N$) the undersampled data in low dimension. To ensure a successful recovery, the sensing matrix (Ψ) must meet the restricted isometry property (RIP), which is defined as follows: if there exists a $\delta \in (0, 1)$ such that the following equation is valid for every vector $v \in \mathbb{R}^N$,

$$(1 - \delta)\|v\|_2^2 \leq \|\Psi v\|_2^2 \leq (1 + \delta)\|v\|_2^2 \tag{8.2}$$

then Ψ has the RIP with isometric distortion constant δ. The notations of all used symbols are summarized in Table 8.1.

8.2.2   Optimized near-isometric embedding

The easiest way to construct a matrix with RIP is to generate a random matrix. The work [292] proves that random matrix is of a very high possibility to satisfy RIP, yet not deterministic. Different from the random Bernoulli sampling matrix that the RIP is probabilistic, an data-driven sampling matrix can ensure the RIP of a finite given data points. One recent work in [289] proposed the **NuMax** framework to construct a near-isometric embedding matrix with deterministic RIP. Given a data set $\chi = \{x_1, x_2, \ldots, x_i\} \in \mathbb{R}^N$, the NuMax produces an optimized continuous-valued embedding matrix Ψ so that every pairwise distance vector v for χ can preserve its norm after embedding up to a given distortion tolerance $\delta_{\max}$.

Once the optimized NuMax sampling matrix Ψ is obtained, the signal acquisition $y = \Psi \Omega x$ can be performed by multiplying the embedding matrix Ψ with signal vector Ωx. The conventional CMOS circuit-based data acquisition front end that performs real-valued embedding is shown in Figure 8.3. The sampling circuit has two major components, the static random access memory (SRAM) memory that stores the embedding matrix and the multiplier-accumulators (MACs) that perform multiplication and addition. For an embedding matrix $\Psi \in \mathbb{R}^{m \times n}$ ($m \ll n$), in each cycle, m MACs multiply one element of input vector x with one column of Ψ, and

Table 8.1   Notation table of used mathematical symbols

Symbols	Descriptions
δ	The isometric distortion of the restricted isometry property
x	Original high-dimensional signal to be sampled by compressive sensing
y	Sampled low-dimensional signal by compressive sensing
Ω	Sparse basis/dictionary
$\hat{x}$	Reconstructed/recovered original signal
Ψ	Sampling matrix
$\hat{\Psi}$	Boolean sampling matrix losslessly quantized from real-valued Ψ
T	Orthogonal RIP preserving transformation matrix for quantization
t_i	ith row of T obtained during row-generation algorithm
$\hat{\psi}_i$	ith row of $\hat{\Psi}$ obtained during row-generation algorithm
χ	Training data set $\chi = \{x_1, x_2, \ldots, x_i\}$ for sampling matrix optimization
$S(\chi)$	Set of all pairwise distances among every two x in χ as input for NuMax
χ'	Testing data set that has no overlap with training data set χ
σ_{LRS}	Standard deviation of ReRAM resistance in LRS
σ_{HRS}	Standard deviation of ReRAM resistance in HRS

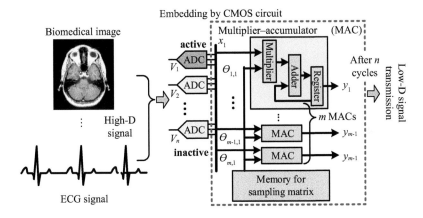

Figure 8.3   The embedding circuit by CMOS matrix–vector multiplier

then add with previously accumulated results. Therefore, it requires n cycles to obtain the embedded signal y.

As NuMax produces real-valued Ψ, the precision of Ψ substantially determines the hardware complexity. For example, a multiplier in MAC with 4-bit resolution, shown in Figure 8.4(a), requires 16 full adders. In fact, the number of full adders required generally quadratically depends on the precision of both Ωx and Ψ. For the typical precision of real-valued elements in sampling matrix, 16-bit (Figure 8.1) resolution may lead to as many as hundreds of full adders for each MAC, which makes the real-valued NuMax embedding less appealing for signal acquisition hardware mapping.

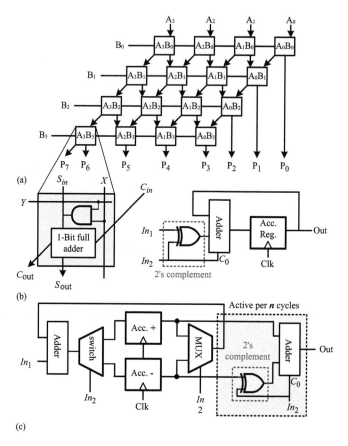

Figure 8.4   The implementation of (a) MAC with multiplier in 4-bit resolution for real-valued embedding matrix; (b) MAC for $\{-1, 1\}^{m \times n}$ embedding matrix; (c) MAC for $\{-1, 1\}^{m \times n}$ embedding matrix with power optimization

8.3   Boolean embedding for signal acquisition front end

8.3.1   CMOS-based Boolean embedding circuit

The mapping of a Boolean embedding matrix can eliminate the usage of multipliers. For a $\{0, 1\}^{m \times n}$ Boolean embedding matrix, the MAC only accumulates signal data when Boolean multiplicand is 1. For a more general $\{-1, 1\}^{m \times n}$ Boolean matrix, the Boolean multiplicand indicates addition or subtraction for the signal data. That is to say, the required resources of full adders are only linearly depending on the precision of signal Ωx. As such, the hardware resource can be significantly reduced.

Specifically for the $\{-1, 1\}^{m \times n}$ embedding matrix mapping, the multiplication by -1 requires the calculation of 2's complement. The intuitive approach is illustrated in Figure 8.4(b). The In_2 signal is 1 for multiplying -1 and 0 for multiplying 1. To obtain the 2's complement, the XOR logic is used to get the complement of each bit and the C_0 (carry 0) is applied as well. However, the 2's complement calculation close to input will incur substantial dynamic power for the combinational logic. Instead, the circuit diagram in Figure 8.4(c) first accumulates all data to be multiplied by 1 and -1 separately, and the subtraction is performed at the very last cycle. Therefore, the 2's complement circuit is only active every n cycles, which can greatly improve the power efficiency.

To be compatible with optimized sampling matrices such as Reed–Muller code [287,288] and NuMax [289], SRAM block is required to store the matrix and provide reconfigurability. For non-optimized sampling matrices such as random Gaussian and Bernoulli, apart from storing the matrix in SRAM, the matrix can also be generated at runtime, which can improve hardware efficiency. In practice, the pseudo-random number generator (PRNG) is used [286,290], which avoids the power-consuming SRAM arrays. As PRNG produces 0/1 sequences with a predetermined pattern, one of the issues for PRNG is the self-coherence. For example, an 8-bit per cycle PRNG has a period of 256 (2^8), and when filling a $n \times 256$ sampling matrix by rows with such 0/1 sequences, all rows of the matrix will be identical. This can be overcome by increasing the number of bits the PRNG produces per cycle at a cost of higher hardware complexity. With limited hardware resources, the pseudo-random numbers generated by PRNG usually lead to performance degradation of signal acquisition compared to stored random sampling matrix.

8.3.2   ReRAM crossbar-based Boolean embedding circuit

The emerging ReRAM crossbar [62,291] provides an intrinsic in-memory fabric of matrix–vector multiplication, which is proposed in Figure 8.5. Compared to CMOS embedding circuit, ReRAM crossbar-based approach can provide three major advantages: (1) embed sensing matrix in-memory without the need of loading Φ externally each cycle, (2) perform the matrix–vector multiplication in single cycle and (3) minimize the leakage power due to its nonvolatility.

A ReRAM crossbar structure is composed of three layers: horizontal wires at top layer, vertical wires at bottom layer and ReRAM devices in the middle layer at each

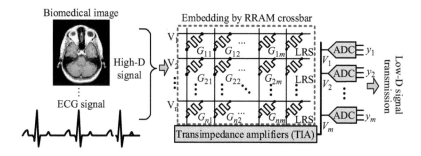

Figure 8.5   The embedding circuit by emerging nonvolatile ReRAM crossbar

cross point. For an $m \times n$ ReRAM crossbar, assume the input signal of ith row is V_i and the conductance of ReRAM device on ith row jth column is G_{ij}, then the output current flowing down jth column $I_j = \Sigma_{i=1}^{m} V_i G_{ij}$. In other words, crossbar structure intrinsically supports in-memory embedding operation

$$\begin{bmatrix} V_1 \\ V_2 \\ \vdots \\ V_m \end{bmatrix} = Z \begin{bmatrix} G_{11} & G_{12} & \cdots & G_{1n} \\ G_{21} & G_{22} & \cdots & G_{2n} \\ \vdots & \vdots & \ddots & \vdots \\ G_{m1} & G_{m2} & \cdots & G_{mn} \end{bmatrix} \begin{bmatrix} V_1 \\ V_2 \\ \vdots \\ V_n \end{bmatrix} \tag{8.3}$$

where Z is the transimpedance of the transimpedance amplifier (TIA). It must be ensured that input $||V||_\infty \ll V$th to avoid accidental value changes of G, in which the Vth is the device programming threshold voltage.

The mapping of embedding matrix is accomplished by the resistance programming of ReRAM crossbar corresponding to Ψ. Intended for memory usage, ReRAM devices are commonly bistable with on-resistance and off-resistance ratio as high as $10^3 \sim 10^4$ [291,293]. Resistance programming with higher resolution has been demonstrated in 4 or 5 levels at most [293,294]. Therefore, resistance programming in continuous (or close-continuous) value resolution is practically challenging due to large process variation under current manufacture technology. In other words, the real-valued sampling matrix does not comply with ReRAM crossbar and Boolean sampling matrix is preferred.

As the ReRAM crossbar is essentially (0, 1) binary in terms of conductance, the mapping of (0, 1) Boolean matrix is as follows: 0 corresponds to high-resistance state (HRS) and 1 maps to low-resistance state (LRS). To map $\hat{\Psi} \in \{-1, 1\}^{m \times n}$, simple linear transformation needs to be considered: $\hat{\Psi}x = (2\Theta - J)x = 2\Theta x - Jx$, where $\Theta \in \{0, 1\}^{m \times n}$, J all-ones matrix and x input vector. The Jx is implemented by an additional all-LRS column that generates Σx as current offset for other columns, as shown in Figure 8.5. The sampling matrices that each type of hardware supports are illustrated in Table 8.2.

Table 8.2 Compatibility of different sampling matrices on various hardware platforms

Hardware	MAC/MEM	ReRAM crossbar	MAC/PRNG
NuMax	✓	✗	✗
This work	✓	✓	✗
Reed–Muller	✓	✓	✗
Bernoulli	✓	✓	✓
Gaussian	✓	✗	✓

8.3.3 Problem formulation

For an sampling matrix Ψ that satisfies RIP with distortion of δ_Ψ, the following equation will also hold true:

$$(1 - \delta_\Psi)\|x\|_2^2 \leq \|T\Psi x\|_2^2 \leq (1 + \delta_\Psi)\|x\|_2^2 \qquad (8.4)$$

if T is an orthonormal rotation matrix. In other words, if we can find an orthonormal rotation matrix that transforms real-valued NuMax embedding matrix Ψ into a matrix that is close enough to a Boolean matrix $\hat{\Psi}$, then the Boolean embedding of $\hat{\Psi}$ can preserve original distortion δ_Ψ. In other words, the resulted $\hat{\Psi}$ is still optimized towards the same training data set as NuMax embedding Ψ, and meanwhile, it can be efficiently mapped to circuits in Figures 8.4(c) and 8.5 with greatly reduced power consumption.

The Boolean sampling matrix optimization can be then formulated as the following optimization problem:

$$\underset{T,\hat{\Psi}}{\text{minimize}} \quad \|T\Psi - \hat{\Psi}\|_F^2$$

$$\text{subject to} \quad T^T \cdot T = I$$

$$\hat{\Psi} \in \{-1, 1\}^{m \times n} \qquad (8.5)$$

where $\Psi \in \mathbb{R}^{m \times n}$ ($m < n$) is the optimized real-valued sampling matrix learned from data set that projects data from high n-dimension to low m-dimension; $T \in \mathbb{R}^{m \times m}$ is an orthonormal rotation matrix that attempts to transform Ψ to a Boolean matrix. $\hat{\Psi} \in \mathbb{R}^{m \times m}$ is the closest Boolean matrix solution where closeness is defined by the Frobenius norm.

Ideally, if an orthonormal transformation matrix T can rotate Ψ to an exact Boolean matrix, i.e., the optimal value of (8.5) is zero, then the distortion δ of optimized Boolean embedding will be exactly the same as the NuMax real-valued embedding. In practice, with a nonzero optimal value, the closeness of $T\Psi$ to $\hat{\Psi}$ indicates information loss degree from Ψ to $\hat{\Psi}$. On the other hand, it can be interpreted as an equivalent near-orthogonal rotation T' transforms real-valued Ψ to an exact Boolean $\hat{\Psi}$. The degree of orthogonality implies the information loss of Ψ.

8.4 IH algorithm

It is intractable to solve the problem formulated in (8.5) considering the orthogonal constraint $T^T \cdot T = I$ and the integer constraint $\hat{\Psi} \in \{-1, 1\}$ simultaneously, as both constraints are nonconvex. When one constraint is considered at one time, (8.5) can be split into two manageable problems: if the orthogonal constraint is considered for T, and $\hat{\Psi}$ a given Boolean matrix, the problem becomes the search of an *orthogonal rotation* matrix for maximal matrix agreement; if the integer constraint is considered for $\hat{\Psi}$ and T a given orthogonal matrix, the problem turns to *Boolean quantization* for maximal matrix agreement. In this section, a heuristic approach is proposed that iteratively solves *orthogonal rotation* problem and *Boolean quantization* problem, and gradually approximates the optimal solution of $\hat{\Psi}$ in each round.

8.4.1   Orthogonal rotation

The problem of finding an orthogonal transformation matrix T that can rotate a given real-valued projection matrix Ψ to another given Boolean matrix $\hat{\Psi}$ can be formulated as

$$\underset{T,k}{\text{minimize}} \quad ||kT\Psi - \hat{\Psi}||_F^2$$

$$\text{subject to} \quad T^T \cdot T = I \tag{8.6}$$

The cost function can be represented by trace function as

$$||kT\Psi - \hat{\Psi}||_F^2 = k^2 Tr \left(\Psi^T \Psi\right) + Tr \left(\hat{\Psi}^T \hat{\Psi}\right)$$
$$-2kTr \left(T^T \hat{\Psi} \Psi^T\right) \tag{8.7}$$

As Ψ and $\hat{\Psi}$ are given matrices, $Tr\left(\Psi^T \Psi\right)$ and $Tr\left(\hat{\Psi}^T \hat{\Psi}\right)$ are therefore two constants. Consider k as constant first, the formulated optimization problem in (8.6) can be rewritten as

$$\underset{T}{\text{maximize}} \quad Tr\left(T^T \hat{\Psi} \Psi^T\right)$$

$$\text{subject to} \quad T^T \cdot T = I \tag{8.8}$$

and with the singular value decomposition $\hat{\Psi}\Psi^T = U\Sigma V^T$, where $\Sigma = diag$ $(\sigma_1, \ldots, \sigma_n)$, the cost function of (8.8) can be rewritten as

$$Tr(T^T \hat{\Psi} \Psi^T) = Tr(T^T U\Sigma V^T)$$

$$= Tr(V^T T^T U\Sigma) \leq \sum_{i=1}^{n} \sigma_i \tag{8.9}$$

The inequality holds as V, T and U are all orthonormal matrices. As such, the trace is maximized when $V^T T^T U = I$, which leads to

$$T = UV^T \tag{8.10}$$

To optimize k, let $\frac{\partial f}{\partial k} = 0$ in which f is the cost function of (8.7), and the best scaling factor can be obtained by

$$k = \frac{Tr\left(T^T \hat{\Psi} \Psi^T\right)}{Tr\left(\Psi^T \Psi\right)} \tag{8.11}$$

8.4.2 *Quantization*

T is a known orthogonal transformation matrix, and Ψ is a given real-valued optimized projection matrix, the problem to find its closest Boolean matrix can be formulated as

$$\underset{\hat{\psi}}{\text{minimize}} \quad ||kT\Psi - \hat{\Psi}||_F^2$$

$$\text{subject to} \quad \hat{\Psi} \in \{-1, 1\} \tag{8.12}$$

It is obvious that the solution for (8.12) is

$$\hat{\Psi}_{ij} = \begin{cases} 1, & (kT\Psi)_{ij} \geq 0 \\ -1, & (kT\Psi)_{ij} < 0 \end{cases} \tag{8.13}$$

This can be seen as Boolean quantization. The quantization error can be defined as

$$e = ||kT\Psi - \hat{\Psi}||_F^2 \tag{8.14}$$

In ideal case, the error would be zero, which means an orthogonal transformation T on optimized real-valued projection matrix Ψ finds an exact Boolean matrix $\hat{\Psi}$. Therefore, the distortion $\delta_{\hat{\psi}}$ caused by $\hat{\Psi}$ will be the same as δ_Ψ. With $e \neq 0$, it can be inferred that $\delta_{\hat{\psi}} > \delta_\Psi$. To reduce the quantization error, it is an intrinsic idea to increase the level of quantization. Consider a modified problem formulation

$$\tilde{\Psi}_{ij} = \begin{cases} 1, & (kT\Psi)_{ij} \geq 1/2 \\ 0, & -1/2 \leq (kT\Psi)_{ij} < 1/2 \\ -1, & (kT\Psi)_{ij} < -1/2 \end{cases} \tag{8.15}$$

with each element of the matrix Ψ normalized within the interval of $[-1, 1]$. It is important to keep matrix Boolean so that it can be mapped to ReRAM crossbar structure efficiently; thus, it requires the matrix $\tilde{\Psi}$ can be split into two Boolean matrices $\tilde{\Psi} = \frac{1}{2}(\hat{\Psi}^1 + \hat{\Psi}^2)$, where $\tilde{\Psi} \in \{-1, 0, 1\}$ and $\hat{\Psi}^1, \hat{\Psi}^2 \in \{-1, 1\}$. With Boolean quantization, only one projection ReRAM crossbar is needed. Two ReRAM crossbars are needed for the three-level quantization case, as a result of trade-off between error and hardware complexity.

8.4.3 *Overall optimization algorithm*

The heuristic optimization process is summarized in Algorithm 8.1. Given some initial guess of $\hat{\Psi}$, the inner loop of Algorithm 8.1 tries to find the local close-optimal solution by improving $\hat{\Psi}$ through iterations. Within each iteration, (8.6) and (8.12) are solved by singular vector decomposition and quantization as concluded in (8.10) and (8.15), respectively. The iterations terminate when the $\hat{\Psi}$ stops improving and converges.

As both integer constraint and orthogonal constraint are nonconvex, the local optimum in most cases is not optimal globally. In other words, the solution strongly depends on the initial guess that leads to the local close optimum. Therefore, the outer loop of Algorithm 8.1 increases the search width by generating numerous initial guesses that scatter within orthogonal matrices space. For each initial guess, it will

---

Algorithm 8.1: IH Boolean sampling matrix optimization algorithm

---

Input: Real-valued embedding matrix Ψ, search width and quantization level
Output: Optimized Boolean embedding matrix $\hat{\Psi}_{opt}$

      initialize $\hat{\Psi}_{opt} \leftarrow$ random $m \times n$ Bernoulli matrix
1: **while** not reach search width limit **do**
2:     seed $\leftarrow$ random $m \times m$ matrix
3:     U, S, V $\leftarrow$ SVD of seed
4:     T $\leftarrow$ U
5:     **while** not converged **do**
6:       $\hat{\Psi} \leftarrow$ quantization of $T\Psi$
7:       U, S, V $\leftarrow$ SVD of $\hat{\Psi}\Psi^T$
8:       T $\leftarrow$ UV
9:       $k \leftarrow Tr\,(T^T\hat{\Psi}\Psi^T)/Tr\,(\Psi^T\Psi)$
10:      **if** $||kT\Psi - \hat{\Psi}||_F^2 < ||k_{opt}T_{opt}\Psi - \hat{\Psi}_{opt}||_F^2$ **then**
11:        $\hat{\Psi}_{opt} \leftarrow \hat{\Psi}$
12:      **end if**
13:     **end while**
14: **end while**

---

gradually converge to a local optimum; thus, the increase in search width will compare numerous local optimal solutions and approximate the global optimum.

8.5   Row generation algorithm

The formulated problem in (8.5) is a mixed-integer nonlinear programming (MINLP) problem, as it has both nonlinear orthogonal constraint $T^T \cdot T = I$ and the integer constraint $\hat{\Psi} \in \{-1, 1\}^{m \times n}$. Although such MINLP problem can be solved by existing algorithms such as genetic algorithm [295], it lacks efficiency and only problem in small size can be managed. For the embedding matrix in compressive sensing, the transformation matrix T could have dozens of rows while matrix $\hat{\Psi}$ may have thousands of Boolean variables, so current solvers may fail in such scale. In this section, we proposed a row generation algorithm that also can efficiently tackle the problem.

8.5.1   Elimination of norm equality constraint

The orthonormality of T in (8.5) implies two specific constraints, the orthogonality of rows of T that

$$t_i^T \cdot t_j = 0, \ \forall \, i,j \text{ that } i \neq j \tag{8.16}$$

and the norm equality that

$$||t_i||_2^2 = 1, \ \forall \, i \tag{8.17}$$

where t_i is the ith row of T. Both imply numerous quadratic equality constraints (non-convex) and therefore it is hard to manage simultaneously. The nonconvex quadratic norm equality constraint of rows of T indicates the normalization of rows after orthogonality is satisfied. In the following, we show how the norm equality constraint can be eliminated without affecting the solution accuracy of problem in (8.5).

Assume we only impose orthogonal constraint on T rather than more strict orthonormal constraint, the original problem can be then relaxed to

$$
\begin{aligned}
& \underset{T,\hat{\Psi}}{\text{minimize}} \quad \|T\Psi - \hat{\Psi}\|_F^2 \\
& \text{subject to} \quad T^T \cdot T = D^2 \\
& \qquad\qquad\quad \hat{\Psi} \in \{-1, 1\}^{m \times n}
\end{aligned}
\tag{8.18}
$$

where $D = \text{diag}(d_1, d_2, \ldots, d_m)$ is a diagonal matrix, and d_i is the norm of ith row of T. That is to say, an additional row scaling operation is introduced during the sensing stage

$$
y = D^{-1}\hat{\Psi}\Omega x
\tag{8.19}
$$

where $\hat{\Psi} \approx T\Psi$ is the optimized Boolean embedding matrix that can be efficiently realized in hardware, Ω is the orthonormal sparse basis of original signal and x is the sparse coefficient.

In fact, the row scaling operation during signal acquisition is unnecessary and can be transferred to recovery stage if an implicit sensing is performed,

$$
\hat{y} = \hat{\Psi}\Omega x
\tag{8.20}
$$

with corresponding signal reconstruction by

$$
\begin{aligned}
& \underset{x \in \mathbb{R}^N}{\text{minimize}} \quad \|x\|_1 \\
& \text{subject to} \quad |D^{-1}\hat{y} - D^{-1}T\Psi\Omega x| \leq \varepsilon
\end{aligned}
\tag{8.21}
$$

where ε is the tolerance for noise on sampled signal data $\hat{y}$. As such, the norm equality constraint is eliminated while the compressive sensing signal acquisition front-end hardware complexity stays the same and recovery quality is not affected.

8.5.2 Convex relaxation of orthogonal constraint

To construct a transformation matrix T with orthogonal rows and minimize the cost function at the same time is challenging, in the following, we propose a convex row generation algorithm that seeks local optimal solution. The idea is to construct each row of T at one time while minimizing the cost function. Assume $t_1, t_2, \ldots, t_{i-1}$ are first $i-1$ rows that are already built with orthogonality, to construct the ith row t_i,

$$\underset{t_i, \hat{\psi}_i}{\text{minimize}} \quad \|t_i \Psi - \hat{\psi}_i\|_2^2$$

$$\text{subject to} \quad \begin{bmatrix} t_1 \\ t_2 \\ \vdots \\ t_{i-1} \end{bmatrix} \cdot t_i^T = \mathbf{0}$$

$$\hat{\psi}_i \in \{-1, 1\}^n \tag{8.22}$$

In other words, each time to construct a new row t_i, it has to be orthogonal with previously built $t_1, t_2, \ldots, t_{i-1}$. The iterative row generation algorithm is shown in Algorithm 8.2. From the geometric perspective, Algorithm 8.2 seeks to find an orthogonal basis in the m-dimensional space iteratively. Initially T is empty so the first direction vector has the greatest freedom to minimize the cost function. After the first basis vector is chosen, the algorithm finds the best basis vector in the left $(m-1)$-dimensional subspace that best minimizes the target function. This is iteratively performed until the last direction is selected in only one-dimensional subspace with freedom for length only.

As T is a square matrix, there always exists a solution for Algorithm 8.2. The MINLP problem with $m \times n$ integer variables in (8.18) is therefore relaxed to m MINLP subproblems integer programming problems each with only n integer variables.

8.5.3   Overall optimization algorithm

The overall algorithm to solve (8.18) is illustrated in Algorithm 8.2. The 0-1 programming problem (8.22) within the loop can be readily solved by branch-and-cut method, under the condition that the number of Boolean variable is kept small. The brand-and-cut method is widely implemented in solvers such as MOSEK [296] and BARON [297].

Algorithm 8.2: Iterative row generation algorithm

Input: real-valued embedding matrix Ψ
Output: orthogonal transformation matrix $\mathcal{T}$, optimized Boolean embedding matrix $\hat{\Psi}$
   1: Initialize $\mathcal{T} = \emptyset$, $\hat{\Psi} = \emptyset$
   2: **for** $i \leftarrow 1$ to m **do**
   3:     get t_i by solving problem in (8.22)
   4:     update $\mathcal{T} = \begin{bmatrix} \mathcal{T} \\ t_i \end{bmatrix}$, $\hat{\Psi} = \begin{bmatrix} \hat{\Psi} \\ \hat{\psi}_i \end{bmatrix}$
   5: **end for**

Without the linearization by row generation, the branch-and-cut method cannot be applied as the orthogonal constraint is strongly nonlinear and thus the evaluation of lower and upper bounds for each subproblem will be extremely complicated. In addition, the linearization by row generation significantly reduces the number of Boolean variables and thus reduces the worst-case complexity from $2^{m \times n}$ to $m \cdot 2^n$. As such, the row generation together with widely available integer programming solvers can find solution for problem formulated in (8.18).

8.6 Numerical results

8.6.1 Experiment setup

In this part, we evaluate different compressive sensing sampling matrices from both software and hardware perspectives. The numerical experiments are performed within MATLAB® on a desktop with 3.6 GHz Intel i7 processor and 16 GB memory. The software performance of sampling matrices is mainly characterized by the signal recovery quality of sampling matrices. For this purpose, both labeled faces in the wild (LFW) image data [298] and biomedical electrocardiogram (ECG) data [299] are used. For both types of data, the NuMax [289] optimization is first applied with varied training parameter δ values ([0.05, 0.1, . . . , 0.35]), NuMax produces optimized real-valued sampling matrices with different ranks. As depicted in the flowchart in Figure 8.2, the proposed algorithms are then applied to Booleanize NuMax sampling matrices. Apart from the above data-driven sampling matrices, random Gaussian, Bernoulli and Reed–Muller [287,288] (non-data-driven optimization) sampling are also compared. The RSNR is used as signal recovery quality metric, which is defined as

$$RSNR = 20 \log_{10} \left(\frac{\|x\|_2}{\|x - \hat{x}\|_2} \right) \tag{8.23}$$

where x is the original signal and $\hat{x}$ is the reconstructed signal.

With respect to hardware cost consideration, above all sampling matrices can be mapped to three different sampling hardware configurations. Specifically, the MAC/SRAM, MAC/PRNG and ReRAM crossbar configurations with their variations are evaluated to examine the hardware friendliness of all the sampling schemes. For real-valued MAC, 16-bit resolution is used as we find that resolution higher than 16-bit will not improve accuracy, as shown in Figure 8.1. For ReRAM crossbar, the resistance of 1KΩ and 1MΩ are used for ReRAM on-state resistance and off-state resistance according to [293]. The area of the ReRAM crossbar is evaluated by multiplying the cell area ($4F^2$) with sampling matrix size plus one additional column to calculate current offset as discussed in Section 8.3.2. Dynamic power of the ReRAM crossbar is evaluated statistically under 1,000 random input patterns following an uniform distribution with voltage ranging from -0.5 to 0.5 V ($|V| < |V_{set}| = 0.8$ V and $|V| < |V_{reset}| = 0.6$ V [293]) and the duration of operation is 5 ns [293]. Both the real-valued and Boolean digital CMOS matrix multiplier designs are implemented in Verilog and synthesized with GlobalFoundries 65-nm low-power process design kit

(PDK). A PRNG design [286] is also implemented and synthesized. The SRAM that stores the sampling matrix is evaluated by CACTI [300] memory modeling tool with 65-nm low standby power process opted.

Table 8.3 shows all valid combinations of sampling matrix and hardware configuration that will be compared in the section. Among all the combinations, we will show in this section that our proposed sampling matrix can achieve both the best signal recovery quality and hardware efficiency.

8.6.2   IH algorithm on high-D ECG signals

For training stage (NuMax), 1,000 ECG periods in dimension of 256 are randomly picked from database [299] as the data set χ, which leads to around 1 million of pairwise distance vectors in set $S(\chi)$. For testing phase, another 1,000 ECG periods are selected as data set χ', which have no overlap with learning data set χ. The ECG signal reconstruction is performed on unseen data set χ' by solving (8.1) with Battle–Lemarie wavelet bases used.

8.6.2.1   Algorithm convergence and effectiveness

The efficiency of Algorithm 8.1 can be examined from two aspects, finding both local and global optima. The efficiency of finding local optimum is assessed by convergence rate. The local search terminates when the approximation error $||T\Psi - \hat{\Psi}||_F^2$ stops improving.

Given specific RIP upper bounds, NuMax [289] provides Ψ with different ranks. With RIP constraint of 0.1, the NuMax produces a $\Psi \in R^{19 \times 256}$ sampling matrix. Algorithm 8.1 is applied to Ψ with total 10,000 repeated local search and the convergence is illustrated in Figure 8.6(a). It can be observed that the relative error reduces dramatically within the first few iterations. The zoomed subfigure shows that local search on average converges within 50 iterations, where convergence is defined as less than 1e-6 error reduction in two consecutive iterations. Generally, the local optimum can be considered found in less than 100 iterations.

The global search is achieved by scattering many initial guesses in the orthogonal matrices space for T, and comparing the corresponding local optima. The errors under varying number of initial guesses are shown in Figure 8.6(b). Considering the Boolean

Table 8.3   Summary of the embedding methods to be compared

Embeddings	Boolean?	Optimized?	Construction
NuMax	✗	✓	opt. on χ
This technique	✓	✓	opt. on NuMax[†]
Genetic algorithm	✓	✓	opt. on NuMax[‡]
Random Boolean	✓	✗	randomize
Gaussian	✗	✗	randomize

[†] Solve (8.5).
[‡] Solve (8.5) by genetic algorithm from [295].

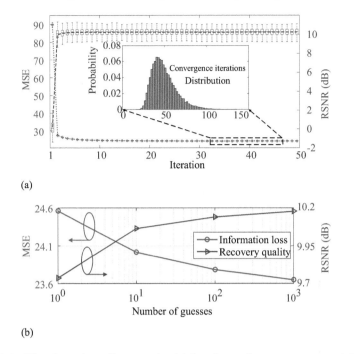

(a)

(b)

Figure 8.6 *The algorithm efficiency for (a) local search convergence and (b) global search convergence*

constraint and the orthogonal constraint, the problem formulated in (8.5) is generally NP-hard. Therefore, the relative error can be improved by scattering exponentially more initial guesses, yet no convergence is observed. Hence, an efficient search policy should be designed in a way scattering as many initial points as possible and limiting the local search for each initial guess within 100 iterations.

8.6.2.2 ECG recovery quality comparison

The ECG signal recovery examples under $\gamma = \frac{19}{256}$ are shown in Figure 8.7. For non-data-driven sampling matrices, both the random Bernoulli and Gaussian show similar reconstruction quality. In other words, the increase of bits in random numbers will not improve recovery quality. This is because, the increase of bits of random number will not gain any additional information.

The PRNG-based Bernoulli exhibits the lowest reconstructed signal quality. This is because, as PRNG produces 0/1 sequences with a predetermined pattern, it has self-coherence issue. For example, an 8-bit per cycle PRNG has a period of 256 (2^8), and when filling a sampling matrix by rows with such 0/1 sequences, all rows of the matrix will be identical.

The Reed–Muller code optimizes the sampling matrix by minimizing the correlations among different rows/columns, which helps to improve sampling performance.

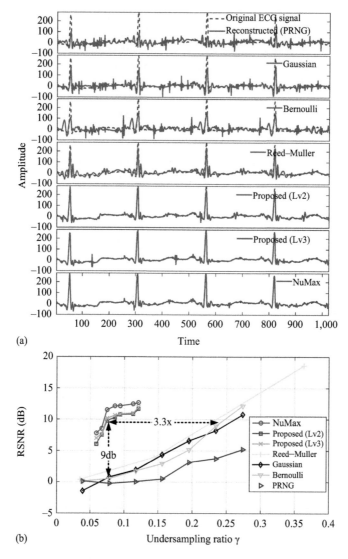

*Figure 8.7   The recovery quality comparison among different sampling matrices:
(a) examples of recovered ECG signals at γ = 19/256 and (b) RSNR
for 1,000 ECG periods*

Being a generic sampling matrix that works with all data types, it cannot exploit the
isometric property of ECG signal, which limits its performance in particular applications. Specifically, it only shows 1 dB improvement compared to random Bernoulli
sampling.

The data-driven NuMax real-valued sampling exhibits the best recovery quality (highest RSNR) as shown in Figure 8.7(b). The proposed iterative heuristic (IH) algorithm quantizes the real-valued NuMax sampling with slight quality loss. Specifically, at the undersampling ratio $\gamma = \frac{19}{256}$, the IH (lv2) exhibits 8, 9 and 10 dB higher RSNR than that of Reed–Muller, Bernoulli and pseudo-Bernoulli samplings, respectively. Also, Level 3 quantization through (8.15) can preserve more information than Level 2 quantization through (8.13). The RSNR of IH (lv3) shows marginal 0.48 dB higher RSNR than IH (lv2). The IH (lv3) sampling matrix $\Psi \in \{-1, 0, 1\}^{m \times n}$ will incur additional hardware overhead compared to IH (lv2) $\Psi \in \{-1, 1\}^{m \times n}$.

Figure 8.7(a) gives a visual effect of quality of recovered ECG signal segments with different sampling matrices. The data-driven sampling matrices, i.e., NuMax, IH (lv2) and IH (lv3), can recover signals that tightly coincide with original signals.

8.6.3 Row generation algorithm on low-D image patches

For training stage (NuMax), 6,000 patches with size of 8×8 are randomly picked throughout all images as the data set χ, which leads to around 18 million of pairwise distance vectors in set $S(\chi)$. For testing phase, another 6,000 patches with size of 8×8 are selected as data set χ' with no overlap with learning data set χ. The image reconstruction is performed on unseen data set χ' by solving (8.1) with 2D discrete cosine transform (DCT) bases.

The genetic algorithm [295] is adopted as the baseline solver for the MINLP in (8.5), which is compared with the proposed algorithm in Algorithm 8.3. Both algorithms are run given same amount of time, i.e., $m \times 500$ s where m is the rank of Ψ that indicates the size of the problem.

8.6.3.1 Algorithm effectiveness

The idea behind the proposed real-valued matrix Booleanization is to preserve the RIP of NuMax sampling matrix, which differs from the truncation-based quantization. The information loss during the quantization is directly related to the RIP preservation. The algorithm effectiveness in this part will be examined by the isometric distortion δ, defined in (8.2).

The distortions of all embeddings are tested on unseen data set χ' (see Figure 8.8). The isometric distortions of both random embeddings are almost invariant. Being optimized on image data set χ, both the NuMax and proposed (quantized NuMax) are significantly better than random embeddings. With focus on the Boolean sampling matrices that are hardware friendly, the isometric distortion of optimized Boolean embedding is $3.0\times$ better than random Boolean embedding on average.

Due to the near-orthogonal rotation, the optimized Boolean embedding experiences some penalty on isometric distortion δ compared to NuMax approach. For genetic algorithm, as it experiences higher distortion than that of the proposed algorithm, it can be inferred that Algorithm 8.3 can find a more precise solution. In addition, it can be observed that the genetic algorithm fails when undersampling ratio $\frac{m}{n}$ increases, and this is because the proposed row generation-based algorithm

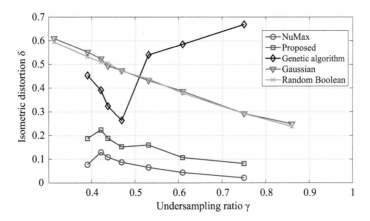

Figure 8.8   The isometric distortion on the unseen data set χ' for different embeddings

---

Algorithm 8.3: Iterative row generation algorithm

Input: real-valued embedding matrix Ψ
Output: orthogonal transformation matrix $\mathscr{T}$, optimized Boolean embedding
   matrix $\hat{\Psi}$
1: initialize $\mathscr{T} = \emptyset$, $\hat{\Psi} = \emptyset$
2: **for** $i \leftarrow 1$ to m **do**
3:     **while** $\mathscr{U}^{\star} - \mathscr{L}^{\star} > \varepsilon$ **do**
4:        **for all** branch with feasible set $\mathscr{S}$ **do**
5:           partition the feasible set $\mathscr{S}$ into $\mathscr{S}_1$ and $\mathscr{S}_2$
6:           evaluate $\mathscr{L}(\mathscr{S}_1), \mathscr{L}(\mathscr{S}_2)$
7:           update lower bound $\mathscr{L}^{\star} = min\{\mathscr{L}^{\star}, \mathscr{L}(\mathscr{S}_1), \mathscr{L}(\mathscr{S}_2)\}$
8:           evaluate $\mathscr{U}(\mathscr{S}_1), \mathscr{U}(\mathscr{S}_2)$
9:           update upper bound $\mathscr{U}^{\star} = min\{\mathscr{U}^{\star}, \mathscr{U}(\mathscr{S}_1), \mathscr{U}(\mathscr{S}_2)\}$
10:          **if** $\mathscr{L}(\mathscr{S}_1)$ or $\mathscr{L}(\mathscr{S}_2) > \mathscr{U}^{\star}$ **then**
11:             cut branch $\mathscr{S}_1$ or $\mathscr{S}_2$
12:          **end if**
13:       **end for**
14:    **end while**
15:    update $\mathscr{T} = \begin{bmatrix} \mathscr{T} \\ t_i \end{bmatrix}$, $\hat{\Psi} = \begin{bmatrix} \hat{\Psi} \\ \hat{\psi}_i \end{bmatrix}$
16: **end for**

---

requires linearly more time when the number of row m increases, while the genetic algorithm needs exponentially more time. Moreover, the solution provided by genetic algorithm is stochastic, which has no guarantee on its effectiveness while the proposed algorithm is deterministic.

8.6.3.2 Image recovery quality comparison

The recovery examples under $\gamma = \frac{25}{64}$ are shown in Figure 8.9(a). The reconstructed images in blue box correspond to Boolean embeddings that have low-power hardware implementations, and images in red box are from optimization-based approaches

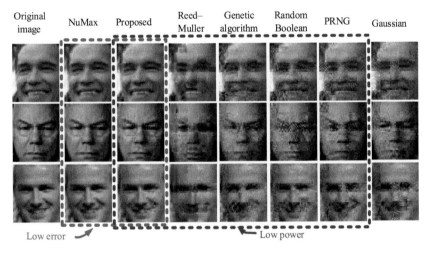

(a)

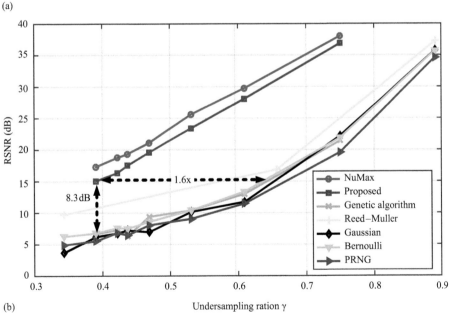

(b)

Figure 8.9   The recovery quality comparison among different embedding matrices: (a) examples of recovered images under $\gamma = 25/64$ and (b) RSNR on 6,000 8×8 image patches

which show lower recovery errors. The genetic algorithm is also optimization based, but the effectiveness is inconsiderable. Therefore, only the proposed can achieve both low power and high recovery performance. The numerical image reconstruction quality is shown in Figure 8.9(b). The two random embeddings show similar reconstruction RSNR, which is averagely 8.3 dB lower than that of the proposed optimized Boolean sampling matrix. The RSNR of optimized Boolean embedding is close to that of NuMax embedding, which is 2.5 dB lower as a result of information loss by near-orthogonal rotation.

On the other hand, the genetic algorithm shows no obvious effectiveness of improving recovery quality even though it optimizes a Boolean embedding matrix. The main reason is that during the conversion of Ψ to $\hat{\Psi}$ too much information loss leads $\hat{\Psi}$ to be close to a random Boolean matrix. In other words, the genetic algorithm is ineffective to solve the problem in (8.5). In addition, the stochastic nature of genetic algorithm makes it necessary to perform the algorithm considerably many times. The proposed algorithm, on the contrary, guarantees to produce a Boolean matrix with high performance with single execution.

8.6.4   Hardware performance evaluation

In this part, the hardware performance benefits of Boolean embedding will be investigated in detail. The evaluation only focuses on the embedding hardware as indicated by red dash-lined boxes in Figures 8.3 and 8.5.

8.6.4.1   Hardware comparison

The matrix–vector multiplier is composed of multiple MACs in parallel. To multiply the signal vector with a 19×256 sampling matrix, 19 MACs are needed and each MAC requires 256 cycles to perform the inner-product with each cycle ($1ns$). To store the NuMax real-valued sampling matrix, 16kB SRAM with 64-bit I/O bus-width is used.

The proposed Boolean optimization quantizes NuMax sampling matrix into a $\{-1, 1\}^{m \times n}$ Boolean matrix. The size of SRAM to store sampling matrix is therefore reduced from 16kB to 1kB. Compared to a Bernoulli $\{0, 1\}^{m \times n}$ matrix, a $\{-1, 1\}^{m \times n}$ multiplication requires calculations of 2's complement of input signal vector, which incurs additional hardware cost for MACs. To minimize the overhead of 2's complement, the MAC design in Figure 8.4(c) is used, which calculates 2's complement only once every 256 cycles.

ReRAM crossbar supports both $\{0, 1\}^{m \times n}$ and $\{-1, 1\}^{m \times n}$ Boolean matrices. As the sampling matrix is embedded into the ReRAM crossbar which also performs the matrix multiplication, no separate memory is required.

The performance of four hardware schemes that support different types of sampling matrices is compared in Table 8.4. Compared to the NuMax real-valued embedding on 16-bit MAC and 16 kB SRAM hardware, the proposed quantized $-1/1$ Boolean embedding on 1-bit MAC and 1 kB SRAM consumes 4.6× less operation energy per embedding, 1.8× smaller leakage power and 1.9× smaller area. This is

Table 8.4 Hardware performance comparison among different sampling matrices (19×256) on varied hardware configurations.

Matrix type	Hardware configuration	Energy (nJ)	Leakage power (μW)	Area (μm²)	Cycle
Real-valued	MAC (16-bit)	116.38	119.63	127,984	256
	MEM (16 kB)	8.08	4.66	31,550	
−1/1 Boolean	MAC (1-bit)	24.81	69.22	73,207	256
	MEM (1 kB)	2.43	0.29	9,800	
0/1 Bernoulli	MAC (1-bit)	21.87	30.40	29,165	~512[†]
	PRNG	8.26e-2	0.04	32	
Boolean	ReRAM crossbar	1.06	—	173	1

[†]PRNG used produces 10 bits per cycle.

because, as mentioned in Section 8.3, the real-valued multiplier generally requires quadratically increasing number of full adders when resolution increases, while Boolean multiplier only needs linearly more full adders.

When the proposed quantized −1/1 Boolean embedding is performed on ReRAM crossbar, it further improves the hardware performance significantly. Specifically, for the operation energy per embedding, the ReRAM crossbar-based embedding outperforms the CMOS circuit-based real-valued embedding by 117×. The area of the ReRAM crossbar-based embedding is nearly 1,000× better than that of CMOS circuit-based real-valued embedding. In addition, the ReRAM crossbar will not experience the leakage power which is at the scale of hundreds of microwatts for the CMOS circuit-based approach. For the operation speed, the ReRAM crossbar embedding executes in single cycle while the CMOS circuit requires 256 cycles due to the reuse of hardware. The overall performance for different sampling matrices on varied hardware platforms is summarized in Table 8.5.

8.6.4.2 Impact of ReRAM variation

One nonnegligible issue of mapping Boolean embedding matrix to ReRAM crossbar is the ReRAM HRS and LRS variations. With high resistance variation, the embedding matrix will deviate from expected values to be represented by ReRAM resistance, and hence the recovery quality may degrade. The sensitivity study of recovery quality on the resistance variations of ReRAM is shown in Figure 8.10. The resistance of ReRAM is assumed to follow log-normal distribution with the mean to be R_{LRS} and R_{HRS}, and standard deviation σ_{LRS} and σ_{HRS} for LRS and HRS cells, respectively.

With varied σ_{LRS} and σ_{HRS}, it can be observed from Figure 8.10 that the performance degradation is more susceptible to resistance variation of LRS, while less sensitive on variation of HRS. In practice, the HRS variation σ_{HRS} is approximately 0.3 [301], and LRS variation σ_{LRS} roughly 0.1 [301]. The real-world σ is annotated in Figure 8.10 and it can be concluded that the proposed Boolean embedding on

Table 8.5 *Comparison of all valid sampling matrices and hardware combinations*

Platform					Construction		Recovery	Energy
Sampling matrix	Sampling hardware	Boolean?	Optimized?	Data driven?	Stage	Effort	quality‡	consumed*
Gaussian	MAC(16-bit) + MEM(16kB)	×	×	×	Off-line	Immediate	1.12	117.4
Bernoulli	MAC(1-bit) + MEM(1kB)	✓	×	×	Off-line	Immediate	1.09	22.9
Bernoulli	ReRAM crossbar	✓	×	×	Off-line	Immediate	1.09	**1.0**
Pseudo-Bernoulli	MAC(1-bit) + PRNG	✓	×	×	Runtime	—	1.00	**20.7**
NuMax [289]	MAC(16-bit) + MEM(16kB)	×	✓	✓	Off-line	~100s	**3.86**	117.4
Reed–Muller [287,288]	MAC(1-bit) + MEM(1kB)	✓	✓	×	Off-line	Fast	1.25	22.9
Reed–Muller [287,288]	ReRAM crossbar	✓	✓	×	Off-line	Fast	1.25	22.9
Proposed†	MAC(1-bit) + MEM(1kB)	✓	✓	✓	Off-line	~100s	**3.18**	25.7
Proposed	ReRAM crossbar	✓	✓	✓	Off-line	~100s	**3.18**	**1.0**

‡ The recovery quality depicts the quality performance ratio of all sampling matrices over baseline pseudo-Bernoulli. The RSNR dB for ECG is converted to mean-squared error. Numbers in bold are ones with good performance.

* The energy consumption is shown as ratio of used energy of all sampling matrices over that of ReRAM crossbar. Numbers in bold are ones with good performance.

† The **proposed** denotes the Booleanized NuMax sampling matrix by proposed Algorithms.

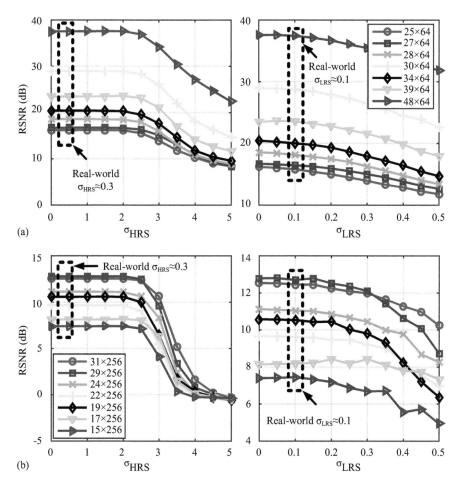

Figure 8.10 *The sensitivity of recovery quality of (a) image signal and (b) ECG signal on the resistance standard deviation σ of ReRAM for both LRS and HRS following log-normal distribution*

ReRAM crossbar is robust against ReRAM device variations when on/off ratio is high ($G_{LRS} \gg G_{HRS} \approx 0$). To further suppress the performance degradation, material engineering [302] and verification programming method [301] can help achieve higher LRS uniformity.

Chapter 9
Conclusions: wrap-up, open questions and challenges

9.1 Conclusion

To conclude, this book has shown a thorough study on resistive random-access memory (ReRAM)-based nonvolatile in-memory architecture towards machine learning applications from circuit level, to architecture level, and all the way to system level.

For the circuit level, on the one hand, we use non-volatile memory (NVM)-SPICE to simulate matrix–vector multiplication acceleration by binary ReRAM crossbar. By programming all the elements of a matrix into ReRAM resistance in the crossbar array, we can use crossbar wordline voltages to represent another matrix, and the multiplication result can be denoted by the merging current on bitlines. In this mapping scheme, both ReRAM resistance and crossbar I/O are in binary format so that the computation accuracy can be guaranteed. Simulation results show that the proposed architecture has shown $2.86\times$ faster speed, $154\times$ better energy efficiency and $100\times$ smaller area when compared to the same design by complimentary metal oxide semiconductor (CMOS)-based application specific integrated circuit (ASIC). On the other hand, we use a Verilog-A model to build an ReRAM-based voltage-controlled oscillator circuit in Cadence. In a coupled network by ReRAM-based oscillator, the simulation results can be fitted as L2-norm calculation. Compared to traditional CMOS-based oscillator circuit, it has a much simpler structure with smaller area and better energy efficiency.

For the architecture level, we have developed a distributed in-memory architecture (XIMA) and three-dimensional (3D) CMOS-ReRAM architecture. For XIMA, we use both ReRAM crossbar for data storage and computing engine. We use a data block and logic block to form a data–logic pair, and all the pairs are located distributively. As a result, the communication bandwidth can be significantly improved because the computing engine only accesses the data from pairs. To achieve the in-memory computing, we design a control bus in each data–logic pair for communication among processor, data and logic block. In addition, communication protocol between processor and control bus is redefined for the in-memory computing implementation. For 3D CMOS-ReRAM architecture, we developed two schemes: single-layer and multilayer. The single-layer architecture uses ReRAM via connecting the top-layer wordlines and bottom-layer bitlines. All the other CMOS logics are implemented in the bottom layer as well. The multilayer architecture uses through silicon via (TSV) connecting the first-layer ReRAM-based data buffer, the second-layer ReRAM-based logic computing and the third-layer CMOS. Such a 3D architecture can significantly improve the throughput as well as the area efficiency for the hybrid ReRAM/CMOS computing system.

For the system level, for the XIMA, we have accelerated three machine learning algorithms. The learning and inference procedures of single-layer feedforward neural network (SLFN) have been optimized and partially mapped on the passive binary ReRAM crossbar. In addition, we mapped the binary convolutional neural network on both passive array and One Selector One ReRAM array with different mapping schemes. Moreover, L2-norm gradient-based learning and inference are also implemented on an ReRAM network with both crossbar and coupled oscillators. For 3D CMOS-ReRAM architecture, we also mapped the optimized SLFN algorithm. All the operations in learning and inference stages are implemented so that it can achieve the online learning. In addition, tensorized neural network is mapped on both single-layer and multilayer accelerators with different mapping scheme. For all the machine learning algorithms mapped on XIMA and 3D CMOS-ReRAM accelerator, we evaluate their performance in device, architecture and system levels. All the implementations show higher throughput, bandwidth and parallelism with better energy efficiency.

9.2   Future work

Based on the above works, there are a few potential future works to enhance this research.

The first potential work is to validate some designs discussed. In this work, we explore the binary ReRAM crossbar as well as oscillator network in device and circuit level by simulation. However, the ReRAM devices in the array are not fully uniform so that the mapping scheme may not be applied in a large crossbar array. In addition, sneak path and thermal effect in the ReRAM crossbar will also occur the inaccuracy during computing. As for the XIMA, this work only simulates a few groups of control bus design, but in the real implementation, there will be thousands of control bus blocks so it is also necessary to optimize all these designs.

The second potential work is to realize neuromorphic computing by the ReRAM network. This work only explores the artificial neural network implementations in the ReRAM-based architecture. All of these algorithms are originally designed for CMOS-based computing systems such as CPU, GPU, CMOS-ASIC and FPGA. The ReRAM-based architecture can perform analog-value computing operations, which is widely applied in neuromorphic applications. For example, it is easier to implement spike-timing-dependent plasticity-based synapse programming algorithm and also spiking neural networks on ReRAM compared to CMOS-ASIC or FPGA. It is possible to explore an ReRAM-based neuromorphic computing system with simpler structure and better scalability than the state-of-the-art works.

References

[1]   Cukier K. Data, data everywhere. The Economist. 2010 Feb.

[2]   International Data Corporation. Digital Universe Study. Dell EMC. 2011.

[3]   White T. O'Reilly Media Inc; 2012.

[4]   Zaharia M, Chowdhury M, Franklin MJ, *et al*. Spark: Cluster computing with working sets. In: USENIX Conference on Hot Topics in Cloud Computing; 2010.

[5]   Apache Flink. Apache Flink: Scalable batch and stream data processing. http://flink.apache.org/. Online.

[6]   Carbone P, Fóra G, Ewen S, *et al*. Lightweight asynchronous snapshots for distributed dataflows. CoRR. 2015;abs/1506.08603.

[7]   Saha B, Shah H, Seth S, *et al*. Apache Tez: A unifying framework for modeling and building data processing applications. In: ACM SIGMOD International Conference on Management of Data; 2015.

[8]   Akidau T, Bradshaw R, Chambers C, *et al*. The Dataflow model: A practical approach to balancing correctness, latency, and cost in massive-scale, unbounded, out-of-order data processing. Proc VLDB Endow. 2015;8(12): 1792–1803.

[9]   LeDell E. High performance machine learning in R with H2O. In: ISM HPC on R Workshop; 2015.

[10] Xing EP, Ho Q, Dai W, *et al*. Petuum: A new platform for distributed machine learning on big data. In: ACM SIGKDD International Conference on Knowledge Discovery and Data Mining; 2015.

[11] Bakshi K. Considerations for big data: Architecture and approach. In: IEEE Aerospace Conference; 2012.

[12] Chen Y, Alspaugh S and Katz R. Interactive analytical processing in big data systems: A cross-industry study of MapReduce workloads. Proc VLDB Endow. 2012;5(12):1802–1813.

[13] Lee KH, Lee YJ, Choi H, *et al*. Parallel data processing with MapReduce: A survey. SIGMOD Rec. 2012;40(4):11–20.

[14] Shvachko K, Kuang H, Radia S, *et al*. The Hadoop distributed file system. In: IEEE Symposium on Mass Storage Systems and Technologies (MSST); 2010.

[15] Magaki I, Khazraee M, Gutierrez LV, *et al*. ASIC clouds: Specializing the data center. In: ACM/IEEE International Symposium on Computer Architecture (ISCA); 2016.

[16]   Caulfield AM, Chung ES, Putnam A, *et al.* A cloud-scale acceleration architecture. In: IEEE/ACM International Symposium on Microarchitecture (MICRO); 2016.

[17]   Gutierrez A, Cieslak M, Giridhar B, *et al.* Integrated 3D-stacked server designs for increasing physical density of key-value stores. SIGPLAN Not. 2014;49(4):485–498.

[18]   Putnam A, Caulfield AM, Chung ES, *et al.* A reconfigurable fabric for accelerating large-scale data center services. SIGARCH Comput Archit News. 2014;42(3):13–24.

[19]   Wess M, Manoj PDS and Jantsch A. Weighted quantization-regularization in DNNs for weight memory minimization towards HW implementation. IEEE Transactions on Computer Aided Systems of Integrated Circuits and Systems. 2018.

[20]   Lechner M, Jantsch A and Manoj PDS. ResCoNN: Resource-efficient FPGA-accelerated CNN for traffic sign classification. In: IEEE International Green and Sustainable Computing Conference (IGSC); 2019.

[21]   Vashist A, Keats A, Manoj PDS, *et al.* Unified testing and security framework for wireless network-on-chip enabled multi-core chips. In: ACM/IEEE International Conference on Hardware/Software Codesign and System Synthesis (CODES+ISSS); 2019.

[22]   Wess M, Manoj PDS and Jantsch A. Weighted quantization-regularization in DNNs for weight memory minimization towards HW implementation. In: International Conference on Hardware/Software Codesign and System Synthesis (CODES+ISSS); 2018.

[23]   Yu H, Ni L and Wang Y. Non-volatile In-Memory Computing by Spintronics. Vol. 2. Morgan & Claypool Publishers; 2016. Available from: https://dl.acm.org/doi/book/10.5555/3086882.

[24]   Yu H and Wang Y. Design Exploration of Emerging Nano-scale Non-volatile Memory. Springer; 2014. Available from: https://www.springer.com/gp/book/9781493905508.

[25]   Song Y, Yu H and Manoj PDS. Reachability-based robustness verification and optimization of SRAM dynamic stability under process variations. IEEE Trans on Computer-Aided Design of Integrated Circuits and Systems. 2014;33(4):585–598.

[26]   Song Y, Manoj PDS and Yu H. Zonotope-based nonlinear model order reduction for fast performance bound analysis of analog circuits with multiple-interval-valued parameter variations. In: Design, Automation Test in Europe Conference Exhibition (DATE); 2014.

[27]   Song Y, Manoj PDS and Yu H. A robustness optimization of SRAM dynamic stability by sensitivity-based reachability analysis. In: Asia and South Pacific Design Automation Conference (ASP-DAC); 2014.

[28]   Wu SS, Wang K, Manoj PDS, *et al.* A thermal resilient integration of many-core microprocessors and main memory by 2.5D TSI I/Os. In: Design, Automation Test in Europe Conference Exhibition (DATE); 2014.

[29] Burger D, Goodman JR and Kägi A. Memory Bandwidth Limitations of Future Microprocessors. SIGARCH Comput Archit News. 1996;24(2): 78–89.

[30] Manoj PDS, Yu H, Gu C, *et al*. A zonotoped macromodeling for reachability verification of eye-diagram in high-speed I/O links with jitter. In: IEEE/ACM International Conference on Computer-Aided Design (ICCAD); 2014.

[31] Makrani HM, Sayadi H, Manoj PDS, *et al*. A comprehensive memory analysis of data intensive workloads on server class architecture. In: International Symposium on Memory Subsystems; 2018.

[32] Makrani HM, Sayadi H, Manoj PDS, *et al*. Compressive sensing on storage data: An effective solution to alleviate I/O bottleneck in data-intensive workloads. In: IEEE International Conference on Application-specific Systems, Architectures and Processors; 2018.

[33] Manoj PDS, Wang K, Huang H, *et al*. Smart I/Os: A data-pattern aware 2.5D interconnect with space-time multiplexing. In: ACM/IEEE International Workshop on System Level Interconnect Prediction (SLIP); 2015.

[34] Hantao H, Manoj PDS, Xu D, *et al*. Reinforcement learning based self-adaptive voltage-swing adjustment of 2.5D I/Os for many-core microprocessor and memory communication. In: IEEE/ACM Int. Conf. on Computer-Aided Design (ICCAD); 2014.

[35] Xu D, Manoj PDS, Huang H, *et al*. An energy-efficient 2.5D through-silicon interposer I/O with self-adaptive adjustment of output-voltage swing. In: IEEE/ACM International Symposium on Low Power Electronics and Design (ISLPED); 2014.

[36] Wang J, Ma S, Manoj PDS, *et al*. High-speed and low-power 2.5D I/O circuits for memory-logic-integration by through-silicon interposer. In: IEEE International 3D Systems Integration Conference (3DIC); 2013.

[37] Manoj PDS, Wang K and Yu H. Peak power reduction and workload balancing by space-time multiplexing based demand-supply matching for 3D thousand-core microprocessor. In: ACM/EDAC/IEEE Design Automation Conf.; 2013.

[38] Manoj PDS and Yu H. Cyber-physical management for heterogeneously integrated 3D thousand-core on-chip microprocessor. In: IEEE International Symposium on Circuits and Systems (ISCAS); 2013.

[39] Manoj PDS, Joseph A, Haridass A, *et al*. Application and thermal reliability-aware reinforcement learning based multi-core power management. ACM Transactions on Embedded Computing Systems. 2019.

[40] Pagani S, Manoj PDS, Jantsch A, *et al*. Machine learning for power, energy, and thermal management on multi-core processors: A survey. IEEE Transactions on Computer Aided Systems of Integrated Circuits and Systems. 2018.

[41] Manoj PDS, Jantsch A and Shafique M. SmartDPM: Dynamic power management using machine learning for multi-core microprocessors. Journal of Low-Power Electronics. 2018.

[42] Manoj PDS, Lin J, Zhu S, *et al.* A scalable network-on-chip microprocessor with 2.5D integrated memory and accelerator. IEEE Transactions on Circuits and Systems I: Regular Papers. 2017;64(6):1432–1443.

[43] Matsunaga S, Hayakawa J, Ikeda S, *et al.* MTJ-based nonvolatile logic-in-memory circuit, future prospects and issues. In: Proceedings of the Conference on Design, Automation and Test in Europe. European Design and Automation Association; 2009. pp. 433–435.

[44] Matsunaga S, Hayakawa J, Ikeda S, *et al.* Fabrication of a nonvolatile full adder based on logic-in-memory architecture using magnetic tunnel junctions. Applied Physics Express. 2008;1(9):091301.

[45] Kautz WH. Cellular logic-in-memory arrays. IEEE Transactions on Computers. 1969;100(8):719–727.

[46] Kimura H, Hanyu T, Kameyama M, *et al.* Complementary ferroelectric-capacitor logic for low-power logic-in-memory VLSI. IEEE Journal of Solid-State Circuits. 2004;39(6):919–926.

[47] Hanyu T, Teranishi K and Kameyama M. Multiple-valued logic-in-memory VLSI based on a floating-gate-MOS pass-transistor network. In: Solid-State Circuits Conference, 1998. Digest of Technical Papers. 1998 IEEE International. IEEE; 1998. pp. 194–195.

[48] Kouzes RT, Anderson GA, Elbert ST, *et al.* The changing paradigm of data-intensive computing. Computer. 2009;(1):26–34.

[49] Wolpert DH. The lack of a priori distinctions between learning algorithms. Neural Computation. 1996;8(7):1341–1390.

[50] Hinton GE, Osindero S and Teh YW. A fast learning algorithm for deep belief nets. Neural Computation. 2006;18(7):1527–1554.

[51] Müller KR, Tangermann M, Dornhege G, *et al.* Machine learning for real-time single-trial EEG-analysis: From brain–computer interfacing to mental state monitoring. Journal of Neuroscience Methods. 2008;167(1):82–90.

[52] Glorot X and Bengio Y. Understanding the difficulty of training deep feedforward neural networks. In: International Conference on Artificial Intelligence and Statistics; 2010. pp. 249–256.

[53] Huang GB, Zhu QY and Siew CK. Extreme learning machine: Theory and applications. Neurocomputing. 2006;70(1):489–501.

[54] Coates A, Ng AY and Lee H. An analysis of single-layer networks in unsupervised feature learning. In: International Conference on Artificial Intelligence and Statistics; 2011. pp. 215–223.

[55] Park S, Qazi M, Peh LS, *et al.* 40.4 fJ/bit/mm low-swing on-chip signaling with self-resetting logic repeaters embedded within a mesh NoC in 45nm SOI CMOS. In: Proceedings of the Conference on Design, Automation and Test in Europe. EDA Consortium; 2013. pp. 1637–1642.

[56] Kumar V, Sharma R, Uzunlar E, *et al.* Airgap interconnects: Modeling, optimization, and benchmarking for backplane, PCB, and interposer applications. IEEE Transactions on Components, Packaging and Manufacturing Technology. 2014;4(8):1335–1346.

[57] Wang Y, Yu H, Ni L, *et al*. An energy-efficient nonvolatile in-memory computing architecture for extreme learning machine by domain-wall nanowire devices. IEEE Transactions on Nanotechnology. 2015;14(6):998–1012.

[58] Akinaga H and Shima H. Resistive random access memory (ReRAM) based on metal oxides. Proceedings of the IEEE. 2010;98(12):2237–2251.

[59] Kim KH, Gaba S, Wheeler D, *et al*. A functional hybrid memristor crossbar-array/CMOS system for data storage and neuromorphic applications. Nano Letters. 2011;12(1):389–395.

[60] Chua LO. Memristor—The missing circuit element. IEEE Transactions on Circuit Theory. 1971;18(5):507–519.

[61] Williams SR. How we found the missing memristor. IEEE Spectrum. 2008;45(12):28–35.

[62] Strukov DB, Snider GS, Stewart DR, *et al*. The missing memristor found. Nature. 2008;453(7191):80–83.

[63] Shang Y, Fei W and Yu H. Analysis and modeling of internal state variables for dynamic effects of nonvolatile memory devices. IEEE Transactions on Circuits and Systems I: Regular Papers. 2012;59(9):1906–1918.

[64] Fei W, Yu H, Zhang W, *et al*. Design exploration of hybrid CMOS and memristor circuit by new modified nodal analysis. IEEE Transactions on Very Large Scale Integration (VLSI) Systems. 2012;20(6):1012–1025.

[65] Liu X, Mao M, Liu B, *et al*. RENO: A high-efficient reconfigurable neuro-morphic computing accelerator design. In: Proceedings of the 52nd Annual Design Automation Conference. ACM; 2015. pp. 66.1–66.6.

[66] Kim Y, Zhang Y and Li P. A digital neuromorphic VLSI architecture with memristor crossbar synaptic array for machine learning. In: International SOC Conference (SOCC). IEEE; 2012. pp. 328–333.

[67] Lu W, Kim KH, Chang T, *et al*. Two-terminal resistive switches (memristors) for memory and logic applications. In: Asia and South Pacific Design Automation Conference (ASP-DAC). IEEE; 2011. pp. 217–223.

[68] Dennard RH, Gaensslen FH, Yu H, *et al*. Design of ion-implanted MOSFET's with very small physical dimensions. IEEE Journal of Solid-State Circuits. 1974;9(5):256–268.

[69] Loh GH. 3D-Stacked memory architectures for multi-core processors. In: International Symposium on Computer Architecture; 2008.

[70] Strenz R. Embedded flash technologies and their applications: Status outlook. In: International Electron Devices Meeting; 2011.

[71] Energy Limits to the Computational Power of the Human Brain. Last Accessed: June, 15, 2020. Available from: https://foresight.org/Updates/Update06/Update06.1.php.

[72] Laughlin SB, de Ruyter van Steveninck RR and Anderson JC. The metabolic cost of neural information. Nature Neuroscience. 1998;1:36–41.

[73] Jiang Z, Wu Y, Yu S, *et al*. A compact model for metal-oxide resistive random access memory with experiment verification. IEEE Transactions on Electron Devices. 2016;63(5):1884–1892.

[74]   Merolla PA, Arthur JV, Alvarez-Icaza R, *et al.* A million spiking-neuron integrated circuit with a scalable communication network and interface. Science. 2014;345(6197):668–673.

[75]   Davies M, Srinivasa N, Lin T, *et al.* Loihi: A neuromorphic manycore processor with on-chip learning. IEEE Micro. 2018;38(1): 82–99.

[76]   Hu M, Graves CE, Li C, *et al.* Memristor-based analog computation and neural network classification with a dot product engine. Advanced Materials. 2018;30(9):1705914.

[77]   Yu S. Neuro-inspired computing with emerging nonvolatile memories. Proceedings of the IEEE. 2018;106(2):260–285.

[78]   Pei J, Deng L, Song S, *et al.* Towards artificial general intelligence with hybrid Tianjic chip architecture. Nature. 2019;572:106–111.

[79]   Yao P, Wu H, Gao B, *et al.* Fully hardware-implemented memristor convolutional neural network. Nature. 2020;577:641–646.

[80]   Roy K, Jaiswal A and Panda P. Towards spike-based machine intelligence with neuromorphic computing. Nature. 2019 11;575:607–617.

[81]   Sherstinsky A. Fundamentals of recurrent neural network (RNN) and long short-term memory (LSTM) network. CoRR. 2018;abs/1808.03314.

[82]   Yu S. Resistive random access memory (RRAM). Synthesis Lectures on Emerging Engineering Technologies. 2016;2:1–79.

[83]   Kim KH, Gaba S, Wheeler D, *et al.* A functional hybrid memristor crossbar-array/CMOS system for data storage and neuromorphic applications. Nano Letters. 2012;12(1):389–395.

[84]   Yang JJ, Zhang MX, Pickett M, *et al.* Engineering nonlinearity into memristors for passive crossbar applications. Applied Physics Letters. 2012 03;100.

[85]   Park S, Kim H, Choo M, *et al.* RRAM-based synapse for neuromorphic system with pattern recognition function. In: International Electron Devices Meeting; 2012.

[86]   Khvalkovskiy A, Apalkov D, Watts S, *et al.* Basic principles of STT-MRAM cell operation in memory arrays. Journal of Physics D: Applied Physics. 2013;46(7):1–35

[87]   Apalkov D, Khvalkovskiy A, Watts S, *et al.* Spin-transfer torque magnetic random access memory (STT-MRAM). J Emerg Technol Comput Syst. 2013;9(2).

[88]   Bi G and Poo M. Synaptic modifications in cultured hippocampal neurons: Dependence on spike timing, Synaptic Strength, and Postsynaptic Cell Type. J Neuroscience. 1998;18(24):10467-10472.

[89]   Hu M, Strachan JP, Li Z, *et al.* Dot-product engine for neuromorphic computing: Programming 1T1M crossbar to accelerate matrix-vector multiplication. In: Annual Design Automation Conference; 2016.

[90]   Kuzum D, Jeyasingh R, Lee B, *et al.* Nanoelectronic programmable synapses based on phase change materials for brain-inspired computing. Nano Letters. 2011 06;12:2179–86.

[91]   Indiveri G, Chicca E and Douglas R. A VLSI array of low-power spiking neurons and bistable synapses with spike-timing dependent plasticity. IEEE Transactions on Neural Networks. 2006;17(1):211–221.

[92]   Chen P, Lin B, Wang I, *et al*. Mitigating effects of non-ideal synaptic device characteristics for on-chip learning. In: IEEE/ACM International Conference on Computer-Aided Design (ICCAD); 2015.

[93]   Wang IT, Chang CC, Chiu LW, *et al*. 3D Ta/TaOx /TiO2 /Ti synaptic array and linearity tuning of weight update for hardware neural network applications. Nanotechnology. 2016;27:365204.

[94]   Angizi S, He Z, Parveen F and Fan D. IMCE: Energy-efficient bit-wise in-memory convolution engine for deep neural network. In: Asia and South Pacific Design Automation Conference (ASP-DAC); 2018.

[95]   Patterson D, Anderson T, Cardwell N, *et al*. A case for intelligent RAM. IEEE Micro. 1997.

[96]   Pudukotai Dinakarrao SM, Lin J, Zhu S, *et al*. A scalable network-on-chip microprocessor with 2.5D integrated memory and accelerator. IEEE Transactions on Circuits and Systems I: Regular Papers. 2017.

[97]   Yong-Bin K and Chen T. Assessing merged DRAM/Logic technology. Integr VLSI J. 1999.

[98]   Deng Q, Zhang Y, Zhang M and Yang J. LAcc: Exploiting lookup table-based fast and accurate vector multiplication in DRAM-based CNN accelerator. In: ACM/IEEE Design Automation Conference (DAC); 2019.

[99]   Courbariaux M, Bengio Y and David J-P. BinaryConnect: Training deep neural networks with binary weights during propagations. In: Proceedings of the 28th International Conference on Neural Information Processing Systems; 2015.

[100]   Courbariaux M and Bengio Y. BinaryNet: Training deep neural networks with weights and activations constrained to +1 or -1. ArXiv. 2016.

[101]   Rastegari M, Ordonez V, Redmon J and Farhadi A. XNOR-Net: ImageNet classification using binary convolutional neural networks. In: Computer Vision – ECCV; 2016.

[102]   Li F and Liu B. Ternary weight networks. CoRR. 2016.

[103]   Wess M, Dinakarrao SMP and Jantsch A. Weighted quantization-regularization in DNNs for weight memory minimization toward HW implementation. IEEE Transactions on Computer-Aided Design of Integrated Circuits and Systems. 2018.

[104]   Li S, Niu D, Malladi KT *et al*. DRISA: A DRAM-based reconfigurable in-situ accelerator. In: IEEE/ACM International Symposium on Microarchitecture; 2017.

[105]   Deng Q, Jiang L, Zhang Y, Zhang M and Yang J. DrAcc: A DRAM-based accelerator for accurate CNN inference. In: ACM/ESDA/IEEE Design Automation Conference (DAC);2018.

[106]   Yin S, Jiang Z, Seo J and Seok M. XNOR-SRAM: In-Memory computing SRAM macro for binary/ternary deep neural networks. IEEE Journal of Solid-State Circuits. 2020.

[107] Sun X, Yin S, Peng X, Liu R, Seo J and Yu S. XNOR-RRAM: A scalable and parallel resistive synaptic architecture for binary neural networks. In: Design, Automation Test in Europe Conference Exhibition (DATE); 2018.

[108] Tang T, Xia L, Li B, Wang Y and Yang H. Binary convolutional neural network on RRAM. In: Asia and South Pacific Design Automation Conference (ASP-DAC); 2017.

[109] Pan Y, Ouyang P, Zhao Y, *et al.* A multilevel cell STT-MRAM-based computing in-memory accelerator for binary convolutional neural network. IEEE Transactions on Magnetics. 2018.

[110] Angizi S, He Z, Awad A and Fan D. MRIMA: An MRAM-based in-memory accelerator. IEEE Transactions on Computer-Aided Design of Integrated Circuits and Systems. 2020.

[111] Taherinejad N, Manoj PDS and Jantsch A. Memristors' potential for multi-bit storage and pattern learning. IEEE European Modelling Symposium (EMS). 2015.

[112] Chi P, Li S, Xu C, *et al.* PRIME: A novel processing-in-memory architecture for neural network computation in ReRAM-based main memory. In: ACM/IEEE International Symposium on Computer Architecture (ISCA); 2016.

[113] Simon WA, Qureshi YM, Levisse A, *et al.* Blade: A bitline accelerator for devices on the edge. In: Proceedings of the 2019 on Great Lakes Symposium on VLSI; 2019. pp. 207–212.

[114] Yang J, Kong Y, Wang Z, *et al.* 24.4 sandwich-RAM: An energy-efficient in-memory BWN architecture with pulse-width modulation. In: 2019 IEEE International Solid-State Circuits Conference-(ISSCC). IEEE; 2019. pp. 394–396.

[115] Bankman D, Yang L, Moons B, *et al.* An always-on 3.8uJ/86% CIFAR-10 mixed-signal binary CNN processor with all memory on chip in 28-nm CMOS. IEEE Journal of Solid-State Circuits. 2018;54(1):158–172.

[116] Si X, Chen JJ, Tu YN, *et al.* 24.5 A twin-8T SRAM computation-in-memory macro for multiple-bit CNN-based machine learning. In: 2019 IEEE International Solid-State Circuits Conference-(ISSCC). IEEE; 2019. pp. 396–398.

[117] Si X, Tu YN, Huanq WH, *et al.* 15.5 A 28nm 64Kb 6T SRAM computing-in-memory macro with 8b MAC operation for AI edge chips. In: 2020 IEEE International Solid-State Circuits Conference (ISSCC). IEEE; 2020. pp. 246–248.

[118] Dong Q, Sinangil ME, Erbagci B, *et al.* 15.3 A 351TOPS/W and 372.4 GOPS compute-in-memory SRAM macro in 7nm FinFET CMOS for machine-learning applications. In: 2020 IEEE International Solid-State Circuits Conference-(ISSCC). IEEE; 2020. pp. 242–244.

[119] Zhang Z, Chen JJ, Si X, *et al.* A 55nm 1-to-8 bit configurable 6T SRAM based computing-in-memory unit-macro for CNN-based AI edge processors. In: 2019 IEEE Asian Solid-State Circuits Conference (A-SSCC). IEEE; 2019. pp. 217–218.

[120] Xue CX, Chen WH, Liu JS, *et al.* Embedded 1-Mb ReRAM-based computing-in-memory macro with multibit input and weight for CNN-based AI edge processors. IEEE Journal of Solid-State Circuits. 2019;55(1): 203–215.

[121] Mochida R, Kouno K, Hayata Y, *et al.* A 4M synapses integrated analog ReRAM based 66.5 TOPS/W neural-network processor with cell current controlled writing and flexible network architecture. In: 2018 IEEE Symposium on VLSI Technology. IEEE; 2018. pp. 175–176.

[122] Eckert C, Wang X, Wang J, *et al.* Neural cache: Bit-serial in-cache acceleration of deep neural networks. In: International Symposium on Computer Architecture (ISCA); 2018.

[123] Seshadri V, Lee D, Mullins T, *et al.* Ambit: In-memory accelerator for bulk bitwise operations using commodity DRAM technology. IEEE/ACM International Symposium on Microarchitecture (MICRO). 2017.

[124] Li S, Glova AO, Hu X, *et al.* SCOPE: A stochastic computing engine for DRAM-based in-situ accelerator. In: IEEE/ACM International Symposium on Microarchitecture (MICRO); 2018.

[125] Sutradhar PR, Connolly M, Bavikadi S, *et al.* pPIM: A programmable processor-in-memory architecture with precision-scaling for deep learning. IEEE Computer Architecture Letters. 2020;19(2):118–121.

[126] Ali M, Jaiswal A, Kodge S, Agrawal A, Chakraborty I and Roy K. IMAC: In-memory multi-bit multiplication and accumulation in 6T SRAM array. IEEE Transactions on Circuits and Systems I: Regular Papers. 2020.

[127] Shafiee A, Nag A, Muralimanohar N, *et al.* ISAAC: A convolutional neural network accelerator with in-situ analog arithmetic in crossbars. In: ACM/IEEE International Symposium on Computer Architecture (ISCA); 2016.

[128] Song L, Qian X, Li H and Chen Y. PipeLayer: A pipelined ReRAM-based accelerator for deep learning. In: IEEE Int. Symp. on High Performance Computer Architecture (HPCA); 2017.

[129] Qiao X, Cao X, Yang H, Song L and Li H. AtomLayer: A universal ReRAM-based CNN accelerator with atomic layer computation. In: ACM/ESDA/IEEE Design Automation Conference (DAC); 2018.

[130] Patil AD, Hua H, Gonugondla S, Kang M and Shanbhag NR. An MRAM-based deep in-memory architecture for deep neural networks. In: IEEE International Symposium on Circuits and Systems; 2019.

[131] Fan D, Angizi S. Energy efficient in-memory binary deep neural network accelerator with dual-mode SOT-MRAM. In: IEEE International Conference on Computer Design (ICCD); 2017.

[132] Angizi S, He Z, Rakin AS and Fan D. CMP-PIM: An energy-efficient comparator-based processing-in-memory neural network accelerator. In: ACM/ESDA/IEEE Design Automation Conference (DAC); 2018.

[133] Yu H, Ni L and Huang H. In: Vaidyanathan S, Volos C, editors. Distributed in-memory computing on binary memristor-crossbar for machine

learning. Springer; 2017. pp. 275–304. Available from: https://link. springer.com/chapter/10.1007/978-3-319-51724-7_12.

[134]   Strukov DB and Williams RS. Exponential ionic drift: Fast switching and low volatility o thin-film memristors. Applied Physics A. 2009;94(3):515–519.

[135]   Joglekar YN and Wolf SJ. The elusive memristor: Properties of basic electrical circuits. European Journal of Physics. 2009;30(4):661.

[136]   Biolek Z, Biolek D and Biolkova V. SPICE model of memristor with nonlinear dopant drift. Radioengineering. 2009;18(2):210–214.

[137]   Wang Z, Joshi S, Savel'ev SE, *et al.* Memristors with diffusive dynamics as synaptic emulators for neuromorphic computing. Nature Materials. 2017;16(1):101–108.

[138]   Midya R, Wang Z, Zhang J, *et al.* Anatomy of Ag/Hafnia-based selectors with 10^{10} nonlinearity. Advanced Materials. 2017;29(12).

[139]   Govoreanu B, Kar GS, Chen YY, *et al.* $10 \times 10 \, nm^2$ Hf/HfOx crossbar resistive RAM with excellent performance, reliability and low-energy operation. In: International Electron Devices Meeting (IEDM); 2011. pp. 31.6.1–31.6.4.

[140]   Kang J, Gao B, Chen B, *et al.* 3D RRAM: Design and optimization. In: IEEE Conference on International Solid-State and Integrated Circuit Technology (ICSICT); 2014. pp. 1–4.

[141]   Fan D, Sharad M and Roy K. Design and synthesis of ultralow energy spin-memristor threshold logic. IEEE Transactions on Nanotechnology. 2014;13(3):574–583.

[142]   Gu P, Li B, Tang T, *et al.* Technological exploration of RRAM crossbar array for matrix-vector multiplication. In: Asia and South Pacific Design Automation Conference (ASP-DAC). IEEE; 2015. pp. 106–111.

[143]   Srimani T, Manna B, Mukhopadhyay AK, *et al.* Energy efficient and high performance current-mode neural network circuit using memristors and digitally assisted analog CMOS neurons. arXiv preprint arXiv:151109085. 2015.

[144]   Wang Y, Yu H and Zhang W. Nonvolatile CBRAM-crossbar-based 3-D-integrated hybrid memory for data retention. IEEE Transactions on Very Large Scale Integration (VLSI) Systems. 2014;22(5):957–970.

[145]   Hu M, Strachan JP, Li Z, *et al.* Dot-product engine for neuromorphic computing: Programming 1T1M crossbar to accelerate matrix-vector multiplication. In: Design Automation Conference (DAC); 2016. pp. 19.1–19.6.

[146]   Xia L, Tang T, Huangfu W, *et al.* Switched by input: Power efficient structure for RRAM-based convolutional neural network. In: Proceedings of the 53rd Annual Design Automation Conference. ACM; 2016. pp. 125.1–125.6.

[147]   Ni L, Wang Y, Yu H, *et al.* An energy-efficient matrix multiplication accelerator by distributed in-memory computing on binary RRAM crossbar. In: Asia and South Pacific Design Automation Conference (ASP-DAC). IEEE; 2016. pp. 280–285.

[148]   Ni L, Huang H and Yu H. On-line machine learning accelerator on digital RRAM-crossbar. In: International Symposium on Circuits and Systems (ISCAS). IEEE; 2016. pp. 113–116.

[149]   Tang T, Xia L, Li B, *et al.* Binary convolutional neural network on RRAM. In: Asia and South Pacific Design Automation Conference (ASP-DAC); 2017. pp. 782–787.

[150]   Yan B, Mahmoud AM, Yang JJ, *et al.* A neuromorphic ASIC design using one-selector-one-memristor crossbar. In: International Symposium on Circuits and Systems (ISCAS); 2016. pp. 1390–1393.

[151]   Jackson TC, Sharma AA, Bain JA, *et al.* Oscillatory neural networks based on TMO nano-oscillators and multi-level RRAM cells. IEEE Journal on Emerging and Selected Topics in Circuits and Systems. 2015;5(2): 230–241.

[152]   Sharma AA, Li Y, Skowronski M, *et al.* High-frequency TaOx-based compact oscillators. IEEE Transactions on Electron Devices. 2015;62(11):3857–3862.

[153]   Maffezzoni P, Daniel L, Shukla N, *et al.* Modelling hysteresis in vanadium dioxide oscillators. Electronics Letters. 2015;51(11):819–820.

[154]   Chua L. Resistance switching memories are memristors. Applied Physics A. 2011;102(4):765–783.

[155]   Pershin YV, Fontaine SL and Ventra MD. Memristive model of Amoeba learning. Physical Review E. 2009;80:1–6.

[156]   Borghetti J, Snider GS, Kuekes PJ, *et al.* Memristive switches enable stateful logic operations via material implications. Nature. 2010;464:873–876.

[157]   Pershin YV and Di Ventra M. Neuromorphic, digital, and quantum computation with memory circuit elements. Proceedings of the IEEE. 2012;100(6):2071–2080.

[158]   Hongal V, Kotikalapudi R and Choi M. Design, test, and repair of MLUT (memristor look-up table) based asynchronous nanowire reconfigurable crossbar architecture. IEEE Journal on Emerging and Selected Topics in Circuits and Systems,. 2014;4(4):427–437.

[159]   Levy Y, Bruck J, Cassuto Y, *et al.* Logic operations in memory using a memristive Akers array. Microelectronics Journal. 2014;45:873–876.

[160]   Ho Y, Huang GM and Li P. Dynamical properties and design analysis for nonvolatile memristor memories. IEEE Transactions on Circuits and Systems I: Regular Papers,. 2011;58(4):724–736.

[161]   Mohammad B, Homouz D and Elgabra H. Robust hybrid memristor-CMOS memory: Modeling and design. IEEE Transactions on Very Large Scale Integration (VLSI) Systems. 2013;21(11):2069–2079.

[162]   Baghel VS and Akashe S. Low power memristor based 7T SRAM using MTCMOS technique. In: 2015 Fifth International Conference on Advanced Computing Communication Technologies (ACCT); 2015. pp. 222–226.

[163]   International Technology Roadmap for Semiconductors—System Drivers; 2011. Available from: https://www.semiconductors.org/wp-content/uploads/2018/08/2011SysDrivers.pdf.

[164]   Niu D, Chen Y and Xie Y. Low-power dual-element memristor based memory design. In: 2010 ACM/IEEE International Symposium on Low-Power Electronics and Design (ISLPED); 2010. pp. 25–30.

[165] Kim H, Sah MP, Yang C, *et al*. Memristor-based multilevel memory. In: 2010 12th International Workshop on Cellular Nanoscale Networks and Their Applications (CNNA); 2010. pp. 1–6.

[166] Zangeneh M and Joshi A. Design and optimization of nonvolatile multibit 1T1R resistive RAM. IEEE Transactions on Very Large Scale Integration (VLSI) Systems. 2014;22(8):1815–1828.

[167] Rothenbuhler A, Tran T, Smith EHB, *et al*. Reconfigurable threshold logic gates using memristive devices. Journal of Low Power Electronics and Applications. 2013;3(2):174.

[168] Biolek D, Di Ventra M and Pershin YV. Reliable SPICE simulations of memristors, memcapacitors and meminductors. ArXiv e-prints. 2013;22(4): 945–968.

[169] Taherinejad N, Sai Manoj PD and Jantsch A. Memristors' potential for multi-bit storage and pattern learning. Proceedings of the IEEE European Modelling Symposium (EMS) Conference. 2015 Oct.

[170] Kvatinsky S, Wald N, Satat G, *et al*. MRL—Memristor ratioed logic. In: IEEE Int. W. on Cellular Nanoscale Networks and Their Applications; 2012.

[171] Zhang Y, Shen Y, Wang X, *et al*. A novel design for memristor-based logic switch and crossbar circuits. IEEE Tran on Circuits and Systems I. 2015;62(5):1402–1411.

[172] Vourkas I, Batsos A and Sirakoulis GC. SPICE modeling of nonlinear memristive behavior. Int J of Circuit Theory and Applications. 2015;43(5): 553–565.

[173] Vourkas I and Siakoulis GC. Memristor-based nanoelectronic computing architectures. Vol. 19. Emergence, Complexity and Computation. Springer; 2015. pp. 9–26. Available from: https://www.springer.com/gp/book/ 9783319226460.

[174] Haykin SS. Neural Networks and Learning Machines. Vol. 3. Pearson Education, Upper Saddle River; 2009.

[175] Wold S, Esbensen K and Geladi P. Principal component analysis. Chemometrics and Intelligent Laboratory Systems. 1987;2(1-3):37–52.

[176] Suykens JA and Vandewalle J. Least squares support vector machine classifiers. Neural Processing Letters. 1999;9(3):293–300.

[177] LeCun YA, Bottou L, Orr GB, *et al*. Efficient backprop. Neural Networks: Tricks of the Trade. Springer; 2012. pp. 9–48.

[178] Werbos PJ. Backpropagation through time: What it does and how to do it. Proceedings of the IEEE. 1990;78(10):1550–1560.

[179] Higham NJ. Cholesky factorization. Wiley Interdisciplinary Reviews: Computational Statistics. 2009;1(2):251–254.

[180] Krishnamoorthy A and Menon D. Matrix inversion using Cholesky decomposition. arXiv preprint arXiv:11114144. 2011.

[181] Cong J and Xiao B. Minimizing computation in convolutional neural networks. In: International Conference on Artificial Neural Networks (ICANN). Springer; 2014. pp. 281–290.

[182] Michalski RS, Carbonell JG and Mitchell TM. Machine learning: An artificial intelligence approach. Springer Science & Business Media; 2013.

[183] Zhang L and Suganthan P. A comprehensive evaluation of random vector functional link networks. Information Sciences. 2016;367:1094–1105.

[184] Bache K and Lichman M. UCI Machine Learning Repository; 2013. Available from: http://archive.ics.uci.edu/ml.

[185] LeCun Y, Bengio Y and Hinton G. Deep learning. Nature. 2015;521(7553): 436–444.

[186] Lawrence S, Giles CL, Tsoi AC, *et al.* Face recognition: A convolutional neural-network approach. IEEE Transactions on Neural Networks. 1997;8(1):98–113.

[187] Krizhevsky A, Sutskever I and Hinton GE. Imagenet classification with deep convolutional neural networks. In: Advances in Neural Information Processing Systems (NIPS); 2012. pp. 1097–1105.

[188] Courbariaux M, Bengio Y and David JP. Binaryconnect: Training deep neural networks with binary weights during propagations. In: Advances in Neural Information Processing Systems (NIPS); 2015. pp. 3123–3131.

[189] Liu Z, Li Y, Ren F, *et al.* A binary convolutional encoder-decoder network for real-time natural scene text processing. arXiv preprint arXiv:161203630. 2016.

[190] Ioffe S and Szegedy C. Batch normalization: Accelerating deep network training by reducing internal covariate shift. arXiv preprint arXiv:150203167. 2015.

[191] Qiu J, Wang J, Yao S, *et al.* Going deeper with embedded FPGA platform for convolutional neural network. In: International Symposium on Field-Programmable Gate Arrays (FPGA); 2016. pp. 26–35.

[192] Plaut DC. Experiments on Learning by Back Propagation. Carnegie Mellon University; 1986. Available from: http://www.cnbc.cmu.edu/~plaut/papers/pdf/PlautNowlanHinton86TR.backprop.pdf.

[193] Hubara I, Soudry D and Yaniv RE. Binarized neural networks. arXiv preprint arXiv:160202505. 2016.

[194] Davis A and Arel I. Low-rank approximations for conditional feedforward computation in deep neural networks. arXiv preprint arXiv:13124461. 2013.

[195] Nakkiran P, Alvarez R, Prabhavalkar R, *et al.* Compressing deep neural networks using a rank-constrained topology. In: INTERSPEECH; 2015. pp. 1473–1477.

[196] Novikov A, Podoprikhin D, Osokin A, *et al.* Tensorizing neural networks. In: Advances in Neural Information Processing Systems (NIPS); 2015. pp. 442–450.

[197] Oseledets IV. Tensor-train decomposition. SIAM Journal on Scientific Computing. 2011;33(5):2295–2317.

[198] Cichocki A. Era of big data processing: A new approach via tensor networks and tensor decompositions. arXiv preprint arXiv:14032048. 2014.

[199] Hagan MT, Demuth HB, Beale MH, *et al.* Neural Network Design. Vol. 20. PWS publishing company, Boston; 1996.

[200]   Bengio Y, Lamblin P, Popovici D, *et al*. Greedy Layer-Wise Training of Deep Networks. In: Advances in Neural Information Processing Systems; 2007. pp. 153–160.

[201]   Tang J, Deng C and Huang GB. Extreme learning machine for multilayer perceptron. IEEE Transactions on Neural Networks and Learning Systems. 2016;27(4):809–821.

[202]   Erhan D, Manzagol PA, Bengio Y, *et al*. The difficulty of training deep architectures and the effect of unsupervised pre-training. In: AISTATS. vol. 5; 2009. pp. 153–160.

[203]   Holtz S, Rohwedder T and Schneider R. The alternating linear scheme for tensor optimization in the tensor train format. SIAM Journal on Scientific Computing. 2012;34(2):A683–A713.

[204]   Oseledets IV and Dolgov S. Solution of linear systems and matrix inversion in the TT-format. SIAM Journal on Scientific Computing. 2012;34(5):A2718–A2739.

[205]   Wright J, Yang AY, Ganesh A, *et al*. Robust face recognition via sparse representation. IEEE Transactions on Pattern Analysis and Machine Intelligence. 2009;31(2):210–227.

[206]   Lee H, Chen P, Wu T, *et al*. Low power and high speed bipolar switching with a thin reactive Ti buffer layer in robust HfO_2 based RRAM. In: International Electron Devices Meeting (IEDM). IEEE; 2008. pp. 1–4.

[207]   Singh PN, Kumar A, Debnath C, *et al*. 20mW, 125Msps, 10bit pipelined ADC in 65nm standard digital CMOS process. In: Custom Integrated Circuits Conference (CICC). IEEE; 2007. pp. 189–192.

[208]   Tan T and Sun Z. CASIA-FingerprintV5; 2010. Available from: http://biometrics.idealtest.org/.

[209]   Chiarulli DM, Jennings B, Fang Y, *et al*. A computational primitive for convolution based on coupled oscillator arrays. In: Computer Society Annual Symposium on VLSI (ISVLSI). IEEE; 2015. pp. 125–130.

[210]   Yogendra K, Fan D, Shim Y, *et al*. Computing with coupled Spin Torque Nano Oscillators. In: Asia and South Pacific Design Automation Conference (ASP-DAC). IEEE; 2016. pp. 312–317.

[211]   Topaloglu RO. More than Moore technologies for next generation computer design. Springer; 2015. Available from: https://www.springer.com/gp/book/9781493921621.

[212]   Xu D, Yu N, Huang H, *et al*. Q-Learning based voltage-swing tuning and compensation for 2.5D memory-logic integration. IEEE Design and Test. 2018;35(2):91–99.

[213]   Xu D, Yu N, Manoj PDS, *et al*. A 2.5-D memory-logic integration with data-pattern-aware memory controller. IEEE Design Test. 2015;32(4):1–10.

[214]   Manoj PDS, Yu H, Huang H, *et al*. A Q-learning based self-adaptive I/O communication for 2.5D integrated many-core microprocessor and memory. IEEE Trans on Computers. 2016;65(4):1185–1196.

[215]   Manoj PDS, Yu H and Wang K. 3D many-core microprocessor power management by space-time multiplexing based demand-supply matching. IEEE Trans on Computers. 2015;64(11):3022–3036.

[216] Manoj PDS, Yu H, Shang Y, *et al.* Reliable 3-D clock-tree synthesis considering nonlinear capacitive TSV model with electrical-thermal-mechanical coupling. IEEE Trans on Computer-Aided Design of Integrated Circuits and Systems. 2013;32(11):1734–1747.

[217] Liauw YY, Zhang Z, Kim W, *et al.* Nonvolatile 3D-FPGA with monolithically stacked RRAM-based configuration memory. In: International Solid-State Circuits Conference (ISSCC). IEEE; 2012. pp. 406–408.

[218] Poremba M, Mittal S, Li D, *et al.* DESTINY: A tool for modeling emerging 3D NVM and eDRAM caches. In: IEEE DATE; 2015. pp. 1543–1546.

[219] Chen YC, Wang W, Li H, *et al.* Non-volatile 3D stacking RRAM-based FPGA. In: International Conference on Field Programmable Logic and Applications (FPL). IEEE; 2012. pp. 367–372.

[220] TaheriNejad N, Manoj PDS, Rathmair M, *et al.* Fully digital write-in scheme for multi-bit memristive storage. In: Conference on Electrical Engineering, Computing Science and Automatic Control; 2016.

[221] TaheriNejad N, Manoj PDS and Jantsch A. Memristor's potential for multi-bit storage and pattern learning. In: European Modeling Symposium on Mathematical Modeling and Computer Simulation; 2015.

[222] Ni L, Liu Z, Yu H, *et al.* An energy-efficient digital ReRAM-crossbar based CNN with bitwise parallelism. IEEE Journal on Exploratory Solid-State Computational Devices and Circuits. 2017;3(1):1–10.

[223] Yu S, Li Z, Chen PY, *et al.* Binary neural network with 16 Mb RRAM macro chip for classification and online training. In: International Electron Devices Meeting; 2016. pp. 16.2.1–16.2.4.

[224] Rastegari M, Ordonez V, Redmon J, *et al.* XNOR-net: ImageNet classification using binary convolutional neural networks. In: European Conference on Computer Vision (ECCV); 2016. pp. 525–542.

[225] Ni L, Huang H and Yu H. A memristor network with coupled oscillator and crossbar towards L2-norm based machine learning. In: International Symposium on Nanoscale Architectures (NANOARCH). IEEE; 2016. pp. 179–184.

[226] Huang GB, Ramesh M, Berg T, *et al.* Labeled faces in the wild: A database for studying face recognition in unconstrained environments. University of Massachusetts, Amherst; 2007.

[227] Vedaldi A and Lenc K. MatConvNet: Convolutional neural networks for Matlab. In: International Conference on Multimedia. ACM; 2015. pp. 689–692.

[228] Goll B and Zimmermann H. A 65nm CMOS comparator with modified latch to achieve 7 GHz/1.3 mW at 1.2 V and 700 MHz/47 μW at 0.6 V. In: International Solid-State Circuits Conference (ISSCC). IEEE; 2009. pp. 328–329.

[229] Zhang C, Li P, Sun G, *et al.* Optimizing FPGA-based accelerator design for deep convolutional neural networks. In: International Symposium on Field-Programmable Gate Arrays (FPGA). ACM; 2015. pp. 161–170.

[230] Chen YH, Krishna T, Emer J, *et al.* Eyeriss: An energy-efficient reconfigurable accelerator for deep convolutional neural networks. In:

International Solid-State Circuits Conference (ISSCC). IEEE; 2016. pp. 262–263.

[231]   Hinton GE and Salakhutdinov RR. Replicated softmax: An undirected topic model. In: Advances in Neural Information Processing Systems (NIPS); 2009. pp. 1607–1614.

[232]   LeCun Y, Cortes C and Burges CJ. MNIST handwritten digit database; 2010. Available from: http://yann.lecun.com/exdb/mnist.

[233]   Krizhevsky A, Nair V and Hinton G. The CIFAR-10 dataset; 2014. Available from: http://www.cs.toronto.edu/~kriz/cifar.html.

[234]   Chen YH, Krishna T, Emer JS, *et al*. Eyeriss: An energy-efficient reconfigurable accelerator for deep convolutional neural networks. IEEE Journal of Solid-State Circuits. 2017;52(1):127–138.

[235]   Huang H, Ni L, Wang Y, *et al*. A 3D multi-layer CMOS-RRAM accelerator for neural network. In: International Conference on 3D System Integration (3DIC). IEEE; 2016.

[236]   Chen PY, Kadetotad D, Xu Z, *et al*. Technology-design co-optimization of resistive cross-point array for accelerating learning algorithms on chip. In: Design, Automation & Test in Europe Conference & Exhibition (DATE). IEEE; 2015. pp. 854–859.

[237]   Ni L, Huang H, Liu Z, *et al*. Distributed in-memory computing on binary RRAM crossbar. ACM Journal on Emerging Technologies in Computing Systems (JETC). 2017;13(3):36.1–36.18.

[238]   Franzon P, Rotenberg E, Tuck J, *et al*. Computing in 3D. In: Custom Integrated Circuits Conference (CICC). IEEE; 2015. pp. 1–6.

[239]   Kim DH, Athikulwongse K and Lim SK. Study of through-silicon-via impact on the 3-D stacked IC layout. IEEE Transactions on Very Large Scale Integration (VLSI) Systems. 2013;21(5):862–874.

[240]   Krizhevsky A and Hinton G. Learning multiple layers of features from tiny images. University of Toronto; 2009.

[241]   GPU specs. Available from: http://www.nvidia.com/object/workstation-solutions.html.

[242]   Chen K, Li S, Muralimanohar N, *et al*. CACTI-3DD: Architecture-level modeling for 3D die-stacked DRAM main memory. In: Proceedings of the Conference on Design, Automation and Test in Europe. IEEE; 2012. pp. 33–38.

[243]   Xue J, Li J and Gong Y. Restructuring of deep neural network acoustic models with singular value decomposition. In: INTERSPEECH; 2013. pp. 2365–2369.

[244]   CPU Xeon-X5690specs. Accessed: 2017-03-30. Available from: http://ark.intel.com/products/52576/Intel-Xeon-Processor-X5690-12M-Cache-3_46-GHz-6_40-GTs-Intel-QPI.

[245]   Han S, Mao H and Dally WJ. Deep compression: Compressing deep neural networks with pruning, trained quantization and Huffman coding. arXiv preprint arXiv:151000149. 2015.

[246] He K, Zhang X, Ren S, *et al.* Deep residual learning for image recognition. In: IEEE Conference on Computer Vision and Pattern Recognition; 2016. pp. 770–778.

[247] He K, Zhang X and Ren S. Identity mappings in deep residual networks. In: European Conference on Computer Vision; 2016. pp. 630–645.

[248] Guo K, Sui L, Qiu J, *et al.* From model to FPGA: Software-hardware co-design for efficient neural network acceleration. In: IEEE Symposium on Hot Chips; 2016. pp. 1–27.

[249] Wang Y, Li X, Yu H, *et al.* Optimizing Boolean embedding matrix for compressive sensing in RRAM crossbar. In: IEEE/ACM International Symposium on Low Power Electronics and Design. IEEE; 2015. pp. 13–18.

[250] Chen T, Du Z, Sun N, *et al.* Diannao: A small-footprint high-throughput accelerator for ubiquitous machine-learning. ACM SIGPLAN Notices. 2014;49(4):269–284.

[251] Wen W, Wu C, Wang Y, *et al.* Learning structured sparsity in deep neural networks. In: Advances in Neural Information Processing Systems; 2016. pp. 2074–2082.

[252] Hashemi S, Anthony N, Tann H, *et al.* Understanding the impact of precision quantization on the accuracy and energy of neural networks. In: Design, Automation and Test in Europe; 2017. pp. 1474–1479.

[253] Dettmers T. 8-bit approximations for parallelism in deep learning. arXiv preprint arXiv:151104561. 2015.

[254] Hubara I, Courbariaux M, Soudry D, El-Yaniv R and Bengio Y. Quantized neural networks: Training neural networks with low precision weights and activations. Journal of Machine Learning Research. 2017;18(1): 6869–6898.

[255] Jacob B, Kligys S, Chen B, *et al.* Quantization and training of neural networks for efficient integer-arithmetic-only inference. In: Proceedings of the IEEE Conference on Computer Vision and Pattern Recognition; 2018. pp. 2704–2713.

[256] Zhou S, Wu Y, Ni Z, *et al.* DoReFa-Net: Training low bitwidth convolutional neural networks with low bitwidth gradients. arXiv preprint arXiv:160606160. 2016.

[257] Bengio Y, Léonard N and Courville A. Estimating or propagating gradients through stochastic neurons for conditional computation. arXiv preprint arXiv:13083432. 2013.

[258] Chi P, Li S, Xu C, *et al.* PRIME: A novel processing-in-memory architecture for neural network computation in ReRAM-based main memory. In: ACM/SIGARCH Computer Architecture News. vol. 44; 2016. pp. 27–39.

[259] Albericio J, Judd P, Hetherington T, *et al.* Cnvlutin: Ineffectual-neuron-free deep neural network computing. In: ACM/SIGARCH Computer Architecture News. vol. 44; 2016. pp. 1–13.

[260]   Fan D and Angizi S. Energy-efficient in-memory binary deep neural network accelerator with dual-mode SOT-MRAM. In: IEEE International Conference on Computer Design. IEEE; 2017. pp. 609–612.

[261]   Wang Y, Ni L, Chang CH, *et al.* DW-AES: A domain-wall nanowire-based AES for high throughput and energy-efficient data encryption in non-volatile memory. IEEE Transactions on Information Forensics and Security. 2016;11(11):2426–2440.

[262]   Sharma A, Jackson T, Schulaker M, *et al.* High performance, integrated 1T1R oxide-based oscillator: Stack engineering for low-power operation in neural network applications. In: IEEE Symposium on VLSI Technology; 2015. pp. T186–T187.

[263]   Chang SC, Kani N, Manipatruni S, *et al.* Scaling limits on all-spin logic. IEEE Transactions on Magnetics. 2016;52(7):1–4.

[264]   Huang H, Ni L, Wang K, *et al.* A highly parallel and energy efficient three-dimensional multilayer CMOS-RRAM accelerator for tensorized neural network. IEEE Transactions on Nanotechnology. 2018;17(4):645–656.

[265]   Deng J, Dong W, Socher R, *et al.* Imagenet: A large-scale hierarchical image database. In: IEEE Conference on Computer Vision and Pattern Recognition; 2009. pp. 248–255.

[266]   Zhu C, Han S, Mao H, *et al.* Trained ternary quantization. arXiv preprint arXiv:161201064. 2016.

[267]   Nair V and Hinton GE. Rectified linear units improve restricted Boltzmann machines. In: International Conference on Machine Learning; 2010. pp. 807–814.

[268]   Xu C, Niu D, Muralimanohar N, *et al.* Overcoming the challenges of crossbar resistive memory architectures. In: IEEE Symposium on High Performance Computer Architecture; 2015. pp. 476–488.

[269]   Kinga D and Adam JB. A method for stochastic optimization. In: International Conference on Learning Representations. vol. 5; 2015.

[270]   Li C, Hu M, Li Y, *et al.* Analogue signal and image processing with large memristor crossbars. Nature Electronics. 2018;1(1):52.

[271]   Lee PC, Lin JY and Hsieh CC. A 0.4 V 1.94 fJ/conversion-step 10 bit 750 kS/s SAR ADC with input-range-adaptive switching. IEEE Transactions on Circuits and Systems I: Regular Papers. 2016;63(12):2149–2157.

[272]   Stathopoulos S, Khiat A, Trapatseli M, *et al.* Multibit memory operation of metal-oxide bi-layer memristors. Scientific reports. 2017;7(1):17532.

[273]   Ma Y, Cao Y, Vrudhula S, *et al.* Performance modeling for CNN inference accelerators on FPGA. IEEE Transactions on Computer-Aided Design of Integrated Circuits and Systems. 2019.

[274]   Kaplan R, Yavits L and Ginosar R. PRINS: Processing-in-storage acceleration of machine learning. IEEE Transactions on Nanotechnology. 2018;17(5):889–896.

[275]   Song L, Qian X, Li H, *et al.* Pipelayer: A pipelined ReRAM-based accelerator for deep learning. In: IEEE International Symposium on High Performance Computer Architecture; 2017. pp. 541–552.

[276]   Mellempudi N, Kundu A, Mudigere D, *et al*. Ternary neural networks with fine-grained quantization. arXiv preprint arXiv:170501462. 2017.

[277]   Zhou A, Yao A, Guo Y, *et al*. Incremental network quantization: Towards lossless CNNS with low-precision weights. arXiv preprint arXiv:170203044. 2017.

[278]   Li F, Zhang B and Liu B. Ternary weight networks. arXiv preprint arXiv:160504711. 2016.

[279]   Dong X, Xu C, Jouppi N, *et al*. NVSim: A circuit-level performance, energy, and area model for emerging non-volatile memory. In: Emerging Memory Technologies; 2014. pp. 15–50.

[280]   Ren F and Markovic D. A configurable 12-to-237KS/s 12.8 mW sparse-approximation engine for mobile ExG data aggregation. In: Proc. 2015 IEEE Int. Solid-State Circuits Conf., San Francisco, CA; 2015. pp. 1–3.

[281]   Zhang Z, Jung T, Makeig S and Rao BD. Compressed sensing of EEG for wireless telemonitoring with low energy consumption and inexpensive hardware. IEEE Trans Biomed Eng. 2013;60(1):221–224.

[282]   Dixon AMR, Allstot EG, Gangopadhyay D and Allstot DJ. Compressed sensing system considerations for ECG and EMG wireless biosensors. IEEE Trans Biomed Circuits Syst. 2012;6(2):156–166.

[283]   Suo Y, Zhang J, Xiong T, Chin PS, Etienne-Cummings R and Tran TD. Energy-efficient multi-mode compressed sensing system for implantable neural recordings. IEEE Trans Biomed Circuits Syst. 2014;8(5):648–659.

[284]   Donoho DL. Compressed sensing. IEEE Trans Inf Theory. 2006;52(4):1289–1306.

[285]   Pant JK and Krishnan S. Compressive sensing of electrocardiogram signals by promoting sparsity on the second-order difference and by using dictionary learning. IEEE Trans Biomed Circuits Syst. 2014;8(2):293–302.

[286]   Ren F and Markovic D. A configurable 12-237 kS/s 12.8 mW sparse-approximation engine for mobile data aggregation of compressively sampled physiological signals. IEEE J Solid-State Circuits. 2015;PP(99):1–11.

[287]   Calderbank R and Jafarpour S. Reed Muller sensing matrices and the LASSO. In: Carlet C, Pott A, editors. Sequences and Their Applications - SETA 2010. Berlin, Germany: Springer Berlin Heidelberg; 2010. pp. 442–463.

[288]   Jafarpour S. Deterministic compressed sensing. Dept. Comput. Sci., Princeton Univ., Princeton, NJ; 2011.

[289]   Hegde C, Sankaranarayanan AC, Yin W and Baraniuk RG. NuMax: A convex approach for learning near-isometric linear embeddings. IEEE Trans Signal Process. 2015;63(22):6109–6121.

[290]   Chen F, Chandrakasan AP and Stojanovic VM. Design and analysis of a hardware-efficient compressed sensing architecture for data compression in wireless sensors. IEEE J Solid-State Circuits. 2012;47(3):744–756.

[291]   Kim S and Choi YK. Resistive switching of aluminum oxide for flexible memory. Appl Phys Lett. 2008;92(22):223508.1–223508.3.

[292]   Baraniuk R, Davenport M, DeVore R and Wakin M. A simple proof of the restricted isometry property for random matrices. Constr Approx. 2008;28(3):253–263.

[293]   Lee HY, Chen PS, Wu TY, *et al.* Low power and high speed bipolar switching with a thin reactive Ti buffer layer in robust HfO2 based RRAM. In: IEEE Electron Devices Meeting; 2008.

[294]   Sheu S, Chiang P, Lin W, *et al.* A 5ns fast write multi-level non-volatile 1 K bits RRAM memory with advance write scheme. In: Proc. 2009 Symp. VLSI Circuits, Kyoto, Japan; 2009. pp. 82–83.

[295]   Costa L and Oliveira P. Evolutionary algorithms approach to the solution of mixed integer non-linear programming problems. Comput Chem Eng. 2001;25(2):257–266.

[296]   ApS M. The MOSEK optimization toolbox for MATLAB manual. Version 7.1 (Revision 28); 2015. Available from: http://docs.mosek.com/7.1/toolbox/index.html.

[297]   Sahinidis N. BARON: A general purpose global optimization software package. J Global Optim. 1996;8(2):201–205.

[298]   Huang GB, Ramesh M, Berg T and Learned-Miller E. Labeled faces in the wild: A database for studying face recognition in unconstrained environments. Univ. of Massachusetts, Amherst, MA; 2007. 07-49.

[299]   Moody GB and Mark RG. The impact of the MIT-BIH arrhythmia database. IEEE Eng Med Biol. 2001;20(3):45–50. Available from: http://www.physionet.org/physiobank/database/mitdb/.

[300]   Wilton SJ and Jouppi NP. CACTI: An enhanced cache access and cycle time model. IEEE J Solid-State Circuits. 1996;31(5):677–688. Available from: http://www.hpl.hp.com/research/cacti/.

[301]   Chen YS, Lee HY, Chen PS, *et al.* Highly scalable hafnium oxide memory with improvements of resistive distribution and read disturb immunity. In: Proc. 2009 IEEE Int. Electron Devices Meeting, Baltimore, MD; 2009. pp. 1–4.

[302]   Wong HP, Lee H, Yu S, *et al.* Metal-oxide RRAM. Proc IEEE. 2012;100(6):1951–1970.

[303]   Bavikadi S, Sutradhar PR, Khasawneh KN, Ganguly A and Sai Manoj PD. A review of in-memory computing architectures for machine learning applications. In: ACM Great Lakes Symposium on VLSI (GLSVLSI); 2020.

Index